There are no easy answers to the complex questions
that arise when parents divorce. But you can turn to
THE PARENTS BOOK ABOUT DIVORCE
for clear and insightful information on:

* Talking to your children about divorce
* Dealing with guilt feelings and avoiding blame
* Staying together "for the sake of the children"
* Meeting your children's emotional needs
* Making the decision to divorce
* Considering mediation vs. litigation
* Reaching a custody agreement
* Monitoring the effects of divorce on young children and
teens
* Adjusting to stepsiblings
* And much more.

NOW REVISED AND UPDATED!
"A lifeline to parents."
—*The New York Times Book Review*

"The best book I know of on the subject."
—Louise Bates Ames, Gesell Institute

THE DIFFICULT CHILD by Stanley Turecki, M.D.
HIGH RISK: CHILDREN WITHOUT A
CONSCIENCE by Dr. Ken Magid and
Carole A. McKelvey
RAISING GOOD CHILDREN
by Thomas Lickona, Ph.D.
NORMAL CHILDREN HAVE PROBLEMS TOO:
HOW PARENTS CAN UNDERSTAND AND
HELP by Stanley Turecki, M.D.
POSITIVE SELF TALK FOR CHILDREN:
TEACHING SELF-ESTEEM THROUGH
AFFIRMATIONS—A GUIDE FOR PARENTS,
TEACHERS, AND COUNSELORS
by Douglas Bloch

THE PARENTS BOOK ABOUT DIVORCE
Revised Edition

RICHARD A. GARDNER, M.D.

Clinical Professor of Child Psychiatry
Columbia University College of Physicians
and Surgeons

BANTAM BOOKS
NEW YORK · TORONTO · LONDON · SYDNEY · AUCKLAND

THE PARENTS BOOK ABOUT DIVORCE

A Bantam Book / published by arrangement with
Doubleday

PUBLISHING HISTORY

Doubleday edition published April 1977
Bantam edition / July 1979
Revised Bantam edition / September 1991
Excerpts appeared in WOMEN TODAY and WOMEN'S RIGHT MAGAZINE.

ISBN 0-553-28632-3

Published simultaneously in the United States and Canada

PRINTED IN THE UNITED STATES OF AMERICA

OPM   0 9 8 7 6

To my three children
Andrew, Nancy, and Julie

Acknowledgments

I wish to express my appreciation and my gratitude to the many people whose support helped make this book a reality. Quite early in my second career as an author, Barbara Wyden, editor and author, encouraged my work by publishing it in the *New York Times*. It was she who recommended this book, while it was still only an idea, to Betty Prashker of Doubleday, who contributed greatly to its editing and publication.

Dr. Jason Aronson graciously permitted me to draw upon material from my *Psychotherapy with Children of Divorce* (Jason Aronson, 1976). My secretary, Linda Gould, cheerfully typed the manuscript and patiently tolerated my scribbles, messy inserts, and seemingly endless modifications. Frances Dubner devoted herself to the editing of the original manuscript and provided me with numerous thoughtful and useful suggestions.

Friends and colleagues in the legal profession saved me much embarrassment by reviewing the sections related to their discipline. Specifically, I am grateful to John Finnerty; my late brother, Ronald Gardner; Arthur Kronenberg; and Michael Sovern, president of Columbia University, formerly dean of the Columbia University School of Law. I wish to point out, however, that the placement of the names of these attorneys here does not constitute an endorsement on their part of everything I have to say about lawyers and the legal profession.

Finally, let me express my deepest gratitude to the children of divorce and their parents, who have taught me most of what is contained here. Although their names have been changed to preserve their anonymity, their stories have enriched this book and will, I hope, help others benefit from their experiences.

Contents

Introduction

The first edition of this book was written in 1976 and published in hardcover in 1977. Much has happened in the years since I wrote the first edition, so much that I could have easily doubled the size of the original with added material. What the reader has here is a distillation of this additional material combined with the revised and updated original.

The deeply gratifying success of my *The Boys and Girls Book About Divorce* (Jason Aronson, 1970; Bantam Books, 1971) prompted me to write this book as a companion volume. Although there was a plethora of books advising the divorcing and divorced, I was not able to find one book specifically advising parents on how to deal with the problems that could arise in their children that I could strongly recommend. Either such guidance was confined to one chapter of a book covering an assortment of issues related to divorce, or the subject was dealt with in ways that I considered superficial and/or incomplete. This book endeavored to fill this gap.

I believe that *The Parents Book About Divorce* provides an in-depth coverage of the most common problems that parents must face when dealing with their children's reactions to separation and divorce. This book does not provide any simple answers. The problems dealt with here are complex. Simple answers to these complicated problems may seem attractive, but they are doomed to failure, and those who rely on them are bound to become disappointed and disillusioned. This book is for those who are suspicious of or fed up with simple solutions and who are willing to expend the effort to deal more realistically with these problems. It describes in detail the ways in which the most common problems arise and are perpetuated. And it provides guidelines and advice for preventing problems before they arise as well as for dealing with them when they do. In spite of the complexity of its subject, this book is oriented toward giving practical advice and attempts to be quite specific about putting into action the recommendations provided. My experience has been that parents who take the trouble to understand and apply these practical solutions often enjoy both immediate and long-standing benefits for themselves and their children.

The text of this new edition reflects modifications of my positions on some subjects—changes resulting from further thought and experience. For example, although trained in both psychiatry and psychoanalysis, as the years have passed I have gradually moved away from the classical psychoanalytic approach. Terms such as oral, anal, and oedipal increasingly seem to me simplistic and misleading. When I wrote the original edition, I was no longer using the first two terms; and in this edition the word oedipal hardly appears. Although Sigmund Freud never directly treated one child (the famous little Hans was treated by the father, under Freud's supervision), Freud did not hesitate to devise a complex theory of childhood psychosexual development. But my own experiences over thirty years of therapeutic work with children have led me to conclude that there is little relevance to Freud's theory of childhood development and that there are many more complex and/or reasonable explanations for the phenomena he described.

This book (like the first edition) takes issue with the classical reliance on strictly separate psychotherapeutic treatment of married people who are in conflict. The notion that each party should resolve his or her own problems and that the marriage will thereby improve is simplistic and dangerous. In fact, as I will clarify in chapter 1, it is one of the causes of divorce. Fortunately, fewer therapists today are committed to this orientation—much to the benefit of their patients.

I do not believe that separation and divorce necessarily cause children to develop psychological problems. However, the situation does increase the risk for the development of such difficulties. Most often parents are aware of this danger and do everything possible to prevent problems from arising. Sometimes one or both parents may be suffering with significant psychiatric disturbance, and the children may develop difficulties as well. This book does not pretend to deal with these situations, which generally require counseling or treatment by a mental health professional. More commonly, parents are relatively free of psychological disturbance but may be handling the children in a misguided fashion and so contributing to their developing psychological troubles. It is to this group of parents that this book is devoted. (Often, of course, the groups overlap; that is, parents with psychiatric difficulties may use misguided approaches in dealing with their children.) My hope is to help prevent and alleviate some of the psychological problems that result from parental inexperience or misguidedness. But I am fully aware, of course, that such disturbances often require much more intensive approaches than mere information and guidance.

About the time of the book's first edition, I began seeing a disorder in children whose parents were litigating for their custody. These children exhibited unambivalent denigration of one parent (usually the father) and unambivalent love and idealization of the other parent (usually the mother). And this was in a situation where there was absolutely no evidence for actual abuse. Initially, I thought I was simply observing children who had been programmed or "brainwashed" by the preferred parent to hate the deprecated one. However, it became clear that the children were introducing their *own* (often absurd) scenarios, which complemented the programmer's. I decided to name this disorder the *parental alienation syndrome* in order to emphasize the point that what I was seeing was not simply brainwashing but a combination of parental programming and children's complementary contributions. My understanding of the causes, development, and symptomatic manifestations of this disorder gave me important insights relative to the issue of gender preference in child custody disputes. After considerable experience with these children and their parents, I drew up a series of guidelines for legal and mental health professionals for making recommendations in custody conflicts. I refer to these guidelines as the *stronger healthy psychological bond presumption*. An understanding of the parental alienation syndrome and its ramifications should prove useful for parents who are divorcing, especially those who have conflicts over the custody of their children.

In the original volume the term *joint custody* appears only once: "A type of custody arrangement that I believe should be tried more frequently can best be called *joint custody*. In this arrangement. . . . ." If ever there was a hope of mine that came to be a reality it was this one. Within a few years of the publication of my book, the joint custodial concept swept the nation. And its popularity is still very much with us. But like all things in this world, joint custody has its advantages and its disadvantages. This new edition contains significant material about joint custody: who are candidates for the arrangement and who are not, when the arrangement is applicable and when not, what are joint custody's advantages and its risks.

My ideas on mediation have not only changed but expanded considerably since the first edition. I have become increasingly strong in my support of mediation—so much so that I have no problem recommending that it be mandated for people who think they can do better by litigating. I have seen so much grief and psychological trauma caused by litigation that I will no longer involve myself as an evaluator in child custody litigation. However, I have not jumped ship entirely. I will still do mediation. I am also devoting myself to promulgating through writing and lectures a three-phase system for parents who are disputing over custody of their children—a procedure that does not allow for the utilization of adversarial proceedings at any stage. The parents can still use attorneys, but they are not permitted to resort to traditional courtroom procedures that hamper the free flow of communication. The system, described in chapter 7, does not deprive parents of any of their Constitutional rights of due process. I hope that this book will help spread the word about this proposed system.

The controversial issue of the homosexual parent was dealt with in the earlier edition. A crucial question is whether a parent's homosexuality should be considered a parenting compromise by legal and mental health professionals who are assessing parental capacity in a child custody dispute. The controversy still rages, although the courts have become somewhat more receptive to custody for homosexual parents. My position has always been that in a custody evaluation a parent's homosexuality should be taken into consideration along with the many other factors that affect parenting capacity. My position here has nothing to do with civil rights. I believe a person's sexual orientation should not be an issue in areas where one's private sexual life in no way affects one's performance. But in a custody assessment, a parent's homosexual orientation—like a wide variety of other personality patterns—has a direct effect on parenting behavior.

The success of the original edition of *The Parents Book About Divorce* and of its companion volume, *The Boys and Girls Book About Divorce*, has been a source of enormous gratification for me. When preparing the second edition I reviewed the first edition word by word. Happily, most of what I read I still considered valid. There were some things, however, that warranted modification or expansion. I believe that the new material adds significantly to the value of the book, and I hope that the reader will agree.

1

Contemplating Divorce

This chapter is written primarily for parents who have not yet made a final decision regarding whether they will divorce.

A central aim of this book is to help parents prevent and alleviate unnecessary suffering for their children. Marital troubles and separation inevitably cause unhappiness for children. Even though divorce may result in less suffering in the long run, the children will still be deprived of the happy atmosphere of a peaceful two-parent home. For this reason, parents often feel guilt—on top of all their other problems—about the decision to divorce. The most effective way for parents to reduce their sense of guilt is to do everything possible to minimize the pain for all concerned.

My purpose here is neither to help parents reconcile nor to help them separate. It is to help couples gain a clearer picture of their situation and to provide information that may be useful to them in making their decision.

Parents who have already made their decision to separate, or who are separated or divorced, may also find much in this chapter of value to them. I hope the information here will prove useful in any involvements parents may now have with lawyers and mental health professionals, and that it will provide guidelines of use in future relationships.

COUNSELING WITH A MENTAL HEALTH PROFESSIONAL

It is important for parents to appreciate that the field of psychotherapy is still very much in its infancy. As is so often true of young sciences, there is much that is uncertain—so much so that no two therapists agree on every point. I express here my own opinions and recognize that they may sometimes differ from those held by counselors whom the reader may be seeing. I do not claim to have final answers, nor is it likely that all the views that I express will be applicable to everyone. I hope that readers will accept and utilize what seems reasonable and reject what does not.

The crucial neutrality of the therapist. I begin with a fundamental point: the importance of the marriage counselor's strict neutrality as to whether a couple is better off remaining married or separating. No one can predict whether a couple contemplating separation will be better off married or divorced. Therapists do well, therefore, to direct their efforts toward helping the parents clarify the issues involved and alleviating inappropriate or disturbed behavior. If they are successful in this regard the parents will then be able to make a healthier and wiser decision. It is most important that, whatever the parents decide to do, they have the feeling it was truly a decision made by one or both of them. If the decision turns out to be an unfortunate one, they must feel that they have only themselves to blame. And if their choice proves to have been a judicious one, they should have no one but themselves to thank. If a counselor takes a strictly neutral position, and the parents see him or her as having done so, they are not likely to react with either gratitude or denunciation of the therapist for their decision. Thanking a therapist for help and dedication is certainly appropriate; thanking him or her for

2

leading one down a particular path regarding separation reflects a deficient counseling situation.

Therapists who boast of never having had a divorce in their counseling practice are probably (either consciously or unconsciously) pressuring some patients into remaining married when they might have been better off divorced. In contrast, therapists with a high frequency of divorces may well be encouraging divorce (consciously or unconsciously) when attempts at working through the marital difficulties might have been preferable. Sometimes the therapist's own marital history may contribute to these inappropriate pressures. Therapists who have been divorced with a resultant improvement in their life situation may tend to exaggerate the value of separation. Therapists whose own marriages are gratifying may encourage patients to maintain their marriages when separation might be more advisable. Finally, therapists who have never been married, their therapeutic assets notwithstanding, are in a poor position to appreciate fully the problems and conflicts of marriage and do well, in my opinion, to involve themselves in therapeutic areas other than marital counseling.

Joint counseling—the best type for the couple considering separation.

I believe that the ideal marital counseling situation is the one in which the partners are seen together by a therapist who has had no previous experience with either. In this way the therapist is more likely to be impartial from the outset. Therapists who see only one of the spouses hears only one side of the story. In joint counseling they can hear both sides—and the differences may be dramatic. Seeing the partners together also provides the counselor with the opportunity to observe the couple's interaction. Therapists who see each partner separately do not get as much information about each partner as the joint sessions can provide. (I am not suggesting that the partners only be seen together; in many situations seeing each separately as well can also be helpful.) Another advantage of joint counseling is that if the partners stay married, they have had a healthy experience in mutual inquiry that should serve them well in their future relationship.

If, however, they divorce, they should have at least become clear about the reasons for their decision. Furthermore, what they have learned in their counseling should help them avoid another injudicious marriage.

In doing joint marital counseling I do not hesitate to express my opinions regarding the appropriateness or inappropriateness of either party's thoughts, feelings, and behavior. Although this may appear as if I am taking sides, it is not the side of the person that I am joining as much as the side of health. In other words, I support psychologically healthy behavior and discourage unhealthy behavior, regardless of who exhibits what. If the therapist is genuinely well meaning and has the parents' welfare as a primary focus, painful confrontations and interpretations will most often be accepted.

In counseling each partner may try to use the therapist as a tool to serve his or her own ends. The competent therapist is generally aware of these tendencies and will refuse to become involved in such manipulations. For example, a wife may try to enlist the therapist's aid in pressuring her husband to spend more time at home when he has little motivation to do so. Or a husband may try to enlist the therapist's assistance in getting his wife to remain in the marriage when she is strongly inclined to separate.

Even when therapists are successful in maintaining a strictly neutral role, the partners may attribute to them motives that are genuinely not theirs. For example, a husband may conclude that the therapist's failure to condemn his wife for an affair served to sanction it. And she too may consider this to be the case. Or a wife may interpret the therapist's neutrality as support for her decision to separate. Her interpretation may arise from her need for support and encouragement to take such an anxiety-provoking step. The therapist, however, was only serving in the proper role of facilitator of understanding—not condemner, imposer of values, or manipulator of people.

The competent therapist appreciates that both parents are usually quite ambivalent about separation and that they may waver between periods when one or both are quite sure that they will divorce and times when they feel that they will be able to work things out. Competent therapists appreciate that even when things are going badly in a marriage it behooves them to refrain from encouraging either party to make the break. They recognize that each of the parents generally needs a period of getting adjusted to the idea of divorcing and that this takes time. The good therapist shows the greatest respect, therefore, for the parents' ambivalence, procrastination, and indecisiveness. Therapists who do not respect this process, who push it along, are doing their patients a disservice. Certain things cannot and should not be rushed by others, and the decision to divorce is one of them. Competent therapists recognize, as well, that while some ambivalent parents may never separate, the ambivalence provides them with hope that someday they may be relieved of their grief. Although this day may never arrive, the hope that it will can be salutary.

There are therapists who tell parents that their "sitting on the fence" about divorce is a disservice to their children. These therapists may advise parents that the longer it takes them to get off the fence and decide one way or the other, the longer both they and their children will suffer. I believe that such advice, although well meaning, is misguided. Sitting on the fence is no more or less a position than being on either side of it. Actually, there are three positions—marriage, divorce, and indecision—each of which has its advantages and disadvantages for all concerned. Specifically, staying together may serve the children's need to have both parents available for them but has the disadvantage of ongoing grief and hostility for the parents, which may then be painful for the children. Remaining in the marriage with great ambivalence again provides the children with two parents but is also likely to expose them to the negative effects of their parents' ambivalence. And separating, although it may decompress the situation for the parents and ultimately give them better lives, deprives the children of the benefits of their parents' living together. To pressure the parents into selecting one of only two of the possibilities is presumptuous on the part of the counselor. It implies that the therapist *knows* which of the three possibilities is preferable. Such advice, if complied with, may deprive the parents and children of the best (its drawbacks notwithstanding) of the three options open to them. A therapist who works with the children of such parents should be as receptive to helping them adjust to parental indecision as to helping them adapt to ongoing marital difficulties or divorce.

Often people feel that the term counseling (and more so the term therapy) implies personality defects or even psychiatric illness. But I do not believe that all troubled marriages result from psychological illness on the part of one or both partners. All of us suffer various traumas and stresses in life, without psychiatric disturbance necessarily being present or playing a role. In some marriages, remaining married is the primary manifestation of the partners' psychiatric disturbances; in others the only manifestation of such disturbances may be their wish to separate. Parents who do not avail themselves of counseling because they fear that it means they are psychiatrically disturbed may be depriving themselves of valuable assistance at a crucial point in their lives. In such counseling they can best learn about what psychological disturbance, if any, exists. If a disturbance is not present to a significant degree, that knowledge can be reassuring. If illness is present, acceptance of it can be the first step toward its alleviation.

The dangers of individual therapy when separation is being considered. When separation impends, individual therapy presents special problems. If the therapeutic work with one spouse is successful, his or her changes may cause a wide variety of painful psychological reactions in the untreated partner. The therapy of one partner tends to unbalance and disrupt unhealthy balances and interactions that may have served to keep the marriage intact. Sometimes untreated partners adapt and involve themselves in healthier forms of interaction. The marriage then is maintained on a new and more secure foundation. On occasion, however, untreated partners may be unable to make such adjustments. They may then seek others to form unhealthy involvements and gain pathological gratifications. In such cases, therapy may contribute to the separation. There is no question that this is one of the dangers of therapy, and married people who enter into treatment should be told of this possibility.

When a marital partner is in individual therapy the intimacy he or she shares with the therapist generally causes some feelings of alienation and jealousy in the other partner—and this can be divisive for a marital relationship and intensify marital difficulties. Whatever benefits the untreated marital partner may hope to derive from the spouse's therapy, he or she suffers a certain amount of invasion of privacy that generally results in some resentment toward both the spouse and the therapist. If the therapist advises a patient not to discuss what goes on in the session with anyone, including the spouse, further feelings of alienation between the partners may result. Therefore, I generally advise my married patients to discuss as openly and as freely as they wish any aspect of their therapy with anyone, spouse or nonspouse. I respect their right to privacy, but I believe that the more open communication there is between people, the less the likelihood of interpersonal and even internal psychiatric difficulties.

Many therapists believe that the ideal therapeutic program for a couple with marital problems is one in which each partner sees his or her own therapist. They hold that the best way of resolving the internal psychological problems that are contributing to a marital conflict is for each partner to work out his or her problems alone with a separate therapist. In addition, they believe that the therapist-patient relationship is automatically compromised if the patient sees another therapist for joint counseling or even if the patient's spouse comes in for one or more joint interviews. I disagree strongly with this position. First, a patient's relationship with a therapist is not necessarily diluted by counseling with a second therapist. Second, it would not speak well for a therapeutic relationship if it could be jeopardized by a single, or a few, or even many meetings with a spouse.

It is difficult, if not impossible, for a therapist working individually with one spouse to avoid siding with the patient in a marital conflict. I do not believe that such therapists can be so objective that they do not become sympathetic with the patient's view. Hearing only one side of a story deprives the therapist of the opportunity to get a balanced and clear picture of the marital conflict. Any therapist who has done marital counseling quickly sees how differently the two partners may see the same situation. Furthermore, the very nature of the therapeutic situation often seduces the therapist into losing some objectivity regarding the patient and increases the tendency to side with the patient in a marital conflict. After all, the therapist cannot but be flattered to have been chosen—over all the other people in the world—as the patient's trusted confidant. The therapist cannot but admire a person who shows such good judgment. And after the relationship has been established, and if the patient starts to consider the therapist the most sympathetic, empathetic, understanding, benevolent, brilliant individual he or she has ever had the good fortune to meet, the therapist's admiration and affection for the patient increase even further. We love most those who have the good sense to appreciate our assets. A mutual admiration society thus develops in which the therapist may become blind to some, if not many, of the patient's defects—defects that are contributing to the marital difficulties. Often this results in the therapist's developing unwarranted antagonisms to the spouse. The result of all this may be the destruction of a marriage that might have otherwise remained intact and even improved had the couple seen a therapist together.

Frank and Ruth's situation demonstrates the disastrous effects of a therapist's siding with a patient against a spouse. Ruth's father died when she was three, leaving her mother with three children: Bob, age seventeen; Jill, age six; and Ruth. Soon after his father's death Bob left school in order to help support the household. Although Bob rose to this obligation admirably, he also tended to be condescending to Ruth and frequently put her down. With Bob as the only father figure she could remember, Ruth grew up tending to view all men as critical of her. This contributed to her difficulties with her husband, Frank, whom she often saw as condescending to her when he wasn't. Accordingly, she became excessively critical of Frank, and often had rage outbursts against him over minor and often nonexistent provocations. Frank took a very loose attitude about his obligations. He was sloppy around the house, expected Ruth to pick up after him, and had not advanced in his profession—social work—to a degree commensurate with his basic intelligence and experience. This was for the most part due to his low drive and low self-assertion. Ruth was a more striving person; she had worked her way through college in order to become a schoolteacher but had interrupted that career in order to raise her and Frank's children. Frank's lackadaisical attitude was irritating to Ruth, and she was constantly on his back to be more assertive and reliable. In spite of these difficulties, both were extremely devoted to their children and shared many common interests.

After ten years of marriage, Ruth decided that her marriage was falling apart and suggested that both she and Frank go into treatment. Frank was unreceptive to the idea but agreed that Ruth needed it and was glad to pay for her treatment. Frank, however, became upset when he learned that Ruth was considering seeing a psychologist with a reputation as a very aggressive woman who was generally hostile to men. Frank communicated his reservations to Ruth, even before her first telephone call to this therapist. Ruth insisted that she was drawn to this woman (she had heard her speak at a PTA meeting) and wanted very much to be treated by her.

And so Ruth proceeded with her treatment. Much of her session time was spent complaining about Frank: his sloppiness around the house, his lack of self-assertion, his provocative condescension, and the numerous other ways in which he was constantly irritating Ruth. Ruth would often come home and relate to Frank how her therapist agreed with her that she had "quite a cross to bear" being married to someone like Frank. Frank admitted that he was a low-drive person and that some of Ruth's complaints were justified, but he also believed that Ruth's distortions about his being condescending toward her were not being appreciated and dealt with by Ruth's therapist. He was convinced that the therapist was being taken in, especially since she had not seen Frank or heard directly his

9

views regarding what was going on between Ruth and himself. Frank requested a joint interview with Ruth and her therapist.

From the earliest minutes of the interview Frank felt that he was on enemy territory. He felt that the therapist's attitude toward him was unsympathetic and hostile. Frank became very upset by the therapist's attitude and concluded that although there might be some justification for her view of him as taking advantage of Ruth, her anger toward him was unprofessional and unwarranted. He discussed this with friends, who urged him to request another joint session in order to discuss with Ruth's therapist his reservations about her. This was arranged, and Frank expressed to the therapist his feeling that she was biased against him and inappropriately hostile. The therapist told him that she was justified in being angry at him for the way he treated Ruth. Then Frank responded that *Ruth* might have a right to feel angry; but that he was not doing anything to hurt or provoke the therapist and that it was therefore inappropriate for *her* to be angry at him. The therapist denied that Frank's complaint had any justification and pointed out that this was just the kind of irrational criticism that Ruth had spoken so much about.

Frank felt helpless. He was convinced that his wife's therapist was inappropriately antagonistic to him and was not being objective. He considered the therapist's failure to have seen Frank for a year, during which time she heard only Ruth's views, had contributed to the marital deterioration. In addition, he suspected that the therapist harbored biases against men that were also contributing to the difficulties between him and Ruth, and now among the three of them. He discussed the problem with friends, some of whom knew the therapist, and they agreed that Frank's view of the situation appeared to be accurate. Frank urged Ruth to quit treatment, but she refused. Frank (exhibiting now more self-assertion than he had in the past) once again asked for a joint interview. During this session he complained to the therapist about his wife's lack of sexual responsivity, to which the therapist replied: "If you don't like it, why don't you go and jerk off!" Frank tried to point out how unsympathetic, unprofessional, and even cruel this response was. But both the therapist and Ruth insisted that this comment had no hostile implications and was entirely justified by the situation. Frank could not convince them otherwise. Accordingly, he informed Ruth that he was no longer paying for treatment. Ruth, he concluded, had developed an attachment to this therapist that defied logic and blinded her to the therapist's obvious defects. Ruth then got a part-time job and combined her earnings with a small inheritance in order to continue paying for her treatment. After about two years, during which time Frank saw his wife's situation continually deteriorating, Ruth's hostility reached unbearable proportions and Frank initiated divorce proceedings. Ruth remained with the therapist for seven more years and became ever more deeply entrenched in her hatred of and disdain for men.

Ruth and Frank's situation may sound unusual—but my experience has been that it is surprisingly common. Not only does individual therapy for marital difficulties present the problem of the therapist's being biased, but the therapist's preexisting attitudes can also have a detrimental effect on the marital relationship of the patient. Therapists are not nearly so free of psychiatric problems as they and many lay persons would like to believe.

But even without the contributing element of therapist's psychiatric problems, therapists who insist on seeing only one spouse have caused many divorces that should never have taken place. Although many such therapists are certainly well meaning, I believe they are misguided in rigidly subscribing to a theoretical principle that not only has not been conclusively validated, but has strong and convincing arguments against it. Accordingly, if a husband, for example, is paying for his wife's treatment and if her therapist absolutely refuses to see him, when a marital conflict is a primary problem, I advise him to refuse to pay the therapist and to do everything possible to get his wife to select a therapist with a more flexible policy regarding joint interviews with spouses. Otherwise, he may be paying a person to contribute to the further deterioration of his relationship.

Nat and Barbara's situation demonstrates how a therapist's refusal to see the spouse of a patient can contribute to a deterioration of a marriage. Nat, a mathematics professor, was a self-absorbed and taciturn man. He was attracted to Barbara's lively and outgoing personality and openly admitted that one of the main reasons he married Barbara was that he could rely on her to enliven a conversation when he could think of nothing to say. Nat was quite dependent on Barbara. In the early years of their marriage she enjoyed making decisions for a man she considered her intellectual superior. But over the years she gradually became more resentful of having to bear the major burdens of running the household and taking care of the children as well as assuming alone many other responsibilities that are usually shared with or done by a husband, such as house repairs, car maintenance, and financial planning. Barbara tended to control Nat at times—a trait that contributed to her willingness to take over these extra household responsibilities in spite of her complaints. Barbara was seductive with men. Although she had had no affairs, she liked to titillate men and would seduce them into propositioning her—only to reject them immediately upon their first sexual overtures.

During their twelfth year of marriage Nat became more withdrawn and depressed. He became fearful of driving, yet he was still able to drive to the university to teach. At this point he went into treatment with a psychoanalyst who was on the faculty of the university where Nat taught. The analyst rigidly adhered to the classical Freudian approach and saw Nat on the couch five times a week. During the sessions the analyst had very little to say to Nat, and there were even sessions when he made no response at all to Nat's associations. During Nat's third week of treatment, Barbara asked Nat if he had discussed with his analyst the fight they had had over Nat's refusing to take his car to the garage for repairs, forcing Barbara to take it herself so Nat could get to work. Nat replied that his analyst suggested they focus on the infantile roots of such problems as this and strictly refrained from providing specific advice. In addition, Nat told Barbara, his analyst had told him that it was against the interests of the treatment for him to discuss what had gone on in the sessions with anyone, even Barbara.

During the ensuing weeks Barbara began to suspect that Nat was not discussing many of their problems. Sexual difficulties were becoming greater; Nat had lost interest completely and Barbara was considering an affair. Nat was becoming extremely irritable with Barbara, had rage outbursts, and had even hit her on a few occasions. When Barbara asked Nat if he had discussed these new developments with his analyst, Nat replied that he had not and had no intention of doing so, and that it was none of her business what he spoke about with his analyst. He then added that he wasn't even supposed to have said what he just had; that telling Barbara he hadn't spoken of the things she wanted him to was, in itself, a revelation of what had gone on in his sessions and was therefore breaking his analyst's rules. Nat told her that he had concluded that she was a very controlling person, that her questions about what went on in his sessions were proof of this, and that she was an important source of his difficulties. Barbara admitted that she had a problem in this area, but also felt that a joint session with Nat's analyst might be useful so that he could gain some picture of what was going on at home. Nat subsequently reported back that such an interview would be impossible because it would be an intrusion on the privacy of Nat's treatment. Ever more frustrated, Barbara asked Nat if the two of them could go to another psychiatrist for counseling. Again Nat returned with a refusal—such counseling would "dilute" Nat's relationship with his psychoanalyst and thereby compromise or destroy his treatment.

The situation deteriorated rapidly after that. Barbara pleaded with her husband to seek treatment from another man, but Nat refused. He quoted his analyst's high credentials, and began speaking of him as if he were all-wise. Barbara pointed out to him that the classical Freudian theory was still very much a *theory,* that a majority of psychiatrists and psychologists do not strictly subscribe to it in every way, and that there are many Freudian analysts who would see a spouse. Her pleas were to no avail. There was no feedback from Nat's analyst; no way for Barbara to communicate with him (a letter she wrote the analyst requesting to see him, either alone or with Nat, was unanswered); and no way of budging Nat from rigidly defending the kind of treatment he was receiving. When asked how he expected to work out their marital problems if his analyst might never even hear her views of their mutual difficulties, she was told that when Nat got better their marital troubles would be reduced. In addition, she was told that if she got her own analyst there would be an even better chance that their marital problems would be solved. Barbara agreed that she might profit from treatment, and that there were problems within her—problems having nothing to do with Nat—that might be helped by individual therapy for herself. However, she could not see how her complaining to a therapist about Nat, a therapist who might never see Nat (because of Nat's therapist's convincing Nat that such a visit would jeopardize his therapy), could help their marital problems. So she did not enter treatment herself.

Within two years of Nat's entering treatment, Barbara asked for a divorce. The marital situation had deteriorated to the point where she felt it was hopeless. And she saw no reason to believe that Nat's treatment was ever going to make things better; in fact, she had every reason to believe that it was making things worse for them.

This story too may sound like a caricature and may seem improbable. But such occurrences are commonplace. Fortunately, as time goes by, fewer therapists are adhering strictly to the classical Freudian theory of treatment, and so such experiences are occurring with less frequency.

I believe that the ideal therapeutic program for a couple with marital problems is one in which both parties can be seen by the same therapist, in both individual and joint sessions. When, however, there is a significant amount of material that each does not wish revealed to the other (whether appropriate or not), then it is probably best for the two to be seen by separate therapists. A patient's therapy is compromised when the therapist has relevant information that cannot be divulged. But when the spouses have separate therapists, there should be joint sessions as well. These are best conducted by the two therapists alternating according to which therapist is best equipped to focus on a particular issue. The therapists should be free to communicate with one another and to reveal to one another what they consider to be indicated and constructive. Each should appreciate that he or she should not burden the other therapist with information that cannot be revealed to the patient. Joint counseling by a third therapist, although a reasonable alternative, is not as advisable as one of the two individual therapists doing the counseling. There are enough potential contaminants with two therapists involved (distortions, communication errors, rivalries); a third can often compound these complications.

Family interviews can sometimes be helpful. Younger children are not generally valuable sources of direct information; however, observing the parents with them can often provide useful data for the therapist. Adolescents, on the other hand, if they are comfortable enough to reveal their opinions and observations, can be a valuable source of information. On occasion, I have also seen one or more of the parents of the couple. At times they play an important role. We never completely outgrow the influence of our parents, and even after they die their wishes and thoughts enter our minds and affect our behavior. Parents of couples anticipating separation are not utilized frequently enough in the counseling process. Their information can often enhance the efficiency of the counseling experience. Of course, therapists should not go overboard with family interviews and bringing in spouses' parents. There are many issues that are justifiably discussed by the couple alone—intimate issues that are of no direct concern to other parties.

Another type of counseling that I have found useful as an adjunct to the individual work or as an alternative to seeing the couple alone is couples' group therapy. I have found three or four couples to be the optimum number for such a group. Two couples do not provide enough variety of opinion and richness of interaction, and when one or more people are absent the group gets too small for efficient work. More than four couples makes the group too large for each couple to get optimum opportunity for airing their difficulties. The couples meet with me for an hour and a half, once a week, and then alternate after-group meetings at one another's homes, where they have the opportunity to observe one another in their natural surroundings. The postgroup discussions are kept on the same therapeutic level and generally last two to four hours. The five or so hours of exposure increases the chances that people will relax and reveal themselves.

Some important suggestions for the couple contemplating separation.

It has been my experience that many couples divorce because they believe that their situation will be immeasurably improved in another marriage. They believe that the euphoria of romantic love should exist continuously and that the failure of intense romantic feelings to persist is evidence of a deep deficiency in the relationship. The mass media have helped popularize this misconception. I believe that a certain amount of romantic euphoria can enrich a relationship and counterbalance some of the pains and frustrations that are an inevitable part of marriage. However, individuals who believe that it is possible to maintain such feelings practically uninterruptedly throughout the course of a lifetime are doomed to disappointment. They will inevitably be disillusioned, no matter how many times they get married. As with the narcotic that romantic love resembles, the individual will ultimately develop tolerance, will require more and more to get the same effect, and will ultimately find that it fails to provide euphoria at all.

Accordingly I generally advise couples who are planning divorce to look carefully at those around them—especially those whom they consider to be enjoying "happy marriages." I suggest that they give special attention to those who have been divorced and remarried. I recommend that they talk as intimately as possible with close friends and relatives who are willing to discuss their marriages and see if they can find anyone *in the real world* who even approaches the kind of marriage they are seeking. It is amazing how few people do this and how many blindly believe they will be able to accomplish what no one off the movie screen has been able to achieve. These people remind me of Samuel Johnson's wisdom: Remarriage represents the triumph of hope over experience.

In addition, I try to help parents appreciate that marriage invariably involves frustration and restriction—its gratifications notwithstanding. I ask them to try to weigh the advantages of the marriage against the misery they may suffer when separated and divorced. I suggest they talk carefully with friends and relatives who have been separated and divorced, and think seriously about whether they wish to suffer such tribulations and privations and whether their present pain is greater.

On occasion, an individual may seek treatment because a spouse threatens separation unless he or she goes into therapy. But such a person's motivation for therapy comes from without—and unless a person is motivated to change within, because of inner pain experienced, he or she is not likely to derive much benefit from a therapeutic experience. Such a person may come with the hope of altering those behavioral patterns that are alienating the spouse or may wish to learn a way to manipulate the partner into remaining in the marriage. Again, with such intentions the therapy is most likely to fail.

I wish to emphasize that I believe therapy can be a very valuable experience for couples with marital difficulties. It may save many marriages and put them on a more secure foundation. It can help couples who are better off getting divorced to do so in the least traumatic and most sane manner. And it can help those so separated make more judicious relationships in the future, both in and out of marriage. As described, however, there are certain therapeutic practices that can be detrimental to a marriage. If one is aware of these practices and avoids involvement with therapists who implement them, then one can gain the advantages of the psychotherapeutic approach.

MEDIATION

Mediation is the best option for parents for resolving disputes relative to their divorce. It is a far more civilized way of dealing with such differences and is likely to prevent the kinds of psychiatric disturbances that so often result from litigation, especially protracted litigation. When the decision is made to divorce, parents today pick up their telephones and engage the services of an adversary attorney. This is a sad mistake. I believe that people in the twenty-first century will look back upon twentieth-century divorcing parents and wonder how they could have automatically and routinely placed themselves in the hands of adversarial attorneys when they had available to them less expensive, more humane, and far less psychologically deranging methods for resolving their divorce disputes.

The legal profession's resistance to mediation. Up until the mid-1980s, the legal profession was generally unsympathetic to mediation and even considered it unethical on the grounds that a lawyer serving as a mediator might be biased. Lawyers had no qualms about serving as mediators in labor and commercial disputes; two business partners who wanted to dissolve their partnership could engage an attorney to mediate their problems, and the lawyer did not risk being considered unethical. Yet two marital partners who wanted to engage an attorney to mediate the dissolution of their marriage contract met with great resistance on the part of the legal profession. Interestingly, the same lawyers who viewed mediation as unethical did not have any conflicts accepting appointments as judges. Somehow, bias at the level of divorce mediation was considered a high risk, but bias at the level of the judge's ruling was not considered to be so. The major reason for this resistance was financial. Obviously, two attorneys involved in protracted litigation can earn much more money than one attorney serving as a mediator. This phenomenon is well illustrated by the old story about a town that needed a lawyer. The people invited a lawyer to move to town, encouraging him with the incentive that he would be the only lawyer available. But the lawyer soon realized that he was not going to make a living in that town and spoke about relocating. The townspeople then decided to bring in another lawyer. This worked. It did not take long before both lawyers became quite wealthy.

In recent years, the legal community's resistance has been reduced significantly, especially by mediation procedures that incorporate independent attorneys as reviewers of the mediation agreement and encourage active communication between the mediator and each party's independent legal counselor. Whereas older lawyers, those more deeply committed to the adversary system, have generally shown resistance to mediation, younger lawyers are more receptive. However, such receptivity has not simply arisen from enlightenment. More mundane considerations have been operative. Because lawyers have been reluctant to do mediation, many other professionals (especially psychiatrists, psychologists, and social workers) have entered the field in order to fill the partial vacuum. A recognition that their reluctance may not be financially wise has led many lawyers to take a more receptive view of mediation.

The advantages of mediation over adversary litigation. When parents litigate over their divorce disputes they are involving themselves in the adversary system. This system of dispute resolution is based on the theory that the best way to find out "the truth," and thereby to resolve disputes that result from differences of opinion, is to let each party present its opinion before an impartial person or group. Each party is permitted to use a representative (generally a lawyer), who presumably will be more effective than the disputants themselves in presenting their arguments before the impartial entity (usually a judge, tribunal, or jury). Each side is encouraged to present, as vigorously as possible, arguments that support its position, and is permitted to withhold, within certain guidelines, information that might weaken its position. On the basis of this presentation of polarized positions the impartials are presumably in the best position to decide what the truth is and thereby to make a judicious decision regarding the resolution of the conflict.

Courtroom procedures utilized in the course of litigation include direct and cross-examination. In direct examination the inquiry is conducted by the attorney who is supporting the witness's position. Accordingly, the witness is allowed wide latitude to present any and all information in support of his or her position. In contrast, cross-examination is conducted by the opposing attorney, the one who supports the position of the witness's opponent. This attorney does everything possible to prevent the witness from revealing to the court any information that would weaken the witness's opponent's position, that is, that of the client of the cross-examining attorney. Frequently the witness is confined to answering either yes or no, even though such simplistic answers may result in providing the impartial with a distorted view of the issue. Interruptions of the examination by the clients are prohibited, and clients often suffer a feeling of impotent rage as they listen to their adversaries' lies and distortions.

In contrast, mediation is much more flexible. It allows the participants to speak directly to one another, rather than through intermediaries, and it is not bound by the constraints of traditional courtroom procedures. I consider the ideal divorce process to be one in which the parents resolve their differences utilizing the services of a mediator. The mediator then draws up a written statement of the agreement. The parents then submit this agreement for review by their two independent attorneys, each of whom works to protect his or her client's best interests. These attorneys should themselves be sympathetic to the mediation process and should ideally be individuals who serve as mediators themselves in other cases. They might be chosen from a roster of lawyers provided to the parents by the original mediator. If there are any differences, these can be discussed among the mediator, the other attorney, and the parents in a relaxed and nonadversarial setting. In this way the interests of each client are protected by independent counsel, while each also enjoys all the benefits to be derived from mediation. The final document then is brought to the court for incorporation into the divorce decree. There are other possible models (to be discussed below), but this is the one that I believe is the best to utilize—as long as we still have adversarial proceedings as the primary method of dispute resolution within our legal system.

One of the most important advantages of mediation over courtroom litigation is that it places control in the hands of the parties in conflict. People who go to court place themselves at the mercy not only of the laws governing child and spouse support, alimony, property division, child custody, and so forth, but of the individual judge. All these laws are subject to differences in judicial interpretation, even by the same judge at different times. Thus, outcomes can be unpredictable at best. In mediation, however, the parents have great flexibility and decision-making power within the confines of the laws. It is the mediator's role to define what the legal restrictions are and to help the parties work within these requirements.

Adversary litigation is invariably an ego-debasing process. Even those who "win" really lose, in that the psychological toll is generally formidable. In mediation, by contrast, no one wins and no one loses. Mediation not only protects individuals from suffering the ego-degrading aspects of courtroom litigation but can even be ego-enhancing in its own right, because it encourages independence and control over one's fate. The adversary system does just the opposite; the clients often become extremely dependent on their attorneys and suffer with a deep sense of powerlessness and impotent rage. In mediation one does not place oneself in such a vulnerable position.

Divorce mediation can also be creative. The process by which the parents work out the final resolution of their problems is a positive one. In successful mediation the parties resolve their differences amicably; and in the process of mediation a weaker party may learn some techniques for negotiating better with the more powerful spouse. Mediation often thereby protects the weaker party from possible future indignities.

Mediation is generally far less expensive than courtroom litigation. Especially if litigation is protracted, the drainage of finances is one of its more devastating psychological drawbacks. Furthermore, mediation ultimately serves the public benefit as well; courts have less pressure on them to hear divorce trials, and the judges' time can be devoted to other kinds of cases.

Another great advantage of the mediation process is that it allows for empirical determinations of the best solutions for the wide variety of problems that confront a specific divorcing couple. In litigation the judge often comes down with a decision that covers many issues, and both parties must adhere to the judge's ruling. But even the most brilliant judge's decision may turn out to have little if any relevance to a particular family. In mediation one can try a plan and then see empirically how it works out. For example, if a support and alimony payment appears reasonable, the parties try it for a month or two and then discuss it again in a subsequent mediation session. In this way they can determine through actual experience—before a final decision is made—exactly what program best fits their needs. The final agreement, then, will reflect what they have previously found to be a reasonable program.

Mediation is likely to reduce hostility between the participants by resolving areas of conflict one at a time and encouraging direct communication and cooperation. Adversary litigation, as described earlier, does just the opposite, bringing hostility to pathological proportions and contributing to the development of psychopathology.

Still another advantage of mediation is that it is private. Divorce proceedings held in a courtroom are generally in the public record. Of course, most divorces do not attract widespread attention, and there are few visitors to the courtroom. However, in most jurisdictions the public is entitled to witness divorce litigation. Most divorces involve personal matters that the individuals would prefer to be kept private. The public exposure of such information can be humiliating. Even the knowledge of the potential for such exposure also produces unnecessary fears and tensions. Mediation provides protection from this kind of publicity. If one or both of the participants are well-known, then public interest may be great, and the privacy that mediation can offer is even more desirable.

After more than thirty years' involvement in forensic psychiatry, I am convinced that many, if not most, judicial decisions in divorce cases are capricious and hastily made and that individuals who *voluntarily* allow judges and attorneys to play an active role in deciding what is just and fair for them are taking a big risk. Judges have overloaded calendars and cannot give as much time to any case as is justified.

With the limited information presented, they are as likely as not to make injudicious decisions. And in practice, the adversary system lessens the likelihood that all the pertinent information will be presented to them in a balanced way. Also, much time in the courtroom is wasted on irrelevancies and digressions. Mediation allows for a much more efficient data-gathering process, and an accompanying custody evaluation provides parents with an even greater opportunity for a detailed investigation into the factors that are important to understand if one is to make a wise decision in a custody dispute.

There is good reason to believe that the agreements that emerge from mediated disputes are more likely to be adhered to than those that have been adjudicated. Having played a role themselves in bringing about the resolutions, the parties may be more committed to the terms of the final agreement. This is in contrast to court-ordered decisions, to which both parties may have little if any commitment. Lacking commitment, the spouses are less likely to adhere to the final decision and are much more likely to abrogate responsibilities, defy the court order, or return to court.

Mediation makes it relatively easy for divorced parents to *come back and reevaluate* their agreement if new situations arise that warrant such reevaluation. This is not the case following adversary litigation. Generally, if a situation arises that warrants revision, couples who have gone through litigation will have to start the whole trial process over again—an extremely lengthy and expensive procedure. Many divorced parents suffer with injudicious decisions rather than expose themselves once again to the terrible traumas of further litigation.

Sometimes there are couples whose original divorce took place at a time when mediation was not generally available. Happily, these couples may now utilize mediation to reevaluate their agreement. For such individuals to forgo the mediation option and return once again to the bloodbath of courtroom litigation is clearly a pathological choice.

Who is best qualified to serve as mediator? Because divorce is primarily a legal matter, I believe that lawyers serve best as mediators. After all, even when another party serves as mediator, he or she still has to incorporate the agreement into a legal document for presentation to the court. There are some mental health professionals who hold that legal training is not necessary for successful mediation and that all a mediator needs to learn are those aspects of the law directly relevant to the divorce process. I believe this is a dangerous position and that much harm has been done by those who subscribe to it. I do not believe, however, that just any lawyer will do. Rather, the lawyer should be someone who has specific training in marital/divorce law and who, in addition, views mediation—rather than adversary litigation—as the preferable mode of resolving divorce disputes.

An important point is that not every lawyer is automatically knowledgeable enough to serve as a divorce mediator. Financial planning and tax law (so important to know about if one is to be a mediator) are not required courses in law schools. Furthermore, law schools do not generally require a course in family law, which obviously, one must know about if one is to mediate divorces. Lawyers, however, are trained in basic legal principles. They are therefore in a better position to gain expertise in these necessary areas than those who have had no such training. This is one of the reasons why I consider the lawyer to be the preferable mediator.

Mental health professionals, however, can play an important role in the mediation process. They serve best as consultants to the mediator. For example, when there is a custody dispute, mental health professionals can help the couple resolve the dispute and have their findings and recommendations incorporated into the final legal papers by the primary divorce mediator. The mental health professional is also sensitive to many of the psychological nuances that may impede the mediation process. For example, the mental health professional may be sensitive to a husband's giving away too much property in order to assuage guilt over leaving his wife. Although the maneuver may momentarily ease his guilt, it is likely to produce chronic dissatisfaction with and resentment about the agreement, and this may ultimately bring about its breakdown. Mental health professionals are trained to appreciate that in divorce disputes the conflict may be present at two levels: the manifest and the latent. The ostensible problems may be only the tip of the iceberg, and there are often hidden agendas. A husband and wife, for example, may seem to be fighting over money. However, they may be unable to resolve their differences or come to compromises because each one is unconsciously fighting for something else, such as power, security, or proof of affection. If there is no resolution of these underlying (sometimes unconscious) factors, there is not likely to be a successful resolution of the ostensible money conflict.

Attorneys are particularly weak in the joint interview situation. The adversary system by definition often rules out joint interviews in which each side has the opportunity to present its position in a relaxed and uncontrived setting. But mental health professionals, especially those who work closely with families and do marital counseling, are particularly skilled in this kind of interview. They recognize that direct confrontations between the parties often bring out more information than is possible to obtain by single interviews. They are trained to pick up the gestures, intonations, or slips of the tongue that are often valuable sources of information. They recognize that as to the knowledge that can be obtained in these kinds of sessions, the whole is greater than the sum of the parts. Because of this particular advantage over attorneys, the mental health professional can play a vital role in the mediation process.

Attorneys are taught that they should be unemotional in their dealings with their clients. In fact, they generally view emotions as compromising objectivity. Mental health professionals, in contrast, are very respectful of both their clients' and their own emotions and consider them to be valuable sources of information. With the exception of some with a strong commitment to the classical psychoanalytic theory, most mental health professionals respect their own emotional responses in their work with patients. The skilled therapist knows how to use these emotions judiciously and sensitively. The mental health professional also, of course, has an advantage when dealing with some of the special psychological problems that affect the mediation process.

Mental health professionals can help reduce animosities, and this can make the mediation smoother and more effective. For example, the mental health professional can help parents understand that children will commonly lie in order to ingratiate themselves to the parent to whom they are speaking at that particular time. Parents in the midst of divorce proceedings may make the mistake of believing these fabrications. The mental health professional can help them appreciate what is going on. This reduces their anger and makes it more likely they will cooperate in the mediation process. Or the mental health professional can help a father whose child is being "brainwashed" by the mother appreciate that part of the scenario of alienation has originated within the child and is not entirely due to the mother's programming. When this problem becomes severe, the child may develop a parental alienation syndrome (chapter 5). The causes and manifestations of this syndrome are important for all concerned in a custody dispute to understand.

The mental health professional can help a mother who is so blinded with rage at her husband that she wishes to cut off visitation to realize that this will harm her children. Similarly, the father who is withholding money as a manifestation of anger and as a weapon of revenge also has to be helped to appreciate that he is hurting his children by this maneuver. A father who is not particularly involved with his children before the separation may propose to the mediator a heavy visitation program that involves frequent visits to the home. Sometimes this kind of proposal reflects a desire for reconciliation, and the mediator has to recognize this desire as a specious motivation for frequent visitation. Supporting such frequent visits may be a disservice to the wife who wants a psychological as well as a physical separation from her husband.

Choosing a mediator.

In the early to mid-1980s, hundreds of courses throughout the United States provided short training programs in mediation for lawyers and mental health professionals. Unfortunately, many others, outside of these two professional areas, were also trained. I believe that some of the trainers did not appreciate that their expertise had come after many years of professional experience and that what seemed obvious and simple to them is really neither obvious nor simple. This is not to say that most of the people who are now functioning as mediators are not properly trained. But there are some who have jumped on the bandwagon who are inadequate and incompetent.

As mentioned, therefore, I believe the ideal divorce mediator is a lawyer with special training in marital/divorce law. In general, the mental health professional is ill equipped to serve as the *primary* mediator in any divorce in which there are significant disputes over property and/or money. And when the mediator is a mental health professional with a classical psychoanalytical orientation, as discussed above, this may compromise the mediation process. Such individuals often take a passive approach to the mediation process; they view their role as being primarily catalytic. This approach can unnecessarily prolong the process and even contribute to its failure. Mediation is not a place for wishy-washy neutrality. I consider the preferable mediator to be someone who is reasonably authoritarian, though not dictatorial. One should be ready to interrupt and to discourage irrelevant digressions. One should be active and confrontational, though always in a benevolent fashion.

In general, mediators who come from the mental health professions make a grave mistake if they believe they can combine mediation with psychotherapy. This extremely risky combination is likely to compromise both the mediation and the therapy. There are mediators who act as therapists during the mediation by interrupting the proceedings and then switching into the role of therapist for one or even both of the parties. They will justify this interruption with the rationalization that the mediation has bogged down and that one or both of the parties need some individual therapy before the mediation can proceed. But a mediator's private therapeutic sessions with one of the parties are bound to compromise the relationship with the noninvolved party. The nontreated party is likely to resent the special relationship that develops between the spouse and the mediator (now serving as therapist). In addition, transferential reactions, which are central to therapy, are likely to evolve. The feelings attendant to this process cannot but compromise the mediation for the patient and possibly even for the therapist, who may develop the countertransferential feelings quite common in treatment.

Therapy and mediation just don't mix. Therapy involves exploration into unconscious processes, and if done properly this can be time-consuming. The mediation process is designed to be short. Also, successful therapy requires a confidential relationship with the patient. Successful mediation requires open communication of all issues between both parties. So if the therapeutic confidential relationship precludes revelations to the other spouse, then the mediation is completely sabotaged. Furthermore, the mediator who brings the client into therapy may justifiably be criticized for using the mediation process as an avenue to earning extra money. This is likely to reduce referrals for the mediator. The whole mediation agreement may even be called into question in subsequent litigation in that the mediator could be accused of having used the process to attract clients for treatment.

Some family therapists believe that they can become divorce mediators after building a therapist-patient relationship. This too is unwise. If the mediation breaks down, at least one of the parties has had to be dissatisfied with the mediation. That party cannot continue beneficial therapy with a therapist toward whom he or she now has these negative feelings. The patient cannot separate the two functions and say, "I dislike him (or her) as a mediator but have confidence in him (or her) as a therapist." Associated with this dissatisfaction are losses of trust and respect, and these feelings will inevitably spill over and compromise the therapeutic relationship.

Choosing the mediator may be very difficult, partly because at present there are no formal requirements and no state certifications. It is legal for any individual to go into the business of mediation, and mediation is still a growth industry. My advice to people is this: If the family is reasonably well off and there are significant holdings (investments, retirement funds, property, etc.), then the divorcing parties *must* utilize the services of one or more individuals who are highly competent in both the law and finance. Again, the ideal person for this would be a lawyer with expertise in both areas. If there is any question about the lawyer's competence in the financial realm, then an expert in financial issues should be brought in as a co-mediator or, at least, as a consultant.

For families with minimal holdings the mediator might well be a person such as a mental health professional. However, this individual must consult an attorney to draw up the final mediation agreement. If the mental health professional mediator can demonstrate significant experience (though this may be difficult, because the field is a young one), then a family may be justified in choosing him or her. If the person has been actively involved in teaching mediation, it is more likely that the person is competent. In recent years a few graduate schools have instituted programs in mediation. A graduate of such a program is probably qualified. Furthermore, law schools now are starting to give courses in mediation, and a lawyer who has taken such a course is likely to be qualified.

People who are candidates for mediation. Not every divorcing couple is a candidate for mediation. Both parties (and I emphasize *both*) must satisfy certain criteria if the mediation is to be successful. If only one of the parties satisfies these prerequisites, there is little if any chance that the mediation will be successful. In fact, in such a situation the ethical mediator will interrupt the process and refuse further services to both clients.

A crucial prerequisite is that both parties be willing to disclose *all* pertinent information. Litigating spouses will often have to resort to court-ordered disclosure in order to obtain information about the other party's financial situation. In mediation each party must be willing to divulge all information freely and openly.

The parties must be willing to *compromise,* rather than be bent on winning. They must accept that "half a loaf is better than none" and that there is no perfect solution to most of their conflicts. Rather, a whole series of compromises will be necessary if there is to be a relatively peaceful and equitable solution to the couple's problems. The couple must appreciate that most of their solutions will involve selecting what is the least painful of a variety of painful options. Furthermore, they must be able to consider the other party's position as possibly valid in spite of the fact that they are filled with unhappy emotions attendant to the divorce process. This may be particularly difficult at this time, as it involves a conscious suppression of emotional reactions in order to allow reasonable and logical thought processes to emerge.

The couple must be able to *communicate* well. It is important that mediators serve as models for good communication. If the mediator does not communicate well, it is likely that the communication capacity of the participants will be compromised. The couple must be able to comply with the mediator's interruptions when communication is fault and must be receptive to the mediator's comments designed to enhance accurate communication. The parents must appreciate that the best kind of communication takes place when the parties focus on concrete issues and avoid generalities. Furthermore, they must appreciate that communication is likely to be impaired if they are overwhelmed by feelings of grief, despair, rage, and so on. It is in this area that the services of the mental health professional may prove useful.

To be successful candidates for mediation, people must have a reasonable capacity to *cooperate*. Clearly, if they could cooperate to a significant degree, they might not have separated. Yet the individuals must have preserved enough capacity to cooperate to involve themselves in the mediation process, a distinction which is possible for some and not for others. Sometimes the mediation process actually improves cooperation and provides the participants with the groundwork for more effective cooperation in the future.

People who are not candidates for mediation.

People who are reluctant to disclose finances are not likely to be candidates for mediation. Struggles over money are at the root of a vast majority of divorce conflicts. With the goal of getting as much money as possible, or paying as little as possible, spouses will often hide money from one another and sequester assets. But without openness and honesty the mediation becomes a farce. Such couples have little choice but to resort to adversary litigation, because the party from whom the information is being withheld is likely to engage an attorney in order to obtain the information.

People with serious psychological problems are not generally candidates for mediation. They may not be able to bring their emotions under control enough to consider logically their various options. In this category, too, are people who are psychologically weak and who therefore may not be as receptive to mediation as those who are psychologically stronger. In order to tolerate divorce negotiations, the weaker person, from feelings of impotence, may need an attorney to provide support and strength. (Psychologically stronger people have greater confidence in their own capacity to mediate successfully.) When severe psychopathological processes interfere with mediation, a mental health professional should be brought in to assess the situation. Only the naive mediator, however, will try to coerce a participant into therapy, as it is relatively rare for a person who is forced into treatment to

31

profit from it. It is inappropriate for the mediator to say, "If you don't go into treatment, I won't continue the mediation." The mediator's position should be: "If you wish to have treatment, you might find that you might benefit from it. You might then find yourself in a better position to profit from mediation. Right now I don't think mediation can be successful. If you decide to go into treatment and if, after that, you think you're in a better position to profit from mediation, I'll be happy to see you again and reassess the situation." This approach places the burden on the client and is noncoercive. The mediator is basically saying to the client: "If *you* want to profit from mediation, you'll have to do something to change yourself." I refer to this as the *ball-is-in-your-court-baby principle*. I recommend it highly.

Where physical abuse and/or physical intimidation is taking place in a marriage, the divorcing parties are not generally candidates for mediation. If a wife, for example, fears that her husband's dissatisfaction with an arrangement may result in his beating her, she may very well agree to an injudicious arrangement. A skilled mediator, of course, will recognize this situation and not agree to the unfavorable "compromise."

Another group of parents who are not candidates for mediation are those whose physical or psychological abuse of the children forces the mediator to report the parent(s) to the authorities. This break in confidentiality, which is required by law, may serve the interests of the children and provide them with protection; however, it is likely to destroy the mediation, because confidentiality has been destroyed. Furthermore, it cannot but produce distrust and resentment of the mediator. Without trust and with significant hostility toward the mediator there can be no mediation.

Individuals who overestimate their chances of winning in litigation are not good candidates for mediation. They are so confident that their cause is a worthy one, and so sure that the judge will rule in their favor, that they are not interested in compromise. Lawyers are often likely to support these expectations—especially because they do not have the opportunity to get full information from the other side. As one who has served for many years as an impartial examiner in custody litigation, I have witnessed this phenomenon many times. Attorneys often gladly enlist my aid as an impartial examiner, so such are they that their client's positions are faultless and unassailable. Many are struck with amazement when my final report comes in. Not having gotten direct input from the other side, the lawyers have been led down the garden path by their clients.

People who are stalling in order to gain certain advantages in the divorce settlement are not candidates for mediation, as mediation is designed to be a short process. Generally, in a custody dispute, the parent with whom the children are living recognizes that the longer the children stay, the greater the probability they will opt to remain where they are. This parent is not likely to mediate in good faith the custody aspect of the separation. Or a mother may recognize that if her husband meets a new woman and wants to marry her, the mother will have more leverage with regard to child support and alimony payments because of the father's eagerness to dissolve the marriage and marry the new woman. She too is likely to stall and not make appropriate use of mediation.

Mediation cannot succeed unless *both* participants desire to end the conflict. This is not invariably the case. There are some individuals who thrive on conflict. This is often the case with a woman whose husband has left her and who has not begun a new relationship. The ongoing conflict can serve as a way for her to remain involved with her former husband. She works on the principle that it is preferable to fight him for the rest of her life than to be lonely indefinitely. There are also men who do not let go, whose lives are left empty by the divorce, and who use the ongoing litigation to give their lives purpose. Court-ordered mediation (discussed below) does not give proper respect to this factor. People who want to continue the conflict are not likely to be successful with mediation. Rather, they litigate for years, clog the courts, and enrich their attorneys.

If there is a significant disparity in the financial sophistication of the two parties, the individuals may not be good candidates for mediation. The disparity may result from differences in intelligence, in education, or in financial experience. One role of the mediator is to help the less sophisticated party appreciate the subtleties of the financial arrangement. But if one party is significantly incapable of grasping such matters, the couple is generally not eligible for mediation, because one person cannot make the requisite decisions. This is especially true when the financial issues are complex.

Couples who have been involved for lengthy periods in adversary litigation are not promising candidates for mediation. Some people can switch from adversary proceedings into mediation. Sometimes attorneys sympathetic to mediation will even advise their clients to interrupt the adversarial proceedings and try to mediate their problems. However, many people in this category become so swept up in the adversary litigation that they become obsessed with winning. And their attorneys may also lose sight of what is going on, so drawn up are they in the war.

People with an inordinate need to gain power over other individuals are not apt to be good candidates for mediation. The struggle for power underlies many divorce conflicts; in fact, it may have been one of the factors contributing to the divorce. This struggle then becomes played out in the divorce proceedings, whether in mediation or in adversary litigation. Some individuals view power as esteem enhancing and consider being overpowered by others to be one of the greatest sources of humiliation—something that should be avoided under any circumstances. Such people may even view a *compromise* as a humiliation. Power-hungry individuals may even attempt to gain power over the mediator. In such cases there is the possibility that the intervention of a skilled mental health professional may salvage the mediation. If this fails, the mediation may not be possible.

The other side of the power-struggle coin is the passive individual who may succumb to an overbearing spouse. Mediation can run into trouble, for example, if a passive-dependent woman is subjugated by her more aggressive, overbearing husband and therefore agrees to a series of compromises that are much to her disadvantage. But in my view it is the role of the mediator to be aware of such imbalances in the mediating parties and to ensure that a weaker party is protected. The fact that the mediator serves as a catalyst or facilitator does not mean that the mediator passively and uncritically accepts every compromise. If this were the case, then the mediator would not need any training or any capacity to assess the judiciousness of each compromise. Furthermore, the memorandum of agreement should be reviewed by attorneys for each of the parents. It is the role of these attorneys to protect their clients from exploitation. The attorneys, as well, generally work with the mediator in order to help resolve inequities.

Mandatory mediation. Many states have instituted mandatory mediation. Like most things, this policy has both advantages and disadvantages. It certainly has the advantage of using court influence to bring into the mediation process individuals who might not have otherwise availed themselves of it. And there is no question that some of these people derive a benefit.

In most states at this time, one must make private arrangements for mediation. It is not provided as a public service. In a few states, however, such as California, it is provided as a public service. In the mediation program in Los Angeles, the mediator first meets with the attorneys to gain information about the parties. The mediator then meets with the parents both separately and together and, if the mediator considers it necessary, interviews the children as well. The mediator may also interview others, such as stepparents, grandparents, or anyone else who has significant involvement with the children. I endorse this approach; I am among the many who hold the view that anyone left out of the mediation who has an interest in its outcome may sabotage the agreement. In Los Angeles the mediation generally takes four to five hours, the agreement is sent to the court, and copies are then made available to the attorneys, who have ten days to respond. If the mediation proves successful, the agreement is incorporated into the divorce decree. The mediator is available for future consultation to work out subsequent problems. If there is no agreement, then no report is sent to the court. The parents then proceed along the adversarial track.

The courts and legislators recognize that mandatory mediation cannot be 100 percent successful. There will always be some individuals who will not be candidates for the mediation under any circumstances. Back in the 1970s I was very unsympathetic to the concept of mandatory mediation, because my psychoanalytic training held coercive techniques to be antitherapeutic and likely to cause more harm than good. Over the years I have changed my position. I have come to appreciate that some individuals can ultimately profit from mediation that may have initially been coerced. I have known situations in which the judge has ordered both clients and both attorneys to sequester themselves in a room in the courthouse and not come out until they have hammered out a mediated program. And sometimes the individuals have been successful in resolving their disputes. Often they reach a point of such weariness that they agree to compromises they would not have previously considered reasonable. Although their weariness may have certainly played a role in their receptivity to compromise, the parties have still had the input and supervision of their attorneys to help ensure that none of the compromises were injudicious.

Final comments about mediation. Mediation for divorce disputes is very much in its infancy. The model I have presented, the one in which the mediated agreement is reviewed by independent attorneys who then attempt to work out all remaining problems, is only one. Other models are also utilized. One such model is co-mediation. Here there are two mediators, instead of one, working with the couple. Generally one of the mediators is a lawyer and the other a mental health professional. Another model is shuttle mediation, in which the mediator meets alternatively with the husband and wife—as is often done in labor mediation. Another approach is for both attorneys to meet with both clients together in the privacy of their offices and attempt to mediate the divorce disputes. This is a common approach, even though it may not be formally labeled mediation. Each of these approaches has its advantages and disadvantages; but they all share the recognition that adversarial proceedings are usually extremely expensive and psychologically detrimental and that mediation, its weaknesses notwithstanding, offers the best hope for parents to resolve their divorce disputes in the most civilized fashion.

ENGAGING THE SERVICES OF A LAWYER FOR ADVERSARY LITIGATION

This section is for those unfortunate parents who have not been able to mediate their divorce disputes. Such couples, under our present system, have no choice but to engage the services of adversarial attorneys and involve themselves in the time-consuming, expensive, and psychologically damaging process of adversarial litigation. Of course, many lawyers try to help litigants resolve their disputes humanely. However, the risk that things will snowball into protracted and emotionally devastating litigation is still high. On many occasions separating couples have said to me that they have no intention of allowing their discussions to degenerate into the kind of debilitating litigation they have observed in friends. At the same time, they eschew mediation—with a wide variety of rationalizations—and place their trust in attorneys who promise them a smooth ride to divorce. I often think (and even say) that these promises are famous last words; that the couple's smooth ride may end up on a roller coaster; and that they may be able to get off only when they run out of money.

When one marries, one enters into a contract and assumes certain obligations that are enforceable by law. In order to dissolve a marriage, one usually signs a new contract. Again, the new obligations are enforceable by law. Most people do not engage lawyers when they marry, because the customary commitments of marriage are understood and expected. However, when the parties wish to add special stipulations to the marriage contract, then they usually engage lawyers. For example, one of the parties may have significant assets that he or she would not want to be available to the other, either within the marriage or if divorce ensues. If the other party accepts this stipulation, then such an agreement might be included in a prenuptial agreement that would be part of the marriage contract.

Although people rarely use the services of a lawyer when they get married, the vast majority of people use lawyers when they get divorced. It is possible to dissolve a marriage without a lawyer, but most recognize that to do so would be a risky business. The divorce contract commonly stipulates lifelong obligations. To agree to such binding commitments without the advice of an experienced professional may be foolhardy. Even when the parties divorce in the most friendly fashion, with no desire to wreak vengeance, it can be dangerous to dissolve a marriage without the contract being drawn by a lawyer. Human beings' feelings toward one another have a way of changing over time: Benevolence changes to malevolence, love turns to hate. Only by a firm contract can even the most well-meaning separating spouses protect themselves from the consequences of later changes of heart.

There are rare situations in which a lawyer may not be needed. For example, if the marriage is an extremely short one, if there are no children, and if there are no demands or requests made by either party regarding property or alimony, then legal services may not be necessary. However, there are very few states in which one can obtain a divorce, even under these circumstances, without the assistance of an attorney. One exception is the state of California, where a couple can obtain a divorce by merely filling out the proper forms and paying a small fee. Obviously, such divorces are usually acquired only by young people who can genuinely remove themselves completely from one another.

There are easier ways for a lawyer to make a living than handling divorce cases. It is important for separating spouses to appreciate that most lawyers do not generally relish the idea of divorce litigation. Especially when the clients are far from resolution of their differences, when there is a likelihood that the case will become prolonged and sticky, lawyers are hesitant to involve themselves. Lawyers whose financial situation is such that they can refer the case on to someone who specializes in matrimonial law, or to someone whose financial position does not warrant being so selective, will often do so. The messy divorce case can consume a vast amount of time, and most clients are not wealthy enough to pay a lawyer an amount that would make deep involvement worthwhile financially.

Accordingly, what frequently occurs is that lawyers do a reasonable job in the simple and straightforward cases; but when complications arise they generally do not devote themselves to the degree that might be in the best interests of their clients. With the recognition that their clients are in no position to pay them for extensive involvement, they work at a minimal level and hope that somehow things will work out. Their clients then find them inaccessible. The lawyer always seems to be in conference or in court when the client calls. And telephone calls are not returned. When the client finally does have the opportunity to speak with the lawyer, he or she is unfamiliar with important facts. Letters that have been sent to the lawyer, sometimes on urgent matters, are still stacked up, unread. The problem is compounded by the fact that the client has generally given the lawyer a sizable advance fee, a retainer, some or all of which may be lost if the lawyer's services are dispensed with. Furthermore, starting all over again with another lawyer, who has to become acquainted with all the details, is a task that the client does not welcome. And so the client feels trapped. Such experiences can exact a terrible psychological toll and add unnecessarily to divorcing parents' problems at this difficult period in their lives.

In order to help my patients avoid adding to their troubles this way, I generally suggest that when seeking a lawyer they should inquire beforehand about accessibility to clients and reliability regarding returning telephone calls. (For obvious reasons such inquiries are better made of previous clients than of the lawyer.)

In addition, I suggest that they discuss the financial arrangements in great detail at the outset. Clients should be willing to pay lawyers for their time (including time spent reading letters and other documents and time spent on the telephone); and the lawyer should be willing to devote such time to the client. Some lawyers will quote one total fee for handling the case; others have an hourly rate. Many will quote one fee if the case is not contested (that is, if differences are resolved without court litigation) and a higher fee if it is contested. Clients who want, and are willing to pay for, the kind of lawyer who will respond to requests for frequent conversations should so state at the outset. The lawyer may agree to this or may prefer not to get involved when such great availability is demanded. In the latter case the lawyer does well to refer the client to another lawyer or to suggest that the client seek one who will satisfy this request.

The important thing is that both lawyer and client clarify and agree to the kind of arrangement they are going to have. Most attorneys do not charge for this type of initial consultation. Clients should request, for example, itemized bills indicating the time and the duration of all services. Unfortunately, lawyers as a group have a very poor reputation for honesty in connection with these itemized bills. Some items, such as telephone call time, can easily be verified, and such entries may add a certain element of credibility to the bill. However, other items, such as "research," cannot be verified. The research may involve matters that the lawyer has done hundreds of times, leading the client to suspect that the services were never really provided. The distrust and sense of impotency that such suspicions produce contribute to the psychological disorders attendant to litigation.

It is important to find out at the outset whether the lawyer will be doing the work in person or assigning the case to associates. It is a common practice for well-known lawyers to give clients the impression that they will be doing the actual work themselves, whereas the client (after providing a large retainer) soon learns that most of the work is being done by a junior associate with far less experience.

In summary, it is important for parents to appreciate that their attorneys are there to serve them. And parents are entitled to know precisely what kind of service to expect. Following preliminary verbal agreement, many lawyers formalize the attorney-client relationship in a retainer letter that sets forth the terms and objectives of their representation and the various factors that will determine the final bill. If the lawyer does not routinely provide such a letter, the client should request it.

The lawyer who discourages clients from divorcing: well meaning, but misguided.

When a person seeks a lawyer's assistance in getting a divorce, it is a common practice for the lawyer to encourage the client to try first to work things out. Ostensibly, this is a rational, humane, and non-self-serving approach. Many lawyers pride themselves on their strict adherence to this practice, consider it proof of their commitment to high ethical standards, and may boast of the number of marriages they have thereby "saved." But the recommendation to "try and work things out" is based on the assumption that marriage is always better than divorce. As many who have been divorced will testify, this assumption is often invalid.

To be sure, the lawyer owes it to the client to inquire into the reasons why divorce is being sought and to consider the possibility that the decision is being requested for frivolous or inappropriate reasons. If the lawyer suspects that there is not a justifiable reason for proceeding, he or she should recommend consultation with a mental health professional. At times the lawyer's suggestion to try to work things out (with or without professional counseling) may in fact be the appropriate course.

What I am criticizing is the blanket suggestion to all clients that they try to maintain the marriage. Such advice may be a disservice to a client. It may have taken the client many years to gain enough courage to institute the divorce proceedings, and this may be a healthy step. The lawyer's discouraging the divorce, under the assumption that maintaining the marriage is automatically in the client's best interests, may squelch this healthy move and may drive the individual back to further years of pain and psychiatric trauma.

The bombastic lawyer: he or she may do you more harm than good.

I often suggest to my patients that they avoid engaging the lawyer who is prone to be bombastic. Many people gravitate toward such lawyers because they believe that when one fights a war, one does better with huge cannons than with rifles. Some lawyers believe this as well; others put on their bombastic act because they sense that this will attract the client. I try to help my patients appreciate that the most effective way to fight a battle is through calm deliberation and that bombast is often resorted to when one's position is weak. The lawyer who subscribes to the adage "Speak softly and carry a big stick" will generally do a far better job for his client than the one who rants. This is especially true in court. Most judges have greater confidence in lawyers who calmly and firmly press their points than in those given to shouting, clowning, and dramatics. In fact, the judge may be so turned off by such antics that the client's case may be seriously weakened.

The lawyer as therapist and the lawyer as lover.

The relationship between lawyer and client can often be a highly charged one—and this is especially true in divorce cases. The stakes are high; the decisions can affect the whole future course of the client's life. Accordingly, the reliance on the lawyer can be formidable, and the need to deny any deficiencies in him or her may be great. Just as very sick patients may have to believe that their doctors are all-knowing, clients going through a painful and difficult divorce may gain strength from believing their lawyers to be more powerful and knowledgeable than they actually are. The more helpless and weak the clients feel, the more dependent they may become on their lawyers. Some lawyers enjoy the position of power they are then placed in, may play the role convincingly (both to themselves and their clients), and may thereby increase the idolization. The situation does not lend itself well to calm deliberation and effective alleviation of the problems at hand. A client in such a situation may attempt to use the lawyer as a therapist. And the lawyer may be grandiose enough to assume the role. The client will get not only poor therapy (lawyers are not trained for such work) but probably inferior legal representation as well— because the lawyer who does not recognize the boundaries of his or her expertise is likely to be deficient within the confines of his or her calling.

A related problem in the lawyer-client relationship is more common among women than among men. A woman whose husband has left her may turn to her male lawyer as a substitute husband. He lends himself well to this role because he is sympathetic to her position, fights for her cause, and may provide solace. The vast majority of lawyers recognize this tendency on the part of some women and keep their distance. However, a small minority of lawyers enjoy the situation and reciprocate their client's wishes for a deeper involvement. Such reciprocity runs the gamut from the purely psychological involvement, to the affair, to actually marrying the client. Whether the gratifications that ensue are deep and lasting or superficial and short-lived, the situation will generally compromise the lawyer's objectivity and thereby make him less useful to his client. (The situation is similar to the one in which a patient becomes socially involved with his or her therapist. Although what may be going on may be a source of deep satisfaction to both, the therapist's loss of objectivity compromises significantly the therapeutic role.) Accordingly, don't use your own lawyer or therapist as the nucleus of a new social life.

THE LAWYER VS. THE MENTAL HEALTH PROFESSIONAL

A true story epitomizes the kinds of problems that often face the therapist who is invited to be of service in divorce litigation. On many occasions I have received telephone calls from lawyers that go like this: The lawyer first introduces him-

or herself, may mention a referral source, then asks me if I would be interested in testifying in custody litigation. The attorney is often quick to tell me that the welfare of the children is first and foremost and that this consideration supersedes all others. And then the lawyer asks me if I would be willing to consider testifying on behalf of his or her client. Most lawyers appear to see nothing inappropriate in asking me to testify on behalf of a client without my even having had the opportunity to see the father or the mother whom the lawyer is representing and decide whether or not I can support with conviction that party's position. My usual reply at this point: "Suppose, as the result of my evaluation, I conclude that your client should not get the children. Will you still use my testimony in court?" After some pause the lawyer will usually hesitantly respond: "I'm sure you appreciate, Doctor, that my first obligation is to my client; so I couldn't possibly use your testimony." To which I respond: "I thought you said before that your first obligation was to the children." The lawyer will usually mumble and fumble and apologetically (and sometimes angrily) concede that the children's welfare may take second place to the lawyer's obligation to support the client's position.

The adversary system from the therapist's point of view. As this vignette illustrates, lawyers and psychotherapists have difficulties in their relationship with one another. The lawyer is deeply committed to doing everything legally possible to support the client's position. In the service of this goal the attorney is obliged to present to the court all information that will strengthen the client's case and to withhold (as far as is legal and ethical) all data that could harm the client's cause. This obligation arises out of a basic assumption of the adversary system: the assumption that an official body is more likely to learn the "truth" about a dispute by having each side present its case as strongly as it can.

Because of its ancient heritage and the deep inculcation central to most law school curricula, lawyers tend to be somewhat blind to some of the defects of the adversary system. They make the assumption that what may be a workable arrangement in a criminal proceeding will prove useful in other situations where there are conflicting opinions. But even back when the grounds for divorce were considered criminal acts, the system was ill suited to divorce conflicts, because divorce laws required that one party be designated "guilty" and the other "innocent," whereas generally both contributed to the difficulties. If both parties were guilty, or if neither one could be proved so, the divorce was not granted. Nowadays, the traditional grounds for divorce (such as adultery, desertion, or cruelty) are no longer considered crimes, and the adversary structure is even less applicable.

Beyond this general problem of the adversary system, the whole procedure of selective revelation of information is totally antagonistic to the psychotherapist's approach. Therapists work on the principle that they must be free to get as much information as possible from their patients and that nothing should restrain them from gaining any relevant data. Although attorneys, as well, profess that they do best when their clients are completely honest with them, there are certain factors intrinsic to the practice of law that get in the way of this principle. A lawyer, for example, may overtly or covertly encourage the client not to disclose to him or her any information that might compromise the client's position—lest the lawyer be placed in an ethically conflictive situation. A kind of tacit agreement is made between the attorney and client that certain things will not be revealed. Such a conspiracy of silence may be necessary to the maintenance of the lawyer-client relationship. In this way lawyers can rationalize that they are being ethical, can avoid lying to the court, and cannot be considered to be encouraging perjury on the client's part or otherwise permitting a fraud to be perpetrated on the court. And not incidentally, such a conspiracy of silence may be necessary if the lawyer is to keep the client and the attendant fee.

Therapists, however, if they suspect that the patient is withholding information, inquire into the particular matter and help the patient appreciate that a therapist is ill equipped to help if deprived of any information relevant to the patient's difficulties. Although, strictly speaking, it is unethical for an attorney to engage in a conspiracy of silence with a client, the temptation to do so is often present. Therapists have no such temptation and can more easily adhere to the principle that they do best for their patients when the whole truth is known to them.

In certain respects therapists tend to be more naive than lawyers with regard to believing a patient's statements. Generally, therapists expect their patients to be truthful with them. They may at times be doubtful about the validity of a patient's statements; their antennae may be out sensing for deceptions; but usually these are the patient's self-deceptions—things that they are trying to hide from themselves. Most often, patients in treatment do not consciously try to deceive the therapist. Lawyers, however, more frequently expect their clients to be untruthful and routinely assume that their adversaries' clients will be even more so. Having more experience with deception, the attorney may often be more astute than the therapist in detecting it. Accordingly, therapists may be poorly equipped to evaluate patients involved in legal proceedings. For example, a therapist may be evaluating a parent in a custody determination. But perhaps it behooves the parent to withhold (consciously or unconsciously) information that might undercut his or her cause. In this case, the therapist's expectations of honesty and inexperience with deliberate deceit may compromise significantly his or her efficacy.

Therapists generally work in accordance with the principle that if they have no conviction for what they are doing with the patients chances of success in the treatment are likely to be reduced. If, for example, the therapist does not have basic sympathy for the patient's situation, if the relationship is not a good one, or if the therapist is not convinced that the patient's goals in therapy are valid, the likelihood of the patient's being helped is small. Without such conviction the therapy becomes boring and sterile—with little chance of anything constructive coming out of it. The lawyer, in contrast, is deeply imbued from law school days with the notion that the obligation is to serve the client and to do the best possible job, even though the attorney may not be in basic sympathy with the client's position and might prefer to be on the opponent's side. Most law schools require their students to have what they call "moot court" experiences where one is assigned to take a side without regard to whether one is basically convinced of that position. In fact, it is often considered preferable for educational purposes for students to take the side that they are not in sympathy with. Whereas such experiences can be education-ally beneficial, and we can all learn from and become more flexible by being required to view a situation from the opposite vantage point, I believe that lawyers are somewhat naive in believing that one's lack of conviction will not affect the kind of job one does. Each of us works less efficiently when we have little enthusiasm for the purpose of the work. And lawyers cannot but plead less convincingly and fight less ardently for clients whose position they do not basically believe has merit. Although lawyers may try to dissuade clients from pursuing a particular issue that they are not in sympathy with, many if not most will still argue that cause if the client insists.

The lawyer and the therapist both deal with human problems and with disputes between people. The orientation of the therapist, however, is generally that of trying to help the individual change the personality patterns and the behavioral manifestations that contribute to such disputes. Although lawyers may be respectful of and sympathetic to these under-lying processes, their orientation is much more toward struc-tured verbal *conflict* through which one party *wins* and the other *loses*. Accordingly, practitioners of the two professions view divorce litigants very differently and may have great difficulty communicating and working with one another.

Lawyers are often criticized for inflaming their clients, adding to their hostility, and thereby worsening the divorcing spouses' difficulties. But of course, the overwhelming major-ity of divorces are uncontested and do not involve the vicious litigation that incurs these criticisms. It may very well be that over 90 percent of divorces are worked out between the attorneys with a minimum of strife. And of course therapists may not be sought by people whose divorces run smoothly. Therapists may get involved only with those whose problems have interfered with their reaching the compromises necessary to successful resolution of a divorce conflict. Therapists see the people who do not seem to recognize that compromises will ultimately have to be made and that they are best made by the individuals themselves—with the help of lawyers as advisers, not as battle leaders.

I tell my patients that they know their situation best and that they have it within their power to settle their differences themselves. The more they involve themselves with litigation, the more they place their fate in the hands of others, the more helpless they will feel with regard to what is happening to them, and the more psychological suffering they are likely to bring to themselves and their children. Sometimes my advice is heeded; often not. The urge to wreak vengeance is strong, the need not to "let him (or her) get away with it" is deep, the readiness of lawyers to get swept up in the fray is ever present, and the resulting psychological devastation of the family becomes commonplace.

The "no-fault divorce." With increased recognition of the psychological toll of divorce litigation and the inappropriateness of the adversary system to divorce proceedings, many state legislatures in the 1960s and 1970s passed *no-fault divorce laws*. As mentioned, divorce laws used to be based on concepts of guilt and innocence, that is, within the context of punishment and restitution. But in recent years there has been greater appreciation by state legislatures of the fact that the traditional grounds for divorce were not applicable to most marital conflicts. There has been increasing recognition that marital breakdown is caused not simply by wrongs and injustices perpetrated by one party against the other, but that both parties have usually contributed to the marital difficulties. With such realization came the appreciation that adversary proceedings (in which one party is found guilty and the other innocent) are not well suited to deal with marital conflicts. Accordingly, an ever-growing number of states have new statutes that do not require designation of guilty and innocent parties; that is, no one must be considered to be *at fault*. Such statutes provide much more liberal criteria for the granting of a divorce. For example, living apart for a period of time is a commonly acceptable criterion. In most states this period is a year, eighteen months, or two years, but sometimes the prescribed period will be shorter if no children are involved. Some states will grant a divorce on the basis of "incompatibility" or "irreconcilable differences." The terms may not be defined any further and it may be quite easy for the couple to demonstrate that they are incompatible or irreconcilable.

The passage of no-fault divorce laws is, without question, a significant step forward. Divorce, by being removed from adversary proceedings, is more readily, less traumatically, and usually less expensively obtained. However, many no-fault laws require the agreement of *both* parties to satisfy the new liberal criteria. If one party does not agree, then adversary proceedings are necessary. In addition, the new laws have not altered the necessity of resorting to adversary proceedings when there is conflict over such issues as splitting of property, visitation, support, alimony, and custody. Also, in most states, traditional "fault" grounds for divorce, such as adultery, cruelty, or abandonment, still coexist with the "no-fault" laws. Spouses and lawyers may attempt to interject these fault grounds to gain leverage when negotiating over property allocation, alimony, or support. The hope is that the party who is guilty of a marital transgression will give in rather than face the ugliness of a courtroom battle and public disclosure.

One of the unfortunate drawbacks of the new laws has been the dissolution of marriages that might still have been viable if the parties had been motivated to stick it out a little longer. With a little more maturity and realization that every marriage has its necessary adjustments and frustrations, the couples might have remained together—with benefit to both themselves and their children—and avoided all the hardship and long-term damage that results from divorce. The disadvantages of the new liberal laws notwithstanding, I am still strongly in favor of the laws in principle. A few families may be adversely affected by them, but this is no reason to deprive the overwhelming majority of the opportunity to extract themselves relatively easily from the anguish of a failed marriage.

Litigation and counseling: a very poor, if not impossible combination.

Because of the differing orientations of the lawyer and the therapist, counseling a couple contemplating divorce becomes difficult, if not impossible, if either party is consulting a lawyer with a view to litigation. Effective counseling requires a basic degree of honesty among the participants. If patients are being advised by lawyers to withhold certain information from the counseling lest their legal position be weakened, the counseling can become worthless. I generally advise couples that they will be seriously hindering our work if they are simultaneously being advised by lawyers about what they should and should not reveal in our sessions. I tell them that I recognize that by being completely honest in the counseling they may be jeopardizing their future legal positions, but that they must decide themselves if the counseling is important enough for them to take their chances regarding this.

There are therapists who will refuse to counsel people who are simultaneously consulting with lawyers. Although somewhat sympathetic to their position, I am not in agreement. The role of a therapist is to help individuals clarify the issues and consider their various options. The patients make their own decisions after such inquiry. They then learn from the results of their own choices. Refusing to see people who are simultaneously consulting with attorneys robs them of this important therapeutic experience.

Also, just as it is inappropriate for the lawyer to play the role of therapist, a therapist has no business providing legal and financial advice. These are the roles of the lawyer and the accountant. Patients in counseling and therapy should be wary of therapists who are grandiose enough to consider themselves capable of providing such advice. Although many issues pertaining to divorce have both legal and psychological implications, it is generally not difficult to draw the lines where each adviser's expertise ends.

STAYING TOGETHER "FOR THE SAKE OF THE CHILDREN"

Parents contemplating divorce generally give consideration to staying together "for the sake of the children." They generally recognize that their unhappy relationship may very well be detrimental to the children, but they fear that the alternative of divorce will even be more devastating. Accordingly, they may decide to remain together, even though unhappy, in order to protect the children from the harmful effects of a separation. Let's look at some of the issues involved.

Does divorce cause a child to develop psychological disorders? I do not believe that divorce necessarily produces harmful psychological reactions in the child. However, the child of divorce is more likely to develop such reactions than the child who grows up in an intact, relatively secure home. In recent years many studies (some involving large numbers of children) have demonstrated conclusively that there are a wide variety of psychological disturbances resulting from divorce.

It is almost impossible to differentiate the effects on children of the divorce itself from the effects of the sufferings they may endure before, during, and after the parental separation. It is the exposure to a wretched environment over time—rather than the acute trauma of the separation—that causes the child to develop unhealthy psychological reactions. Of course, years of separation from a parent could constitute a chronic psychological trauma; however, it need not be. If the parent who lives away from the home maintains a good, consistent relationship with the child *and* relates reasonably to the former spouse, the child may be spared the development of unhealthy reactions to the divorce.

Certain aspects of the divorce situation do increase the risk that a child will develop psychological difficulties. Obviously, two parents can provide children with far more guidance, sustenance, and protection than one, and are more likely to prevent the kinds of psychological disturbance that may result from deprivations of these necessities. I often compare the need of the child for two parents with the need of the human being for two eyes or two kidneys. Nature seems to have provided us with a "spare" for each of these organs. People who lose one may still get by with the other, although the individual with one eye does lose depth perception, and there may be some compromise of kidney function for the person with only one kidney. The loss of both organs, however, like the loss of both parents, can be devastating. When one parent is temporarily absent from the intact home, it is likely that the other will be available to gratify the child's needs in a loving way. This is not so readily the situation in the divorced home.

In addition, most will agree that children need an intimate relationship with both a male and female adult. A boy needs a father as a model for identification, and a girl needs a mother for the same purpose. The child of each sex has to learn to relate to adults of both sexes if he or she is to get along optimally in life, and growing up in a home with a mother and a father is probably the most effective way to accomplish this. Accordingly, children who are significantly deprived of one parent are more likely than those who have good relationships with two parents to exhibit impairments in their psychological development and interpersonal relations.

There are inevitably times when children are frustrating and a source of resentment to a parent. Having a second parent available in the home lessens the chances that children will suffer during the periods when they are at odds with the first parent. Deprivation of parental affection is one of the most common and predictable causes of childhood psychiatric disturbance. And children of divorce, having only one parent available in the home, are more likely to experience such deprivation.

Last, it is not difficult to see how children of divorce often come to view human relationships as basically unstable. From their vantage point, the significant individuals in one's life may suddenly abandon one forever. With such distrust of human relationships, the offspring of divorced parents tend to show unstable psychological development and often have trouble forming strong emotional bonds.

It is not surprising then that many psychological studies find a greater frequency of psychiatric disorder in children of divorced parents than in those from intact, stable homes. If such children were not found to be a greater risk for the development of psychiatric disturbance, then one would have to reevaluate the assumption that a child's living with two parents is preferable to a child's living with one. The studies, however, indicate that such reevaluation is not warranted.

There does not appear to be any specific kind of disorder produced by marital discord. Similarly, there is no typical psychological disturbance exhibited by children of divorce; rather, there is a whole range of possible reactions, as chapter 4 will explain.

Pros and cons of "staying together." Mental health professionals have conducted numerous studies that attempt to determine whether children are better off living in a home in which the parents are unhappy than in one in which the parents have separated. Such studies are difficult to conduct, and few claim that their results constitute anything like proof. When one studies large groups of children, however, it does appear that *on the whole* children living in an intact but unhappy home suffer more psychological disorder than children living in a peaceful home with only one parent. Nevertheless, it would be a serious error to conclude that unhappily married parents will always do best for their children by splitting up. Even though these studies indicate that *more* children do better in single-parent homes than in unhappy *intact* homes, there were still some children who probably did better in the unhappy intact home than they would have had their parents divorced. One cannot predict which of the two situations would be preferable for a particular child. Although the statistics may support the decision to separate, there are still children in separated and divorced homes who are worse off than they would have been had the parents remained together.

There are mental health professionals who recommend that parents not consider the divorce's effects on the children when making their decision. They suggest that the parents make the decision as if the children were not being affected. Although they agree that the outcome may harm the children, they consider concern for the children's welfare to be a contaminant to decision making and advise the parents to make the best choice for them and to hope that what will be in their best interests will be in the children's as well.

My own belief is that the effects on the children should be one of the considerations in the divorce decision, but not the major one. The major determinant should be whether the parents feel that there is enough pain in their relationship to warrant its being broken. However, in addition to considering the frustrations and privations each will suffer following the separation and divorce, they should also try to imagine the effects on their children. They should not just assume that their children will be better off it they divorce, or that whatever will be best for them will automatically be best for the children as well.

Sometimes parents will claim that they are staying together "for the sake of the children," when in reality the relationship is being maintained for other reasons—such as fear of the unknown, fear of criticism of relatives and friends, reluctance to suffer the financial pressures that the divorce will entail, fear of being alone, fear of the increased responsibilities that will result from the divorce, and so on. Professions of concern for the children may even be rationalizations to buttress various psychopathological interactions. For example, the couple may have a sadomasochistic relationship in which one partner gets morbid gratification from suffering pain and the other has a pathological need to inflict it. Or one may need a marital partner who serves as a parental figure while the other enjoys infantilizing the spouse. Or perhaps both are basically fearful of sexual encounters and would be made anxious by a more sexually assertive partner. The couple may complain bitterly about their frustrations with one another and vow that if not for the children they would have split long ago. But actually, the children may be serving as a convenient excuse for their staying together and maintaining the sick gratifications that they provide one another without their having to admit that this is the case.

James and Carol's situation provides an example. Carol had always been a shy girl who dated infrequently. She met James when she was in nursing school and he was a medical student. From as early as the first grade James had always been an obsessive student, invariably being among the highest in his class but never having many friends. James and Carol married when James graduated from medical school, and she worked in nursing to supplement his small salary as an intern and resident in surgical training. Throughout this period they saw little of one another because of the long hours of work that James's training required. And when James was home he was absorbed in studying his medical books and journals.

When James opened his practice, Carol quit her job and began having children. Again, building up a practice kept James away from the home for long periods. He gradually gained the reputation of being one of the most dedicated doctors on the hospital staff. No patient's problem was too small for him to give his complete attention. He was not only devoted to caring for his patients' surgical needs but spent much time with them as well, reassuring and counseling them and discussing in detail other matters that they would confide to him. Nurses and patients alike commented admiringly how he was one of the first doctors to arrive in the morning and one of the last to leave. Meanwhile, back at the ranch house, Carol completely devoted herself to the upbringing of their children. She and James had little social life, because they never knew when James would have an emergency. Since they were living in a town distant from both of their families, there was little contact with relatives either.

My first contact with the family came when Linda, the oldest of their children, developed severe facial tics and grew obsessed with fears that harm might befall her parents, especially her father. Her fears for her father's welfare became especially prominent when his work load was particularly heavy—when, for example, he had to work all day Sunday, rather than his usual half day. I considered Linda's symptoms to be related to the anger she felt both toward her father, for essentially abandoning her, and toward her mother, who, although attentive and caring, was not a very warm or affectionate person. The anger could not be directly expressed, and as it built up Linda became tense—and her tension caused her facial tics. Obsessive fears often reflect unconscious hostile wishes. Although consciously Linda very much wanted her father to be safe, another part of her was deeply angry at him. Experiencing her angry thoughts as fears lessened the guilt she would have felt if she accepted such thoughts as desires.

In my interviews with James, it became apparent that he had little interest in Carol. He found her dull and boring. Their sex life was practically nonexistent. He had affairs from time to time that provided him with an adequate sexual outlet, though denied any deep emotional involvement with any of these other women. Yes, he had thought of separation but felt that it would be bad for the children, even though he admitted that they might see more of a stepfather than they were seeing of him.

Carol saw no problems with her marriage. She denied any resentment over James's long absences from the home, stating that she knew when she married him that she would be leading this kind of life. She had never had strong sexual urges and so was quite content that James didn't "bother her" about sex. She considered the possibility that he might be involved with other women, especially when he would come home at two or three in the morning after "emergency operations," but denied any jealousy. She did not fear that he might leave her for another woman, because she did not see him as the kind of man who got emotionally involved with women in that way. Yes, James had talked to her on occasion about separation, but she could not see why he would want to, considering that this might be upsetting to the children.

It was clear that James and Carol were two people who were essentially remote from others and from one another.

Psychologically they had never really been married. They were incapable of involving themselves deeply with one another or with their children—and this was especially true of James. When I asked James if he could see a way to spend more time with the children, he made feeble attempts to do so. However, his medical obligations always seemed to pull at him, and he was soon back to his original schedule. Carol too was unable to relax enough to cuddle, play with, or involve herself more with her children. I finally recommended that the parents hire a very warm housekeeper as well as a teenager to come and play with the children a few times a week. In addition, I worked with Linda and attempted to help her to recognize and accept her parents' emotional deficiencies, to get what affection she could from them when it was available, and to seek compensatory gratifications elsewhere from both peers and adults. Under this program there was a diminution of her anger and the symptoms that were caused by it.

It was clear that, for James and Carol, staying together for the children's sake served as an excuse to remain in a marital situation that each was essentially comfortable with. Both being quite distant people, they would have been made anxious by partners who were capable of deeper involvements.

Effects of separation on children at different ages.

Some mental health professionals consider there to be certain periods in a child's life when a divorce can be particularly harmful. Accordingly, they suggest that parents contemplating divorce wait until a child has passed the particular developmental period before separating. Some consider the period that psychoanalysts refer to as the oedipal phase to be a time when children are particularly vulnerable to the effects of separation. This is the period, usually between ages three and five, when a child develops a strong possessive attachment to the opposite-sexed parent and a desire to take over the role of the same-sexed parent. At times the attraction can take on mildly sexual overtones, and the child may demonstrate rivalrous hostility toward the parent of the same sex. The sexual desires are generally not for intercourse but for more generalized physical-sexual gratification. For example, a boy may become very affectionate with his mother, become hostile toward his father, and even entertain wishes that the father leave the home so that he will have his mother all to himself. A girl may entertain similar possessive fantasies toward her father and jealous resentment toward her mother.

According to the theory, healthy children pass through this phase without incident and grow up to direct their attentions toward more appropriate and available love objects. If, however, a parent leaves the home during this period, the child may develop what some psychoanalysts call oedipal problems. The little boy, for example, may believe that his father left because the boy wished he would do so. Accordingly, the child may develop unrealistic ideas about the power of his wishes and guilt over bringing about such a catastrophe in his home. He may develop feelings of inferiority because he is not capable of assuming all the responsibilities he believes are his, now that he has won possession of his mother over his rival. And the daughter of such a father may develop difficulties in her relationships with males, both present and future, because her basic model for males is not so readily available. Males become to her strange creatures with whom she cannot relate in a comfortable manner. Or she may come to expect rejection from males. Similarly, when it is the mother who leaves the household, her daughters may develop the kinds of problems related to the fantasy that they have won the oedipal rivalry, and her sons may develop the kinds of difficulties that may result when a female figure is not available to them. An extension of this theory holds that there is a reactivation of the oedipal conflict in the early- to mid-adolescent period. Accordingly, this phase is also considered to be one in which the youngster is especially vulnerable to the psychological effects of parental separation.

Some claim that the couple should wait until the youngest child has started school. In this way, the mother will not be left with the burden of having to take care of young children at home and will have greater opportunity to earn money and to avail herself of various activities that may enrich her life and compensate her for the pains and frustrations of the divorce. Others advise parents not to separate at the time school starts, because then the child is exposed to two separations simultaneously.

On the basis of my own experiences as a therapist I am not convinced that there are particular periods during which the child is especially vulnerable to the effects of parental separation. Rather, I believe that from the day of birth the child needs both parents and that the removal of either is likely to have harmful effects on a child's psychological development. Although a boy may not need his father as a model for identification during the first few months of life, he does from then on, possibly even until the time that the father dies. I do not see the three- to five-year-old period or adolescence to be particularly crucial with regard to such identification; rather I view identification as a continuing process that may taper off in late adolescence and early adulthood but that may continue to a lesser degree throughout a person's life.

With regard to the little boy's interest in his mother, I believe that her role as the model woman begins at his birth and continues throughout life. Because she is the model to which all other women are compared, her loss can result in difficulties in the boy's relationship with females. The earlier the boy is deprived of his father and/or his mother, the greater the likelihood that psychological disorder will result. With regard to the girl, I believe the same considerations hold. The earlier a girl is deprived of her father, the greater the chances she will have difficulties relating to men. Similarly, the earlier she is deprived of her mother, the greater the likelihood she will not only suffer problems in identification with females, but other difficulties as well—difficulties associated with the generalized emotional deprivation resulting from the mother's loss. For both the boy and the girl, I am in agreement that parental loss during the oedipal and adolescent period can be very detrimental; but I am not convinced that parental loss during these periods is more harmful than loss during other phases.

One fundamental reason for my belief that younger children suffer more from a divorce than older ones is based on the child's ability to understand what is actually happening when parents divorce: the younger the child, the less the child's understanding. The child is therefore more likely to develop a wide variety of cognitive distortions; that is, distortions and misconceptions about reality. And these cognitive distortions contribute to the development of psychological problems. Older children, being more conversant with the world, are less likely to develop such distortions and are therefore less likely to develop psychiatric problems attendant to the divorce.

Another factor is that younger children, by virtue of their age, are far more dependent on parents than older ones. The sense of impotence that they feel cannot but contribute to the development of psychiatric difficulties. An older child, especially an adolescent, moves much more independently following a separation. For example, when a divorced father is late to pick up his three-year-old for a visit, the child may pace nervously back and forth, hoping that Daddy will come soon. And the disappointment the child may feel if the father does not appear—especially if such failures to appear are frequent—may be profound and can contribute to the development of psychological disturbances. In contrast, adolescents after waiting a reasonable period, can take off on their own. Adolescents have much more freedom to acquire and avail themselves of substitute gratifications, making them less vulnerable to the psychological difficulties that younger children may suffer.

In general, I believe that the younger the children are when the loss occurs and the longer they are exposed to the loss, the greater the harmful effects may be. However, I do not suggest that parents wait until the children get older so that they may be less affected by the separation. I explain that I believe that the older the children are at the time of separation the more opportunity they will have had for the beneficial effects of living with two parents. However, I quickly add that the parents must take into consideration the harmful effects of an unhappy home, as well as the many other factors of importance in making their decision. I do not recommend that they consider the ages of the children to be the most critical issue.

Even if there were certain critical periods in children's lives, it is not likely that trying to avoid those periods would be useful or practical for most families. Most families have two or more children, so it is likely that after one child passed the critical period, a younger child would be entering it. It is possible that parents who took such advice very seriously and decided to stay together until all the children had passed beyond the various critical phases might have to wait ten to fifteen years before getting a divorce.

A more serious reason why the critical-period theory is misguided is that it fails to take into account other considerations that are important at the time when a couple is contemplating divorce. It may have taken the parents many years to have reached the point where they have finally decided to separate—the point where the pain of their remaining together outweighs its advantages. To advise such parents to maintain their relationship for months and even years to allow a child to grow past a critical phase gives priority to a theoretical and unproven need of the child over an actual need of the parents. Heeding the advice may result in years of further misery. And if the parents do not follow the advice, they may add an additional burden to the guilt they already suffer over the effects the divorce may have on their children. In addition, it is quite common for one or both parties already to have become deeply involved with a third person. By following advice to wait, the parties may miss the opportunity for a new relationship that could serve to lessen some of the pains associated with the divorce.

PARENTAL PRESEPARATION SHAME AND GUILT

Guilt and shame are two different things. *Shame* can be defined as the feeling of low self-worth that one experiences when one is "discovered" doing an unacceptable thing. It requires an audience of finger pointers. *Guilt* also involves a sense of low self-worth; but with guilt the "finger pointer" is oneself. A feeling of guilt doesn't require an audience of accusers.

Shame over counseling. Even in this so-called enlightened time, some parents are quite ashamed to seek predivorce counseling with a therapist. Those who are considering counseling would do well to appreciate that the benefits that they can potentially derive more than outweigh any embarrassment or other discomfort they may experience as a result of the experience. In addition, such parents should appreciate that it is often more courageous to admit that one has psychological difficulties and needs the assistance of a trained impartial person than to deny one's difficulties.

Shame over telling the children about the real reasons for the separation. A parent may not wish to tell the children about the true reasons for a divorce because of shame. Most commonly an extramarital affair is the reason which the parent is ashamed to disclose. Other problems, such as alcoholism, obsessive gambling, and drug addiction, are common causes of divorce that may also be a source of great shame to the afflicted parent. In the latter cases the children are usually aware of the problem anyway. And when an affair is the cause, they may or may not have become aware.

Because I believe (as discussed in chapter 2) that children should be given information about the *major issues* that brought about the separation—and I would consider infidelity to be in that category—I hold that the parent does the child a disservice when withholding such vital information. To help reduce the parent's sense of shame, I generally try to help the parent appreciate some of the problems with the word infidelity. Strictly speaking, it refers to one's being unfaithful or disloyal. If the infidelity was the result of significant difficulties in the marital relationship and was an attempt to gain some solace and affection when there was little at home, then I try to help the parent appreciate that the affair was human and almost predictable. If the faithful spouse exhibits condemning intolerance for the infidelity (and especially if it was an infrequent occurrence and/or unassociated with deep involvement), and if that spouse is unwilling to try to work out any problems that may have contributed to such infidelity, then I try to explain to the unfaithful spouse the inappropriateness of the partner's attitudes. I describe to the parents what I consider to be the social, moral, and religious condemnation that is the lot of the unfaithful.

And I try to impress upon both parties that human beings' desire for variety is deep-seated and that marriage demands a greater degree of tolerance for frustration of desires for variety than practically any other situation. Some people are willing to accept the frustrations associated with the inhibition of their desires for sexual variety because they are not willing to tolerate the repercussions of infidelity. Others choose to gratify these desires, either openly or secretly, to greater or lesser degrees. In short, I try to lessen shame to the point where the parent is willing to divulge the infidelity to the children as a reason for the divorce. This is not to say that I suggest necessarily divulging the identity of the individual or individuals involved, or details of the parents' sexual life—either with each other or with the third party(ies). There may still be some shame left, and appropriately so, because, whatever the circumstances, a trust has been broken.

In sum, my aim is to lessen exaggerated and inappropriate shame to the point where the parent can provide the children with a proper degree of information concerning the reasons for the separation.

The healthy, concerned parent feels guilty about the separation. Most parents feel significantly guilty about a divorce. They generally appreciate that no matter how much they and their children may benefit from the divorce, the children are still likely to suffer. Perhaps they will suffer less than they would have had the marriage remained intact, but the children will still experience certain deprivations. There is a sense of guilt not only over what has gone before (the preseparation parental conflict) but over what is to come (the harmful effects of living in a home without one of the parents.) But we have to expect some feelings of guilt. In fact, if a parent did not feel some guilt over the divorce, I would consider there to be a deficiency in that parent's affection for the children and/or an unrealistic understanding of the potentially harmful effects of the divorce on the children.

There are therapists who take the position that it behooves them to reduce guilt feelings in their patients, regardless of the guilt's source or appropriateness. They may even believe that all guilt is pathological. I am in sharp disagreement with this position. I believe that the therapist should make differentiations between guilt that is appropriate and inappropriate, that is warranted and unwarranted. After all, without guilt we would not have civilized society. Without guilt there would be anarchy; the world would be a predatory place where people would impose themselves on others with little concern for the effects of their behavior. There are, of course, people with an exaggerated sense of guilt, and therapists have to help them reduce their inordinate feeling of guilt. But there are others who do not have enough guilt. It behooves a therapist to help these people feel *more* guilty. I believe that one of the world's problems is that not enough people have enough guilt. If a patient does not exhibit any guilt whatever over a separation, then, the therapist should do whatever possible to help the person understand the impact of his or her past and present actions.

Reducing excessive guilt over separation. When counseling parents I attempt to help them differentiate between two kinds of guilt. I compare them with the man who buys an automobile and because of a manufacturing defect has an accident in which someone is hurt. This driver is treated quite differently by the courts from the one who purposely injures someone with his car. The first man is not considered a criminal, whereas the second is. Although the victim's pains and injuries may be identical, and it may make little difference to him or her whether the injuries were accidentally or purposely caused, the appropriateness of guilt in the two situations is very different. I often try to help parents appreciate that their marriage was an error and that the suffering their mistake has brought to them and their children resulted from a well-meaning but ill-advised union. In some situations the marriage may not initially have been a mistake, but the partners have grown apart. They may have been quite compatible at first, but one spouse may have matured more than the other, or both may have developed in different directions. I try to help such partners appreciate that this is another kind of mistake that might not have been anticipated or prevented. I try to reassure them that to the best of my knowledge they have both endeavored to do what they considered best for their children. I attempt to impress upon the parents that I see them as similar to the man driving the car with the factory defect. Although it may be true that the victim would not have been injured had the man not been driving the car at that time, it is also true that the driver was in no way at fault. Neither the driver nor the separating couple inflicted pain through malicious intent.

I do not stop there, however. I try to impress upon the parents that the best thing they can do to reduce their guilt is to take constructive action to interrupt any perpetuation of an unhealthy atmosphere to which they may have been exposing their children. They must do everything possible to help their children pick up the pieces and make the best of a difficult situation. To the degree that they can actively contribute to the improvement of their children's situation, their sense of guilt will be reduced. If the parents continue to embroil the children in their problems (if that has been the case), then they can expect the children to continue suffering and can anticipate a continuation of their own guilt.

Many parents are so swept up in their antagonisms that they lose sight of the effects of the conflict on their children. For most, however, the fighting finally dies down, and then parents may see for the first time how harmful the hostilities have been. One could argue that I am providing such parents with unnecessary additional guilt with my warnings. I am producing guilt; but I believe it is justified. There are many individuals whose psychological difficulties include a deficiency in guilt-producing mechanisms—with the result that many around them suffer needlessly. Fostering a consciousness of guilt in some divorcing parents may not only help them reduce their incessant conflicts but can have a healthy effect on their children as well.

Encouraging therapy to reduce guilt. Reasons for entering or recommending therapy may vary—and some reasons are invalid. Sometimes a husband (often previously unreceptive to his wife's going into treatment) will encourage such a step around the time of the separation. Generally, the husband's change of heart is not particularly motivated by the desire for his wife to gain increased insight into her underlying psychological processes but by his desire to lessen his guilt over leaving her. (Although it is less common, a woman who initiates the separation may encourage her husband's involvement in treatment for the same reason.) The husband may fear that his wife will fall apart; he hopes that if he puts his wife "into good hands," the therapist will prevent the impending calamity. Or he may hope that the therapist will substitute for him and help fill the void in the wife's life. Wives themselves often consciously or unconsciously seek therapy for this reason. If this is the primary motive for a wife's being in treatment, the likelihood of anything beneficial coming out of the therapy is quite small. Therapists' primary role is to provide therapy. If, incidental to that function, they provide some solace from the pains of loneliness, fine. If solace, however, is a therapist's primary function, the patient is paying a heavy price for something that she might obtain equally well and at no cost from a friend.

Using money to reduce guilt. Although divorce imposes formidable economic hardships on the majority of parents, there are some who will use money in an attempt to assuage the guilt they feel. Of course such guilt alleviation is most readily utilized by the wealthy. Alimony laws in most states are particularly well suited to assist wealthy individuals. We are all familiar with the astronomical settlements, common among the rich, that enable the woman to live in the style to which she was previously accustomed. The wives of very rich men can generally be relied upon to help their husbands reduce their guilt in this way. But even poorer individuals may offer (or allow to be taken) more money than they can reasonably afford in order to lessen their guilt. Again, alimony laws generally help implement, and wives can generally be counted upon to comply with, an offering based upon psychopathological guilt feelings.

Getting the children's permission to separate.

There are occasional parents who will actually ask their children for *their* opinion as to whether the parents should divorce. Since the children will be directly affected by the divorce, such parents argue, they should have a democratic say in it. I am not a believer in such a democratic system, believing as I do that the judgment of children is not as good as that of most adults. Often, such parents are essentially asking for the children's permission. The hope is that this permission will lessen the parents' guilt over the breakup of the home. Others who are frightened of anyone's anger—regardless of the age of the angry person or the appropriateness of the anger—may ask permission in the hope that the children will not be angry. Such children may have long since learned of the parents' ultrasensitivity to their angry responses, and so they may comply with the parental wish that no anger be expressed. Accordingly, they may provide the permission and squelch their real disapproval, lest they hurt their parents even more. Healthy parents recognize the inevitability of children's angry responses to divorce and have enough personality strength to tolerate such hostility.

2

Telling the Children

As with many issues surrounding divorce, the problem of telling the children has no simple answers. As a general rule, however, parents should appreciate that they do their children more harm by withholding information than by revealing it. Children are far less fragile than many parents appreciate.

HOW AND WHEN TO TELL THEM

In my experience, children are usually very much aware that their parents are unhappy. Still, there are many questions about just when and how to break the news of divorce.

How old the children should be before being told. Is there a certain age below which children are too young and/or psychologically fragile to tolerate the news of parental separation? This question reminds me of a question asked an ear, nose, and throat specialist who was an instructor of mine in medical school. A student asked: "How old should a baby be before one would prescribe a hearing aid?" The instructor's response: "If it were a breech delivery, I would wait until the head came out." Obviously, one cannot tell a newborn infant, or one a few months old, about a parent's forthcoming separation from the home. I would, however, allow a toddler access to such conversations with older children. Certainly by eight to nine months of age most babies differentiate their parents from strangers and, I believe, are significantly affected by a parent's departure from the home. The child who is old enough to recognize the existence of a parent is old enough to be told (at whatever level of communication is proper) that that parent will no longer be living in the home. The fact that the child may not be able to comprehend fully the import of what is being said is no justification for not trying to impart the information. The child is entitled to the message, and it will be appreciated at some level, no matter how primitive.

The situation is analogous to providing children with information about sex. Most mental health professionals agree that children who are old enough to ask a question about sex, are old enough to get an answer commensurate with their developmental level and capacity to understand the response. A three- to four-year-old who asks about how babies are born might be told about the growth of the baby in the mother's "belly" and its birth through the vagina. One would not, of course, attempt full explanations of anatomy, menstrual cycles, and so on. More important than the child's understanding is the child's experience that the question has been answered honestly. The child thereby comes to view the parents as people who can be relied upon to provide direct and honest answers to these important questions. The child will have plenty of time to question the parents again in the future and correct any misunderstandings. But what cannot be easily rectified are the psychological effects of parents' not responding openly and honestly to sexual questions. It is in a secretive or dishonest atmosphere that guilt and inhibition are created— attitudes that are the foundation of many sexual problems. Similarly, for children whose parents are separating, if the children are old enough to appreciate that one of the parents is no longer going to live in the household or are old enough to ask about the absent parent's whereabouts, they are old enough to be given an honest explanation.

There are parents who do not tell preschoolers (or occasionally even older children) about an impending separation because "they're too young to understand." This excuse is often a way to avoid the embarrassment or guilt the parents would feel upon revealing to the children their plans to separate. By convincing themselves that the children are too young to understand what is happening, they do not have to face the children's tears and pleas for the parents to reconsider. Some parents justify withholding the information with the excuse that young children would be so pained by the disclosure that psychological damage might result. Again, the excuse is actually a means to enable the parents to avoid the psychological discomforts they might suffer by revealing the separation. Furthermore, such withholding is shortsighted. The children ultimately will learn of and appreciate the parental separation. In some cases, children may never be told, with the parents' continually providing excuses for the absent parent's failure to live in the household: "He's away on business," or "The place where he lives now is closer to work." But the immediate pain of learning of a coming separation is far less traumatic psychologically than the anxieties associated with an atmosphere of secretiveness. If the divorce is kept secret, the children see that things are not right, but because they have not been given any information about what has gone wrong, they generally view the situation as worse than it really is. Furthermore, their trust in the parents is reduced at a time when they can least afford it.

When they should be told. The timing of the announcement is another issue. Telling children long in advance may provide them with the opportunity to adjust to and work through their reactions with the departing parent still available. It is a generally accepted psychological principle that it is preferable to work out a problem one may have with another individual in a setting in which one has direct access to that person. For example, it is extremely difficult, if not impossible, to resolve completely problems one may have had with a parent who has died. There is no opportunity for feedback, compromise, or experiences that correct distortions. While the parent is still in the home and available to them, children not only have greater opportunity for discussing their questions and reactions to the forthcoming separation, but can have living experiences that mean far more than words. For example, a father who is preparing to leave may tell the children that he still loves them and will continue to love them after moving to the new home. This statement is far more convincing when the children have had the living experience that the father is still relating in a loving way—and this is best accomplished while he is still living with the children. They will be left with greater confidence that his affection will be maintained after the departure.

An analogy with the death of a loved one is applicable here. If one has advance notice, one has the opportunity for anticipatory mourning, and this increases the likelihood that one will adjust adequately and in a reasonable period after the person dies. When there has been no expectation—when one has been shocked by the news—the grieving period becomes more difficult. Because it is the purpose of grieving to help the survivor adjust to the death, anything that hinders its progress interferes with the bereaved person's ability to become accustomed to the loss.

However, long periods between the divorce announcement and the actual departure may serve to deepen and fix the child's denial mechanisms. Observing the departure makes it harder for the child to deny its occurrence. But when a long time elapses after the announcement of the separation, it is easy for the child to conclude that the departure will not take place. In addition, younger children do not appreciate time passage the same way adults do, so significant advance notice is of little value. To a two- or three-year-old there is little difference between five weeks and five years. It is similar to the adult's trying to comprehend the difference between stars five trillion miles and fifty trillion miles away. Furthermore, a long waiting period may prolong children's agony and thereby increase their chances of developing psychological disturbances.

Giving the children extremely short notice does have the advantage of reducing the painful waiting period. However, it may deprive the children of the opportunity to work through their reactions and desensitize themselves to the trauma. There are some parents who tell the children at the last possible moment, ostensibly to shorten the children's grief as much as possible. My experience has been that in such cases it is more likely the parental agony that is of concern. With bags packed, the departing parent informs the children that he or she is leaving—and then rushes out of the house. Concern for the welfare of the children and "getting it over quickly" for their benefit is used as an excuse for covering up parental cowardice, shame, and lack of concern for the children's need to work through the separation. Any advantages there may have been to getting it over quickly are more than counterbalanced by the disadvantages of depriving the children of the opportunity to work out their reactions in advance.

Usually the most appropriate time to tell the children is when a *definite* decision for separation has been made. I emphasize the word definite because it is cruel and psychologically detrimental to subject children to the numerous tentative decisions that often precede the final one. Most couples go through many such cycles before making their final decision. These cycles of dashed and then raised hopes can only be psychologically harmful to children. It is as if a ticking time bomb were placed in the house and the children never knew if and when it would explode. Of course there may be instances when the parents have made a definite decision to separate, tell the children about it, and then decide to try again to salvage the marriage. The children must be told about the changed plan, and they will probably not suffer from one such cycle. The more frequent the cycles become, however, the greater the likelihood of increased traumas. If the parents have decided upon a trial separation, the child should be told about this. Although this presents the danger of the back-and-forth situation, their not being told may result in new problems arising—problems relating to loss of trust and other effects of parental secretiveness and dishonesty.

If the time between the decision to separate and the actual time of separation is to be long (many weeks, or even months), then one might wish to withhold the information until a few weeks prior to the separation. This is justifiable in that it protects the children from prolongation of their pain and yet provides them with an adequate opportunity for working through their reactions.

Because of the range and variations in the capacity for human beings to adjust to a trauma, one cannot have any hard-and-fast rules regarding the optimum time between disclosure and departure. But there is less danger in the child's being told in advance, and much to argue for it. And a few weeks in advance appears to be the optimum time for this disclosure in most families.

Who should tell them? I have found that it is preferable for the parents together to tell the children. Such an approach lessens the likelihood that one parent will try to make the other solely responsible. Although there certainly are divorces in which one parent is more responsible than the other for the deterioration of the marriage, the more common situation, in my experience, is that both partners have contributed. The children's erroneously thinking that the separation was caused by only one parent can contribute to some psychological difficulties. Also, both parents' telling can help lessen the inevitable insecurities that befall children at such a time. Implicit in the fact that both parents are providing the painful information is the notion that, although soon to be separated, they will both continue to be available. Having two parents available for consultation, support, and discussion is certainly better than having just one and may lessen the chances that the children will feel abandoned. In addition, when both parents conduct the discussion, the stage is set for similar talks with each one of them alone in the future. Each one at that point is establishing a reputation for being receptive to and available for such conversations.

Sometimes one parent may want the other one to tell the children. At times the reluctant parent is ashamed of what may be revealed, fearful of the children's probable angry response, or guilt-ridden over the impending separation. Such a parent may also try to talk the other parent into withholding vital information from the children. (Generally, this is done in the service of preserving the uncommunicative parent's image.) Sometimes a parent who wishes to provide more information complies with the withholding parent's demands because of passive dependency on the spouse. Although recognizing the value of the disclosure, the parent is too fearful of invoking the anger of the partner to do what would be in the best interests of the children.

I generally advise the parent who still wishes to communicate such information to consider doing so. That is, the main issues of the separation should be divulged to the children. One need not provide every specific detail, but only those general issues that explain the cause(s) of the separation. The parent who withholds information from the children (information that they should know if they are to deal optimally with the separation) in order to protect the image of the spouse is doing the children and the spouse a disservice. Such "protection" causes the children to lose trust in the parent who is withholding the vital information (because they generally sense that the parent is holding back) and confuses them about the parent whose real or imagined failings are being covered up.

How should they be told? The best arrangement is for both parents to sit down with all the children together and tell them about the impending separation. There are some who believe that children are best told separately because different age levels require explanations of varying sophistication. Although I agree that separate explanations may very well be necessary, I think these can be provided in the presence of the other children. Although it may take more time to repeat the explanation in order to adapt to the children's various levels of appreciation, there is much to be gained by the children's hearing the news together. They gain a sense of closeness with one another, and this sense of closeness is especially important at the time of impending parental separation. Being told separately, too, invariably involves children's "comparing notes" and the likelihood of errors being introduced.

Separate discussions create an atmosphere of secretiveness and distrust toward the parents. The child who is waiting outside is not likely to accept the explanation that he or she is not old enough to understand what is being told an older sibling behind locked doors. The child is more likely to conclude that things are being withheld that he or she would like to know—and has a right to know. Or the child may conclude that he or she is being talked about—not an unreasonable conclusion when one is prevented from being party to a conversation. From this secretiveness develops distrust of the parents and even the siblings. At this time the children can ill afford further compromises in their relationships with their parents. Telling them together avoids this drawback.

If, in the attempt to avoid these consequences of separate discussions, the parents decide to tell each child at a time when the others are not around, difficult logistics may be required. Even if this difficulty is overcome, the chance of A saying something to B before the parents do is great. (Children, like adults, are not famous for their abilities to keep secrets or withhold burning information.) This system, then, contains the risk of the child's being told first by a sibling, rather than by a parent—a situation that is bound to undermine the child's confidence in the parents.

Many parents hesitate to involve themselves in such discussions for fear that they will break down in front of their children. A parent may exclaim, "I just don't want them to see me crying; it will just make them even more upset." There are even professionals who advise parents to make sure that they tell the children at a time when they are so composed that they will not show how upset they are, lest the children become upset as well. I believe that this advice is naive and misguided. Dealing with divorce (for both parents and children) is an experience analogous to grieving after a death. Vital to adequate grieving is the expression of the various feelings that inevitably arise. The parents must serve as models for the children. If the parents hold back their feelings, the children are likely to as well; and bottled-up thoughts and feelings are among the most common causes of psychological problems. Parents do well then to express, in moderation, the emotional reactions they have to the separation.

I am not suggesting that the parents begin telling the children about the forthcoming separation at a time when they are overwhelmed by their feelings. It is preferable that they wait until their feelings are at a relatively low level and they can discuss the situation with some degree of objectivity. However, they should appreciate that their expression of emotion *in front of their children* can be a healthy experience for all concerned. It is healthy for the parents because they are expressing their feelings and thereby lessening the chances that they will develop psychological problems in reaction to the separation. And it is healthy for the children because their parents' example will enhance the likelihood of the children's expressing their emotions as well. Of course hysterical outbursts are not in order. This would be substituting one inappropriate way of handing emotions with another.

Some parents hesitate to discuss the reasons for the divorce with the children lest their bitter, angry feelings toward the spouse be revealed. They fear that such expression will undermine the child's respect for and relationship with the partner. But as I've noted, children are usually already aware of anger between the parents; it is rare for the separation to come as an absolute surprise. Furthermore, if no angry feelings are exhibited, then the child may wonder why the parents are getting separated. Such suppression can only serve as a model for the children to suppress their own anger, and inhibition of anger is a common cause of psychological trouble. Finally, children who grow up in an atmosphere in which they have been protected from criticisms of a parent may develop unrealistic views about that parent, and this will interfere with their identification process, as well as their ability to relate healthily to others.

WHAT SHOULD THEY BE TOLD?

Be appropriately truthful. Parents do best when they describe to their children the *basic reasons* for the divorce. It is surprising how frequently parents do not provide their children with this important information. I believe that some of the disturbances that children of divorced parents suffer result from the fact that their parents, often with the best intentions and even supported by professional authority, are not *appropriately* truthful about the divorce. I use the word *appropriately* because parents' lives should not be an open book to their children. Still, many parents hide from their children things that, if disclosed, would help them deal more effectively with the separation. Such information is usually withheld because the parents think its divulgence would be psychologically harmful to their children.

When telling the children about the forthcoming separation, it is important that parents communicate *concrete* information rather than vague statements. For example, the children should be told (to the degree possible) exactly when the departing parent will leave and exactly where he or she is going to live. As early as possible, the children should have the opportunity to visit the new home of the departing parent. Optimally this should be done before that parent's departure. Having a mental image of exactly where the departing parent will be going lessens anxieties—especially abandonment anxieties. Detailed information should also be provided (if possible) regarding the planned frequency of visitation and the settings in which the visits will occur. This kind of information can also help the children feel more secure about a continuing relationship with the parent who is leaving the home. If the custodial parent and the children are planning to move (to a smaller apartment or to the home of grandparents, for example) the children should be given as much detailed information as possible (when, where, etc.). Furthermore, the children should be told that a telephone will be available and that direct communication will be given the highest priority.

The effects of deceit on children. Children are much more capable of accepting painful realities than is generally appreciated. What is difficult for them to handle (and this is true for adults as well) are the anxieties associated with ignorance and parental furtiveness; fantasies run free and the worst anticipations can be neither confirmed nor refuted. Truth, even though painful, produces trust and gives children the security of knowing exactly what is happening to them. They are then in a better position to handle situations effectively.

If the parents are being deceptive—even though well meaning—regarding the primary reasons for the separation the children will sense the parental dishonesty. This will undermine their trust in the parents at a time when they are most in need of a trusting and secure relationship with them. In addition, deception creates a new burden for the parents. Generally, one lie begets another. If, for example, the children are told that Daddy is away on a business trip, new lies must be created to explain the failure of the father to return, and as time goes on these become even less credible. When the children learn the truth (and they ultimately do), they are bound to become disillusioned with those who have lied to them about such an important issue. But a child's basic trusting relationship with his or her parents is at the foundation of healthy personality development. Parental dishonesty can predictably shake this foundation.

In the situation in which parents provide little or no information about the separation, the children become curious about the causes. They may question each parent alone and gradually extract information. They may then compare notes with one another. Whatever excitement there may be to such an investigation, having to gain information in this way can only be humiliating to the children. It is as if they have become spies on their parents. Furthermore, the chance of their accurately determining what has been going on is small, and with false and distorted data they will be less equipped to cope adequately with the situation.

Consider a case reported by a colleague of mine. Rather

than tell her three-year-old daughter that her parents were separated, the mother informed the child that her father had gone to work in another city and would not be returning home. The child's first assumption was that she and her mother would soon join the father. She repeatedly asked the mother, "When are we going to Daddy?" As time passed and such a visit did not materialize, the child began to assume that her father was dead and entered into a mourning period. She stopped asking questions and began repeating to her dolls, "My daddy's dead. I'll never see him any more." Although the mother knew that sooner or later there would be some contact with the father, she did not correct the child's mistake.

Suddenly, one day, the father appeared. The little girl went into a state of shock. She became apathetic and listless and demonstrated no affection for him. Whereas previously she had been gay and outgoing, she became withdrawn. The experience was totally incomprehensible to the child—it was as if the dead had come back to life. She protected herself from the anxieties of her incomprehensible world by withdrawing into a state of apathy. It was only through psychiatric treatment that the child was able to come out of this state.

Telling about affairs and other touchy subjects.

One can provide children with the basic reasons for the separation without necessarily divulging personal intimacies that are not their business. Because these touchy subjects generally involve criticisms of parents, it is best to present them as balanced by positive aspects. Furthermore, it is best to present the positive qualities first. This emphasized, I will focus here on ways of dealing with the parental failings that are generally difficult to discuss with children.

For example, perhaps parents are getting divorced because the mother is having an affair with another man and no longer wishes to remain married to her husband. The children can be told, "Mommy doesn't love Daddy very much any more. He has done many things that have hurt her. She loves another man much more and wants to spend her time with him." If frigidity is a problem, the child can be told, "Mommy doesn't like to hug and cuddle with Daddy very much and this makes Daddy feel very bad. For a long time we have tried to solve the problem, but we can't. So we are getting divorced." A similar explanation will generally suffice for a husband's impotency. An older and more sophisticated child may ask questions that the parents may justifiably not wish to answer. I generally suggest that the parents respond in this vein: "There are certain things that Mommy and Daddy consider personal and we do not wish to discuss these things with you. As you grow older you'll have more and more personal things that you will not want to talk about with us. We still want you to ask all the questions that come to your mind. We will answer most of them. However, if there is a question that we do not wish to answer, we will tell you so. We will not make believe we are answering it when we really aren't." If the parent does not state directly that the question is not being answered, but responds evasively or with a nonanswer, the child's further questioning will be discouraged, and this will deprive him or her of the benefits of accurate information.

What to reveal to the children when an extramarital sexual involvement has been the precipitating cause of the separation? This is a complex issue, and I do not claim to have any final answers. There are those who claim that jealousy over a spouse's affair(s) is immature—a residuum of childhood needs for exclusive possession of loved ones. When both spouses fully subscribe to this view they may be able to accept each other's extramarital sexual activities without resentment. They do not look upon these affairs as signs of infidelity, because no trust has been broken, and they would not consider such involvements reasons for divorce. Such couples are in a very small minority. In most marriages at least one (and more often both) becomes deeply pained when the spouse's extramarital sexual involvement is revealed. The liaison is viewed as infidelity because the partner has broken a vow made (explicitly or implicitly) at the time of the marriage. Most couples today do not quickly separate when such an affair becomes divulged. They often try to determine if there have been difficulties in the marriage that contributed to the infidelity. If such problems cannot be resolved, then divorce may result. In some cases the partner who has had the affair does not believe it to have been caused by any major deficiencies on the part of the spouse and may consider the spouse's inability to tolerate the infidelity as his or her only defect. But if such individuals cannot resolve their conflict or come to tolerate their differences, divorce may still ensue.

When extramarital involvements have been a central cause of the separation, as explained in chapter 1, the children do best if they are told. (I am not suggesting that the identity of the third party need necessarily be revealed.) In the situation where both partners consider the infidelity to be a symptom of more basic difficulties in their relationship, difficulties that they have been unable to resolve, they do well to present to the children the fundamental contributions of each and to describe the affair as a possible outcome of such problems. As I have stressed before, to withhold the information may make the parent more comfortable, but it will handicap the children in their ability to deal with the trauma of the separation. Knowing the exact causes of the separation helps the children learn about the kinds of things that can bring about marital discord. Also, learning about parental deficiencies makes it more likely that the children will tolerate deficiencies within themselves and others. An inability to live up to unreasonably high standards in oneself is a common factor in insecurity and self-esteem problems. And unrealistically high expectations from others can result in lifelong disillusionment in one's interpersonal relationships, as each person fails to live up to one's expectations.

In the situation in which one parent is quite comfortable with extramarital sexual involvements and the other finds such liaisons intolerable, the children do best when told about their parents' different philosophies on this matter. If an affair results from one spouse's inability or refusal to engage in sexual relationships, every detail need not be revealed. While the children have the right to know the basic problems, the parents still have the right to certain privacies.

I have focused here on just a few of the more common

types of conflict over extramarital liaisons that may contribute to divorce. Whatever the exact nature of the problem, however, these general guidelines and qualifications apply.

In recent decades many homosexual parents have openly revealed their homosexuality. Some have led a double life, and now proclaim that they refuse to live in this way any longer. They divorce in order to lead more freely the homosexual life with which they basically feel more comfortable. More homosexual men than women have taken this course, so I will discuss this issue from the man's point of view, but the principles that I suggest are, I believe, equally applicable to the female homosexual.

Before such a man and his wife can decide whether the children should be told about this reason for the separation and, if so, exactly what they should be told, the homosexual man must first decide whether he is going to divulge his homosexuality to others besides his wife. I believe that the healthiest choice that such a man can make is to reveal the homosexuality to friends and relatives in a manner similar to that which one would use when describing other reasons for divorce. Although the alternative of hiding the homosexuality may protect the man from the persisting stigma of homosexuality, concealment is not without its drawbacks. Living with the fear of disclosure is anxiety provoking and degrading. Also, the man must rely on his wife to comply with his request for secrecy. If she is willing to this, then the parents are likely to give the children an explanation that is false or evasive. And when others learn of or even suspect the father's homosexuality, the children ultimately hear about the father's homosexuality from others or come to suspect it themselves. It is far preferable that children learn directly about a father's homosexuality than that they have it revealed by others or figure it out themselves.

I recognize that there are men whose very livelihood may depend upon their concealing their homosexuality. Their concealing the information may be the most judicious choice, but the advantages they gain from concealment are somewhat counterbalanced by the potential psychological complications of concealment—for them, their wives, and their children.

If the joint decision is made not to reveal the homosexuality to the children, then the parents should tell the children about the causes of the divorce that are not specifically related to the homosexuality and should mention that there are other reasons that are personal and private. Although such an explanation produces curiosity, it is preferable to evasions, alibis, or reasons that have no validity.

What if the wife refuses to respect the father's desire for secrecy? She then has a choice whether she is going to disclose the information to her children or just to others. If the children are younger than four or five, informing them of their father's homosexuality is likely to be confusing. However, such a mother ought to tell the children when they get older. To choose the course of telling others but not the children creates the risk of their learning it from others or their sensing it themselves. But before telling the children, a wife does well to try first to decide whether she believes her husband's homosexuality to be a normal human variant or a psychological disorder. This will not be an easy decision for her to make, because mental health experts themselves are sharply divided on this subject.

A mother who believes that her husband's homosexuality is a manifestation of psychiatric disorder might say: "Most men love women and want to be married to a woman. Daddy really likes men more than women and doesn't want to live with Mommy any more. And he doesn't want to live with any other woman either. I think that this is a sickness. Although I am very sad and angry about this, I also feel very sorry for Daddy that he has this illness." Older children, especially adolescents, should be given a more specific explanation.

If the mother believes that homosexuality is not a psychological disorder but a normal sexual variation, she might say: "Some men like to be with women and others like to be with men. Daddy has decided that he no longer wants to live with Mommy. Rather, he wants to spend more time with his men friends. I feel very sad that Daddy is this way, because he will no longer be living in the house." Again, older children can be provided a more specific and sophisticated explanation.

If the mother has no firm conviction about the nature of homosexuality, she would probably do well to try to communicate to the children that there are two opinions on the subject. She should explain as best she can what the two viewpoints are (at the children's level of comprehension) and say to the children that as they get older they will be in a better position to decide which explanation seems most reasonable to them. If the two parents disagree on this issue, they can explain to the children that even Mom and Dad have different opinions regarding the causes of homosexuality.

In my opinion, it is premature for anyone at this point, considering our present knowledge, to state that he or she knows with certainty what is the cause of homosexuality. And this is especially the case with regard to the question of whether it is genetically determined or environmentally induced. My own belief is that in most cases homosexuality results from a combination of genetic predisposition and environmental factors. As I see it, in some people the genetic loading is so great that minimal environmental influences are necessary, while in others, the genetic loading is extremely small or even nonexistent. If both the doctor and the patient believed that environmental factors were significantly operative, then they might agree, that the homosexuality was primarily a psychiatric disorder and that psychotherapy might be useful. Note that I use the word *might*. There is some evidence that psychotherapy may be an effective therapeutic modality in some instances of borderline homosexuality.

The members of the American Psychiatric Association are in sharp disagreement on this issue. The *Diagnostic and Statistical Manual of Mental Disorders* (DSM) of the APA generally reflects the position of the majority (or possibly the most politically powerful) of its members. The manual utilized before 1980, DSM-II, viewed homosexuality as a psychiatric disorder. In the 1980 DSM-III, the basic position was that homosexuality is not per se a psychiatric disorder but a normal human variation. However, there was a category called "Egodystonic Homosexuality," which referred to discomfort with one's homosexuality. In other words, if the homosexual doesn't like being homosexual and wishes to change sexual orientation, then he or she can justifiably be treated by a psychiatrist, even though no psychiatric disorder is present. Like many compromises, this one leaves much to be desired.

In 1987 DSM-III was updated with DSM-III-R. DSM-III-R does not include a diagnosis of homosexuality at all but has a category, "Sexual Disorder Not Otherwise Specified," for the individual with "persistent and marked distress over one's sexual orientation." DSM-IV is scheduled for publication in 1992. Conflicts are still raging, but I doubt if the pendulum will shift back to the concept of homosexuality as a purely psychiatric disturbance.

My own view, at this point, is that obligatory homosexuals, that is, homosexuals who have never experienced a heterosexual interest, probably (and I am not saying this with certainty) are suffering with a psychiatric disturbance. Even if there is a high genetic loading, then I would still hold that it is a psychiatric disturbance, but one with strong genetic components. People who have always found themselves to be bisexual—who say that if it feels good they'll do it, regardless of the sex of the partner—may not be suffering with a psychiatric disorder (but they may be).

Considering all this confusion, parents must decide for themselves which theory seems most reasonable to them. And this theory should be the one they present to the children, if they decide to discuss the subject with them.

There is no question that the social stigmatization homosexuals have suffered has been cruel and inhumane. It is understandable that a homosexual father might not wish to have his sexual orientation generally known. He might want the children to be among the intimate few who were told, once they were old enough to understand the significance of the divulgence and could be trusted to respect their father's wish not to reveal his homosexuality to others. As the reader can well appreciate, telling children about a parent's homosexuality is always difficult. Parents must simply do the best they can in their specific circumstances. Chapter 5 includes a discussion of homosexuality in connection with child custody, and this further discussion may offer some helpful ideas.

Sally's experiences provide an example of the way in which divulging the cause of a separation, no matter how touchy, can be psychologically valuable to a child. Sally was referred to me at age seven because of disruptive behavior in the classroom. She was then in the second grade and extremely bright. However, she was functioning at first-grade level.

Her parents had separated about one year before Sally's first visit with me. Her mother had initiated the separation because of her husband's alcoholism. He totally denied that he had a drinking problem. He agreed with his wife that he did indeed consume large volumes of alcohol, but felt that the alcohol had absolutely no effect on him. Sally's mother claimed that her husband's hostile outbursts and sadistic behavior toward her occurred primarily when he was drinking; the father either denied the outbursts or justified them as warranted by his wife's nagging behavior and other unspecified provocations.

The mother decided that it would not be in Sally's best interests to tell her that her father had a drinking problem. Rather, she said nothing about the causes of the separation. When Sally asked for reasons she received evasive answers like "Your father and I just don't get along" and "We just don't love one another any more." On a few occasions Sally pointedly asked her mother about her father's drinking. (She had overheard many arguments over the father's alcoholism.) Sally was emphatically told by her mother that her father did not have a drinking problem. Her father, of course, claimed that there was no such difficulty at all or told Sally that it was all her "mother's imagination." Not surprisingly, Sally was confused about the reasons for her parents' separation and distrustful of them because of their evasiveness and dishonesty. In my early work with Sally it became apparent that these were important contributing factors to her problems at school.

From what I could learn from a detailed inquiry, I concluded that the father did indeed have a significant drinking problem and that it was not merely his wife's imagination. I then explained to Sally's father that in my opinion to admit the drinking problem would be not only in his best interests but in Sally's as well. He angrily responded that my advice proved to him that I was incompetent and that he would no longer pay for treatment. If his wife wanted to waste her money on me, he could not stop her.

Sally's mother told me that she thought telling about the drinking problem would cause Sally to lose respect for her father. I explained to her that it would reduce somewhat Sally's image of him, but that this would be less harmful than the atmosphere of confusion and deceit that had been created. After further discussion she agreed to tell Sally the truth—which she did the same day. Within the next three weeks Sally asked her mother many questions about her father and became clear regarding not only his drinking problem but his denial difficulties. The mother tried to convey a sense of compassion for the father, which she was able to do in spite of her anger toward him. I too worked on these issues in my sessions with Sally. Over this period there was a marked improvement in Sally's classroom behavior. Although other problems still had to be worked on, telling Sally the truth about her father's difficulties played a significant role in reducing her own psychological problems. She became less confused and more secure in her relationships with both parents. She now knew she could rely on her mother to provide honest answers to her questions. And she became more knowledgeable about what kind of person her father was—about the areas where she could count on him and about those where she could not.

Withholding the identity of the initiator. It is common for the person who initiates the separation to request that his or her identity not be revealed to the children. The initiator fears that the children will place all the blame on him or her no matter how justifiable the decision was and no matter how much the reluctant spouse contributed to the marital difficulties. Such an anticipation is realistic, because it is quite common for children to blame the parent who takes the initiative and to view the other parent as the innocent party.

The reluctant spouse often reinforces this notion. The children generally believe that if the initiator *really* loved them he or she would tolerate the pains and indignities of the marital relationship. They have difficulty putting themselves in the parents' positions and appreciating the grief the marital difficulties are causing their parents. Initiators must accept the fact that their identities are not easily hidden from the children. It is far better for the parents to reveal this information themselves than to risk the distrust and distortions that result from concealment. The initiator must also accept the fact that he or she is going to be viewed as the bad guy—no matter how justifiable the decision—and that the reluctant spouse is going to be seen as "Mr. or Mrs. Innocent." If the parent who takes the first step apprises the children of his or her identity and informs them of the reasons for the decision, there may be some lessening of their tendency to put full blame on the initiator. Hearing the opinions of the rejected spouse as well can help the children correct any distortions that may have arisen. Also, as the children grow older they will become more competent to make their own decisions about each parent's role in the marital conflict.

Even with discussions in which the children hear both sides, it is likely that the parent who initiates the separation decision will be considered to be more at fault than the hesitant spouse. Such an eventuality should not be a reason for a parent's remaining in a marriage considered to be miserable. Nor does it justify withholding this important information from the children.

Repudiated spouses, then, should not comply with a spouse's request not to tell the children who first decided to separate. Simple, straightforward statements of a spouse's deficiencies may result in some loss of respect for the criticized parent. But, as mentioned, there are many benefits to be derived from openness. Any undesirable psychological effects caused by children's exposure to and appreciation of parental deficiencies are generally less than those resulting from campaigns of vilification and endless hostilities between the parents. This is what should be avoided; not accurate communication of parental assets and liabilities.

Creating an atmosphere of open communication.

Having repeated opportunities to question their parents about the separation enables children to adjust better to the trauma of the separation. More important than the information that the children gain from their questioning is the open atmosphere of communication that such interchanges foster. The children cannot fully comprehend all at once what they are being told. They will need to repeat their questions over time. They must be given the feeling that their questions will be welcomed at any reasonable time and that the parents will make every attempt to answer them directly and honestly. The children will then gain trust and security. And there is nothing that will more predictably squelch this important experience than parental dishonesty and evasiveness.

It is not the gaining of information that makes repetitious questioning so beneficial, but the *process* of repeating the questions. It is as if each time the children discuss the separation, it becomes a little more bearable. This desensitization to the pain of the separation is central to the children's adjusting to it. The children's repetitious questioning can also provide them with reassurances about the parents' interest and availability. Parents who are too quickly put off by repetitious inquiries will deprive their children of important opportunities to work through their reactions to the separation in a healthy way. Parents should understand that such questioning may extend over a period of months, even years. As the children mature they become more appreciative of the many factors that may have operated in bringing about the separation. Regardless of when a child asks a question, the very fact that it has been asked indicates that some issue has not yet been fully resolved.

When providing information, however, remember that it is unwise to confront the children with too many facts at once. There are parents who will, in their desire to communicate, dump a barrage of facts on the children. The children then become overwhelmed and confused. For this reason I generally suggest that there simply be ample opportunity for open, relaxed discussion. Parents can then provide information in piecemeal fashion in accordance with the children's ability to comprehend and absorb it, letting the children guide them as to how much should be given and at what pace.

When it is appropriate not to reveal certain information. There are times when it may be appropriate that the parents not provide a child with information. For example, if a father has been involved in criminal behavior and if legal proceedings are under way, the children may justifiably be given only partial information. For example, they might be told, "Mommy doesn't love Daddy any more and no longer wishes to live with him." The statement is true, as far as it goes, and so the children have not been lied to. However, vital information has been omitted and so the truth has been compromised. As the children grow older, and once the disclosure will no longer jeopardize the father's legal position, then the children can safely be given further information.

There are also times when identifying a third party involved in the divorce may be inappropriate and undesirable. For example, a man is having an affair with a married woman and decides to separate. He chooses not to divulge the identity of his lover to his wife because his lover has not decided whether she wishes to break up her marriage. Under these circumstances it may very well be appropriate for the father not to reveal the identity of his lover to the children. This advice is not commonly applicable, because the situation itself is not common; most often the wife, and often even the children, have a very good idea who the lover is. Still, the father here, although not disclosing certain information, at least is not lying to the children.

When a parent suffers with significant psychiatric disturbance. When the divorce comes about because one of the parents is suffering with a significant psychiatric disturbance, it is important for the nonafflicted parent to try to communicate to the children a sense of sympathy for the disturbed parent. For example, a mother has decided that she can no longer tolerate her husband's gambling. In addition to telling the children about some of the father's gambling, she should try to communicate to them the notion that the gambling is an illness that cannot simply be cured by willpower. She would do well to tell the children about how much she has tried to be helpful. A similar approach can be useful when the divorce is the result of a parent's chronic depression, drug addiction, or criminal behavior.

The marriage as a mistake. I often advise divorcing parents to communicate to the children that they realize now that their marriage was, or somehow developed into, a *mistake*. All too often children look upon their parents as perfect. Unfortunately, there are parents who try to perpetuate this myth. Although such a practice generally stems from parental insecurity, it is usually justified as being in the best interests of the children. Nothing could be farther from the truth. Children do best when they grow up with realistic expectations from others. Admitting the marriage to have been a mistake is one way in which the parents can provide their children with a healthy sense of their imperfection.

When the "mistake" relates to the fact that the parents have grown apart—without any particular parental defect being the cause of the marital failure—the children should be helped to understand what has happened.

Reassuring the children: love and other matters.
When parents tell their children about the forthcoming separation, I generally advise them to mention that they *did* love one another at the time of their marriage (if this was the case, and it generally is). Appreciating that they were the products of love—that they were born at a time when their parents wanted them and anticipated that they would be living together—can give children some security and enhance their feelings of self-worth at a time when their self-esteem is most likely to be damaged. I also urge the parents to explain to the children that

although they do not love one another any more, each of them still loves the children. The children must be helped to appreciate that in any triangle consisting of three individuals, A and B may not love one another, but A and B can each love C. Although this may seem like an obvious statement, it may not be obvious to the children. Children tend, more often than not, to feel that if the parents don't love one another, they too may become unloved. This is not a totally irrational supposition. If Daddy, for example, can stop loving Mommy, won't he stop loving his children too? The child in a stable home may not consider the possibility that anyone is going to stop loving anybody. For children of divorce, however, such an eventuality is very much in their scheme of things.

I also generally recommend that the parents impress upon the children that the divorce was not the children's fault. Children commonly develop the notion that the divorce was due to their own misbehavior, so this reassurance should be communicated. In chapter 4 I discuss in detail the guilt reactions of children of divorce and the more definitive approaches to the alleviation of this form of guilt, which is extremely common.

Many children fear that following the separation they will suffer deprivations of vital necessities such as food, clothing, and shelter. Often the children will have overheard parental concerns and conflicts over their forthcoming financial arrangements that will add to their insecurities in this area. It is important, therefore, for separating parents to reassure their children that although things may be tighter, they will all still have enough to eat, a reasonable supply of clothing, and a place to live.

It is important, too, to encourage emotional expression. When children become very upset and cry on being informed of the forthcoming separation, parents sometimes make such comments as "See how brave you can be" or "Big boys and girls don't cry." But to inhibit the children's natural emotional reactions can interfere with their adjusting adequately to the separation and can contribute to the formation of problems later on. Parents during this period should be encouraging their children's expression of feeling, not squelching it.

I have attempted in this section to cover the common issues that arise when parents discuss separation with their children. It is important for parents to go beyond what I have discussed and invite their children to raise whatever questions may be on their minds. A child may have special concerns, and these should be taken seriously. The open airing of problems, mutual inquiry, and cooperative discussion that can ensue often serve to reduce the disruption of parent-child relationships that divorce so often brings about.

3

Early Postseparation Adjustment

In the first months following the divorce, the whole family has to make adjustments. There are many ways parents can help their children meet the challenges of this difficult time.

TELLING FRIENDS AND NEIGHBORS

Telling people outside the family about the divorce can be stressful for all concerned. There was a time when divorce was generally looked upon as disgraceful. Although social attitudes toward the divorced person have improved significantly, there are still remnants of this unfortunate attitude. Rather than being looked upon as someone who has suffered an unfortunate experience, the divorced person is still occasionally viewed as being somewhat less righteous, less psychologically healthy, or less moral than those who have never been divorced.

First, parents must come to terms with their own sense of shame. Because of the mar on their reputations that some divorced people anticipate, they may try to hide the fact as much as possible. This is an unfortunate attitude and can only add to the divorced person's burden. Individuals who try to conceal divorce reveal that they are basically in agreement with those who are prejudiced toward divorced people— that there is indeed something to be ashamed of. The healthiest attitude to take is that there is nothing to be ashamed about and that those who would think less of a divorced individual have some problem of their own. The divorce should be disclosed and discussed at appropriate times and in appropriate places, in as matter-of-fact a manner as possible.

If divorced parents deal with the divorce in this way, it is likely that their children will do so as well. I would go farther and say that the most important determinant of whether the children will be ashamed of the divorce is parental shame. Even if the parents do not directly tell the children how ashamed they are, the children are bound to pick up the parental feelings. The first thing that divorced parents must do is to get it clear in their own minds that there is absolutely nothing shameful about the breakup of a marriage. It is a sad event, but in no way is it a blot on one's reputation. When the parents believe this with conviction, then the children are likely to do so as well. In contrast, the parents who are basically ashamed of the divorce are not likely to be very effective in helping their children reduce their shame. A parallel is the cigarette-smoking parent who warns a youngster about the dangers of the habit: The child is not likely to take the warning very seriously. Even when a parent tries to hide feelings of disgrace, the child will generally sense the parent's underlying shame.

The reactions of the children's peers. Once the parents have straightened things out in their own minds, they should advise their children to tell their friends about what has happened. It is inadvisable for parents to attempt to discuss in advance with the children any inappropriate reactions that their playmates may have. To do so is to cause the children to anticipate problems that may never materialize and may add to their fears. Parents do well also to appreciate that their children's friends will generally feel threatened by the news. For the friends, divorce may be something that they have heard takes place elsewhere. However, when it happens to one's own neighbor, it gets too close to home; the friends may fear that the same calamity will befall them. One way children often deal with such fears is to become oversolicitous of the child whose parents are separating. A boy, for example, may reveal a surprising degree of sympathy for a little girl whose parents are divorcing, much to the amazement of observers who may never have thought of the youngster as particularly sensitive. Actually, what is going on in such a situation is that the boy has identified himself with the girl and sees himself in her. By consoling her he is really consoling himself. The boy's unanticipated benevolence serves more the needs of the consoler than the child who is being consoled—although basic concern for the suffering child may still be present.

The problem that may arise from these consolations, especially if the child is the recipient of such attentions from a number of children, is that each consoler may tell the child not to worry and may even enumerate all the things the child need not worry about. Accordingly, the child may be introduced to concerns that never entered his or her mind before. When this occurs the parents can only attempt to reassure the child that the particular concern is not valid (if, of course, such is the case). If it is a reasonable concern, then the parent should discuss the matter and try to help the child deal with it as effectively as possible. Most, if not all, of the problems described in this book would serve as examples of the kinds of difficulties that the child may learn about during such periods of consolation by friends.

Taunting is another reaction from friends that may derive from the sense of threat that the child of divorce produces in peers. A girl, for example, may respond with a "there but for the grace of God go I" attitude after learning of the breakup of a little boy's home. She may bolster her self-reassurance by emphasizing the differences between herself and the boy. "His parents are getting divorced and mine are not" quickly becomes "Ha, ha, your parents are getting divorced and mine are not." The more she mocks the boy, the more she hopes to reassure herself that his plight will not be hers. It is difficult for divorcing parents to explain to their children what is really going on. The best one can do is to try to help the taunted children appreciate that it is not nice to laugh at a person who has had a sad experience. Children who are so teased also have to be helped to appreciate that they are not necessarily what others claim them to be. And at times, mocking children are expressing the intolerant attitudes of their parents; in such cases the divorcing parents can point out the distortions of thinking that exist in the minds of the adults concerned.

On occasion, the divorce will have occurred because of parental behavior that is socially alienating, such as chronic alcoholism, drug addiction, or promiscuity. When such problems become known to the community (as they often do), the children may be subjected to terrible ridicule and mockery. It is very difficult to help children rise above such derision. Such children have to be helped to appreciate that guilt by association is unjust, that a defect in a parent does not warrant a child's being scorned similarly; and that there is something significantly deficient in someone who would ridicule a child for the behavior of a parent. The children have to be helped to understand that if they are kind, friendly, and fun to be with, they will be accepted by most for what *they are* and not rejected because of what their *parents are or were*.

Dealing with the child who tries to hide the separation. There are children who may try to hide the divorce from their friends. Such children may compare themselves unfavorably with those who have an intact home and feel different from them. Obviously, such a reaction is more common in situations in which the child encounters few, if any, children from divorced homes. Many children equate *difference* and *inferiority* (many adults do so as well) and will therefore feel inferior to peers whose parents are married. Such a child might go to great lengths to keep the divorce a secret. A boy, for example, may tell friends that his father takes numerous lengthy business trips and that is why they never see him. Or he may refrain from inviting friends to his home, lest they become aware of his father's absence. Children who deal this way with the divorce add to their burden, because they live under the constant threat of disclosure of their secret. A parent should suspect that the child may be resorting to secrecy when there is a sudden reduction in visitors to the home and/or when the child starts finding all kinds of flimsy excuses for not having friends over. Such children have to be helped to appreciate that being different does not mean that one is inferior and that they are no better or worse than a child whose parents are living together—just perhaps a little less lucky. I say *perhaps* because such children also have to be helped to recognize that not all parents who stay together are living in bliss. Many children in intact homes are exposed to continual strife and chaos, whereas for children of divorce the conflict has most often ended.

Problems of discretion with friends and neighbors.

Parents who follow my advice that they be open and honest to their children about the basic reasons for the divorce may be confronted with the problem of what their children will then transmit to their friends and neighbors. This is a difficult problem. I believe that one's first obligation should be to do what is in the children's best interests. The problems that may arise from possible leakage of information to others are generally not so great that parents should refrain from telling the children the basic reasons for the separation. As previously mentioned, I do not suggest that the children be given *all* information. Children should be given the basic facts; they should *not* be given information that, if spread, might cause harm to the parent or other parties. Children can be encouraged not to discuss with others some of the things that they have been told, because certain family matters are private. Of course, the younger the children, the less likely they can be trusted to respect such a request. But all children have to learn that there are private family matters that are not appropriately discussed with outsiders, and the reasons for a divorce come under this category. Parents should recognize, however, that their children may still divulge some or all of what has been told to them. They should be willing to risk some embarrassment, because withholding the basic facts will contribute to their children's difficulties.

TELLING THE TEACHER

Some parents argue against the teacher's being told about parental separation. They fear that the teacher will treat their children differently and make a special case out of them. And special attention and indulgence from the teacher, they fear will invite the ridicule and alienation of the children's classmates. Or the parents may anticipate such spectacles as a child's being brought up in front of the class and asked to tell everyone how it feels when one's parents separate. Or they may fear that the teacher will be prejudiced against the child. Although intolerant reactions by teachers certainly occur, I believe they are becoming increasingly rare. Their possible occurrence, however, does not warrant depriving the child of the benefits of the teacher's being told.

Some believe that the teacher should not be told unless the children's reactions to the separation draw attention to them in the classroom and disrupt their work there. But I find it hard to imagine a child's not reacting strongly to parental separation— even when the separation provides a respite from continual domestic unhappiness. To wait until children exhibit symptoms may deprive them of valuable early intervention—intervention that might reduce and even prevent the development of more serious reactions. When teachers have been told in advance about the separation, they, possibly more than anyone else, can substitute for the departed parent. Even teachers of opposite sex to the parent who has left can still serve as a second adult to compensate for the loss the child has suffered. The teacher is with the child six or seven hours a day, five days a week, and is in an excellent position to keep the child happily busy and to provide support, reassurance, and advice.

To try to withhold the information from the teacher not only deprives the child of important support but is naive. It is practically impossible to keep such an event from a child's teacher for a long time. Neighborhood children learn of the event and it soon spreads to classmates. The other children worry that the same calamity may befall them. And a common way of reducing such fear is to discuss the matter at length— among themselves, with their parents, and with other individuals, such as their teachers. It is far better, therefore, for the parents to tell teachers themselves so they will have the most accurate information and be in the best position to be of assistance. Furthermore, when teachers are not told about parental separation they are not likely to be as understanding of the child's abnormal behavior as when they are forewarned.

It is true that some teachers may handle the situation inappropriately. But this does not justify a blanket policy of never telling the teacher. Teachers who the parents suspect might deal inappropriately with the situation might be forestalled from doing so by the parents discussing their concerns with them beforehand. My experience, however, has been that most teachers are sympathetic and understanding.

ADJUSTING TO TWO HOUSEHOLDS

Children whose parents separate not only must adjust to the fact that one parent will be absent from the home but also must become accustomed to the departed parent's new living arrangement. Immediately following the separation the departed parent's absence becomes very acute. Little things that were taken for granted now loom large, with a kind of deafening silence. Father is no longer shaving in the bathroom, and there's no commotion about when he'll be finished. The child wishes Dad were in there and would welcome the traditional battle for priorities. Or Mom is no longer in the kitchen making breakfast, and somehow Daddy just doesn't know how to cook things right. Dad's new home looks so small. The new place where Mom is living is all right, but the bed isn't very comfortable. These adjustments make formidable demands upon the child, even with the most sensitive and judicious advance warnings and discussions. Hearing that something is going to happen and experiencing the actual occurrence are two very different things, especially for a child.

Not too many changes at once. Separating parents should try not to complicate matters further by making other changes in the child's life at the same time. For example, if Dad leaves the house and Mom plans to move, she does well to wait at least a few months. Parents must appreciate that a move does not simply involve a change in home atmosphere; it generally involves a change in school and a loss of friends. It should not be taken lightly, and the children do best when they have had some chance to recover from the trauma of the separation before being required to adjust to these additional stresses. When a new home has been chosen, the custodial parent should show the child the new dwelling at the earliest possible time (even though it may be weeks, and even months, before the move). Having a visual image of exactly where they will be living lessens children's anxieties. Similarly, visiting the new school, seeing the new neighborhood, and if possible meeting the new neighbors, can also reduce the child's fears. The more knowledge one has about an anxiety-provoking situation, the less anxiety one generally has about it. And after the move has been made, the parent does well to invite old-neighborhood friends (if practical) as soon as possible in order to smooth the transition.

Visiting the departed parent's new living arrangements. Before the separation, it is good for the children to visit the new living quarters of the departing parent. A concrete image of where the parent will be lessens fears of abandonment. After the parent leaves, actually seeing the parent in the new home can further reduce the children's fears of never seeing that parent again. The sooner such a visit can be arranged the sooner this aspect of the children's anxieties will be lessened. The children should be provided with the telephone number of the departed parent's new home and be encouraged to call with reasonable frequency. Although the content of such calls may appear trivial, they generally serve the more important purpose of fostering the children's reassurance that the absent parent will still be available to them. In addition, phone calls can provide the children with opportunities to ask questions and discuss other aspects of the separation.

Following the departure, the parent with whom the children live should also keep open the lines of communication. It is hoped that the children will continue asking questions and discussing what has been going on. The custodial parent, as well as the absent parent, has the obligation to be available to the children for such interchanges, because they are among the most effective ways of preventing psychological problems.

Tolerating the children's hostility in the postseparation period. Both parents should appreciate that during this early period considerable hostility on the children's part is a common reaction. Parents must increase their tolerance for their children's anger during this period and must allow for more disruptive and rambunctious behavior (within limits) than normally would have been permitted. Not to do so fosters the development of excessive guilt over and suppression of anger, and this sets the stage for the formation of various unhealthy psychological reactions. In addition, the children must be helped to direct their anger into appropriate and constructive channels. For example, a girl who is angry because her absent father does not consistently return her telephone calls should be encouraged to speak with her father about this rather than have temper tantrums as she awaits the call.

The child's assuming the role of the absent parent. Soon after the separation, children of the same sex as that of the parent who has left may attempt to assume the role of the absent parent. Boys may try to take over the role of their fathers and girls of their mothers. Generally, it is only when the parents comply with these tendencies (because of their own problems in this area) that difficulties may arise. For example, after a father has left, a boy will have to assume some of his father's obligations, and to encourage the assumption of some responsibilities is appropriate. However, the mother must not encourage such identifications to an unreasonable degree. Comments such as "Now that your father has left, you're going to be the man of the house" and "From now on you're going to be like my husband" are inappropriate. They constitute excessive encouragement of the boy to assume the father's position.

It is reasonable to allow a little boy some cuddling and short periods of resting together in his mother's bed (as is inappropriate, in my opinion, when the father is present). However, if a boy begins sleeping in Mom's bed throughout the night, every night, trouble can ensue. Both mother and son are entitled to some compensatory affection, physical contact, and solace with one another. However, when such contact and involvement become intensified and prolonged, and when seductive elements are introduced, then the likelihood is great that psychological problems will result. And what I have said about the relationship between a mother and son holds equally for a father and daughter. The same problems can also arise when a child visits an opposite-sexed noncustodial parent, and the same warnings hold.

The perpetuation of parental hostilities. Immediately following the separation there is likely to be some continuation of the same hostilities that brought about the separation. During this period, frequent contact between the parents is necessary in order for them to work out the innumerable arrangements associated with the divorce. Generally, hurt feelings and resentments color practically every negotiation. But I cannot emphasize strongly enough the importance of parents attempting to resolve their difficulties as soon as possible. The longer the hostilities continue, the greater the likelihood their children will become disturbed. I am not simply suggesting that parents suppress their resentments or argue outside of the children's presence (both of which have a place in reducing the child's exposure to their hostilities). Rather, the parents must do everything possible genuinely to resolve their remaining difficulties in the most civilized fashion. The failure to do so is one of the most predictable ways of producing psychological disturbances in children.

TIME ALONE TOGETHER

The most potent preventive and one of the most effective cures for psychological disturbance is the parent's spending time alone with each child. I recommend to all parents, regardless of whether their child is in therapy and regardless of whether the parents are divorced, that they set aside a time every day when they can be alone with each child without distraction or interruption. Each sibling should have his or her own time, from which the others are excluded unless invited by mutual agreement. And this time alone together should be cancelled only under unusual circumstances. It should have the highest priority for both parents and child.

These periods are most effective when both parent and child are genuinely enjoying themselves. If the parent only *pretends* enjoyment of a game or activity, the child will sense the resentment stemming from the parent's reluctant involvement, and the time spent together will become compromised and even a detrimental experience for the child. This time can be profitably used for talking about feelings and for sharing the day's experiences—for finding solace, commiseration, and understanding, and for relating anecdotes, achievements, and disappointments. Or the parent and child might spend the time reading together, playing games, or listening to music. It is during these moments of shared feeling and empathy that loving feelings flourish, and both the child and the parent become enriched by them. Such experiences deepen the relationship between the parent and child and thereby serve to protect the child from developing the kinds of difficulties that arise from impairments in the parent-child relationship. Such time alone together can also be most effective in assuaging the pain and frustration of children whose parents have just separated. These shared times are even more vital during the postseparation period than at other times. For the custodial parent such times alone together should take place every day. And for the parent who lives away, every day of visitation. I cannot recommend them strongly enough.

4

Dealing with Children's Postseparation Problems

The more one understands about the causative factors underlying a child's adverse reactions to divorce, the greater the likelihood these reactions can be dealt with effectively. We not only want to know the causes that are at the foundation of the symptoms, but mechanisms by which unhealthy reactions develop. This is indeed a situation in which knowledge is power. The focus here will be on those untoward reactions that parents can either prevent or alleviate themselves. But if these problems become deeply entrenched and are not alleviated by the measures described here, then, of course, consultation with a mental health expert may be warranted.

DENIAL OF THE SEPARATION

Denial is one of the most primitive psychological mechanisms that people use to protect themselves from mental pain. What easier way is there to avoid suffering the pain of a trauma than to deny its existence? Generally, an individual does not consciously decide to resort to denial; it is an unconscious process. The person does not recognize that blindness to the painful situation has been self-induced. The ease with which one turns to denial is often dependent on how frequently it is resorted to by people around one, especially family members. Accordingly, the family pattern plays a significant role in determining whether the child of divorce will utilize this protective mechanism.

Parental contributions to children's denial. Certain parental personality characteristics and ways of dealing with children may contribute to children's developing the denial mechanism as a way of handling the separation trauma. There are parents, for example, who believe that fighting in front of their children will necessarily be detrimental to them. Continual squabbling in front of the children is certainly harmful to them. However, witnessing occasional arguments between their parents, arguments that are neither violent nor sadistic, can be a useful experience for children. It helps them appreciate that no one is perfect and that in every marriage there are times of conflict and fiction. Parents who never fight in front of their children provide them with a continuous lesson in inappropriate suppression of angry feelings. Although a fight may represent a failure in the parents' ability to settle their differences in a more civilized manner, it should inevitably occur, at times, in the healthy marriage, because no one can handle all conflicts in an ideal and judicious way. This is the normal and expected environment in the relatively intact home.

There are parents who are basically silent and noncommunicative people. The general atmosphere in the home is quiet, and people may communicate only about matters that are essential to the functioning of the household. Such parents may be especially inhibited in expressing feelings, and they will serve as models for similar suppression in their children. When a separation takes place, they are not likely to communicate very much about what is going on, especially about their emotional reactions. In such an atmosphere it is hard to imagine their children's not developing denial patterns themselves.

As previously described, there are parents who will justify not giving their children information about the separation with excuses such as "They're too young to understand" and "They're too young to have it affect them." For example, a father may leave the home with absolutely nothing said to the children. But such withholding of vital information is likely to contribute to children's denying their own thoughts and feelings about the separation.

The denial mechanism is an extremely powerful one. Human beings' ability to blind themselves to the obvious is at times astounding. There are people who will take a few days to acknowledge that a loved one has indeed died. Many soldiers will enter combat with the delusion that others around them may be killed but that they somehow are immune. Similarly, there are parents who will actually separate and then, amazingly, act as if the separation has not taken place. Each goes about his or her business as if life is just as before. Father's empty chair is ignored and supper is served without any reference to the fact that an important family member is missing. Such parents will usually concede, if asked, that they are living separately, but will deny that there are any other effects of the separation. The children are likely to follow the parental pattern and deny that they have any untoward reactions. They too may continue living as if there were no changes.

Parents who actively encourage their children to suppress their emotional reactions contribute to the development of the denial mechanism. But parents often have to make a conscious effort to encourage children's emotional responses, because reacting stoically to a traumatic experience is admired in our culture. The woman who doesn't cry when her husband dies is said to have "taken it well." At the time of President Kennedy's assassination, hardly a television announcer did not compliment the President's wife, Jacqueline, on her forbearance; and people in high places serve as models for the rest.

There are also parents who, following the separation, will act as if the spouse who is no longer living in the home has never existed. But even if an absent parent has totally abandoned the family, he or she still exists in memory. To deny this contributes to denial and deprives children of the opportunity to express their reactions and work them out. In the more usual situation, where the absent parent is very much involved, the utilization of this reaction by the remaining parent requires an even greater denial of reality; yet the remaining parent may strictly avoid any mention of the absent parent and act not only as if the former spouse no longer exists but as if he or she had never existed. And the children, in order to remain in the good graces of the parent with whom they live, may react similarly.

Common ways in which children deny the separation.

There are children who will deny the separation without significant parental contribution. Because denial is such a primitive mechanism and so easily utilized, it is not surprising that children may resort to it with facility.

For instance, a child may react to the announcement of the separation with such calm that the departing parent may question the child's affection. Generally, such a reaction is not related to the absence of a feeling of loss. Rather, it may be a manifestation of the child's failure to appreciate time lapses. To the average preschooler, there is little if any difference among waiting periods of three days, three weeks, or three months. Or a child's calm may relate to an inability to appreciate fully an occurrence until the child actually observes it. ("If I don't *see* it happening, then it's *not* happening.") Or it may be a sign of the child's wish to deny that the separation will take place. Even after a parent has left and the remaining parent repeatedly invites the child to express emotional reactions, there may be none forthcoming. Even though the child may be told that the departed parent is no longer going to be living in the home, the child may repeatedly ask when the parent is going to return. Each time the child questions as if he or she had never before been told the answer. The situation is similar to one occasionally seen after the death of a parent. The children of the deceased may frequently say, "I know Daddy's (Mommy's) dead and in the ground in the cemetery, but when is he (she) coming home for supper?"

There are children who are explicitly told the facts of the separation and who still will speak and fantasize about the absent parent's returning. They make such statements as: "Daddy comes home very late, after I fall asleep. He leaves very early in the morning, before I wake up." "Mommy's living at Grandma's house. Grandma told me." "Daddy's working late." "Mommy's coming home very soon."

On occasion children will hide their anxieties by viewing the separation as a newsworthy event. They will excitedly tell their friends about their calamity, but do so in such a way that it seems that the pleasure they get from the attention they receive while reporting the news far outweighs any grief they may be suffering. Such a denial mechanism is most frequently seen before the actual separation. Once the child has the living experience that the parent is no longer in the home this "laughing on the outside, crying on the inside" mode of adjustment generally breaks down and the tears may burst forth. Here again, children's reactions to parental death are often analogous. Following the funeral services and burial, there are children who will play such games as "Cemetery" and "Funeral." This may appear macabre to adult observers, but such games serve to help children deny and work through their reactions to the parents' death.

Or a child may appear oblivious to the separation, but may become obsessively concerned over the welfare of another person or a pet. Such children are displacing onto a substitute their worries over the well-being of the departed parent. This type of denial mechanism also occurs in patients suffering fatal diseases; when visited in the hospital they talk little about themselves, but become excessively concerned over the most minor illnesses of their friends and relatives.

In a related type of denial, the child takes an attitude of "It's their problem, not mine." In this attitude of "I couldn't care less," children deny their concerns and consider the problem to be entirely that of the parents. Rather than show sympathy for the parents, the children exhibit disdain and scorn—an expression of the anger they feel toward the parents.

Sometimes a child's denial may relate to fear of and guilt

over expressing anger. What appears to be denial is actually evidence of inhibition in expressing the angry feelings that the separation has produced. Such children fear saying anything about the separation lest they reveal their angry feelings in the process. Often, these inhibitions are the result of parental attitudes toward the child's expressing hostile feelings.

Some children involve themselves in play and fantasy that serves the function of restoring the absent parent. A boy, for example, may play the role of the absent father in such games as "house." Although to a certain degree this is normal, the child of divorce may become obsessed with such a role. By identifying with the absent parent the child hopes to regain him or her. On occasion, this mechanism may operate following the death of a parent. A child or even an adult may suddenly take on many of the qualities of the absent parent: vocal intonations, gestures, personality characteristics, and even opinions. At times the overnight transformation is almost uncanny.

Following the separation some children will fantasize that they are actually with the departed parent. This usually occurs at ages two to four, the time when children most commonly develop imaginary friends. These children will talk to the invisible parent as if he or she were still in the home and become involved in prolonged games with the fantasized parent. In addition, the child may exhibit many of the other behavioral patterns that typified involvement with the fantasized parent. When someone sits down in the parent's former chair the child may loudly exclaim, "Get out of that chair. You're sitting on my mother." When leaving home the child may cry out, "We forgot to take Daddy. He's still inside." The child may even run back into the house and bring along the fantasized father.

Idealization of the absent parent, with an associated denial of any deficiencies, is a common reaction. (Parents strictly refraining from criticizing one another can foster such idealization.) Related to idealization is the denial that an absent parent has lost interest in the child. In the extreme, some children may insist that the departed parent still loves them even though the parent has not been seen or heard from in many years. The notion is obviously a means to avoid the painful realization that the absent parent no longer loves them. A mother whose husband has not been heard from in years may foster such denial with comments such as "Your father still loves you, he just can't show it." Although such a comment may be well meaning, it is misguided. The parent is obviously trying to protect the children from trauma. Such a mother does better, however, to help the children appreciate that there is something seriously wrong with a parent who cannot love his own children. In addition, she should encourage the children to involve themselves with others, both peers and adults, who will demonstrate that they are still lovable. The children must be helped to realize that although one of their parents may not love them, it does not follow that no one else in the whole world can either.

Commonly, children will react as if they were denying having any reactions to the announcement, because it has not come as a surprise. For months and even years, they may have been witnessing their parents fighting and talking of divorce. (Parents are often amazingly oblivious to their children's awareness of their altercations.) Accordingly, when the announcement is finally made they do not exhibit strong reactions because they have been accommodating themselves to the event for a long time.

Dealing with children's denial. It is important for parents to appreciate that the goal of the denial mechanism, although it is most often maladaptive, is to produce a certain degree of psychological stability. To a degree, all of us must build a psychological wall around ourselves as protection from the multiple painful stimuli that bombard us. Were we to see clearly every danger and were we to react emotionally to all traumas—past, present, and potential—it is unlikely that we could preserve our sanity.

So there are times when it is a disservice for a parent to attempt actively to remove a child's denial mechanism. The most obvious example is the way we deal with a person who is dying. The woman with a fatal disease who displaces fears of her own well-being onto others should not be told that her concerns for her friends and relatives are merely displacements of her concerns about herself. I am not suggesting that one routinely support denial mechanisms exhibited by a person who is dying. Sometimes denial may deprive the person of lifesaving treatment, and at such times denial mechanisms should not be respected. But at other times, no purpose is served by attempts to get the person to see reality.

In contrast, it is generally not cruel to attempt to remove the denial mechanism in a child of divorce. Most often, the utilization of denial by children of divorce is maladaptive, because denial interferes with the development of healthier adjustments to the separation. Direct discussion of the child's denial, however, is generally anxiety provoking. Parents who try the direct head-on approach, repeatedly confronting a child with his or her distortions, may find that the child responds with even more adamant adherence to the denial mechanisms. In such cases I recommend pulling back and allowing time and experience slowly to help the child see the reality of the situation.

Parents whose children exhibit the kinds of denial I have described do well to examine their own behavior and ask themselves if they have been contributing to their children's denial. Parents who utilize denial themselves are not likely to be effective in helping their children give up the denial form of adjustment to the divorce.

Child therapists appreciate well that children discuss their difficulties much more readily when talking about third parties, animals, and other symbols of themselves. Children's self-created stories and verbalized fantasies can be a valuable source of information about underlying problems. Often, the particular concerns that children may be denying, both to themselves and to others, may be thinly disguised by such stories. Although it may be obvious to adults that children are really talking about themselves in such stories, it is generally not apparent to younger children—especially those under the age of seven or eight. By discussing with children the events in the lives of the symbolic figures one can say important things without the children's experiencing the anxiety they would have if they knew they were talking about themselves.

Sometimes children's stories are so obvious that parents without any special mental health training can readily interpret them and be in a better position to help. For example, a boy who appears unperturbed by his father's departure may tell a story in which a dog's father runs away and the dog is left starving and can get food only by hunting for it in garbage cans. I will respond to such a story with one in which the same dog fears that collecting food from garbage will be his fate after his father departs, and he even spends restless nights dreaming of himself searching for food in garbage cans. However, he is reassured by his older-brother dog that they still have their mother, who then proves to be an adequate provider. In this way, I affirm that the absence of this father does not mean that the child is totally abandoned. My hope is that when such a child is reassured that his mother will still take care of him *and when she proves to do so,* he will more readily accept the separation. When working with such a child I may or may not try to help him understand the true underlying meaning of his story. We may talk entirely about the dog, for example, and how *he* can best deal with *his* father's departure. If the child can tolerate discussions of the real issues, of course, I am happy to engage him in such conversations. Although dealing with such stories and fantasies is best done by a trained therapist, these stories are often so transparent that many parents should be able to make use of them for the benefit of their children. The basic principle is that if one can alleviate some of the fears that underlie the child's denial, the child is less likely to deny. And when the denial is reduced the child is in a far better position to deal effectively with the separation.

GRIEF

Similarities between grief following divorce and grief following death. Although there are definite differences between the reactions children may experience following a divorce and those they may suffer after the death of a parent, there are certain similarities as well. One such similarity is the occurrence of a grief reaction. An understanding of the grief reaction following a death can be helpful in understanding the grief children may feel at the time of separation.

Generally, after a death the mourners become preoccupied with thoughts of the departed person. This preoccupation provides for a piece-by-piece desensitization to the trauma. Each time one thinks about the dead person the pain associated with the loss becomes a little more bearable. The phenomenon is similar to the kind of reaction soldiers may suffer in response to extremely traumatic combat conditions. In shell shock (the World War I term), or combat neurosis (the World War II term), or post-traumatic stress disorder (the term used since the Vietnam War), the individual relives in fantasy and dreams the battlefield traumas. Most of us have seen war movies in which a soldier in a military hospital wakes up at night in panic at the sound of shells that only he hears. Although each repetition may bring terror, there is a gradual reduction in the intensity and frequency of the panic states. Such repetition appears to be part of the natural process of accommodating to a trauma. Although such a soldier appears to be "sick," the sickness in this case is actually the curative process. The doctors can do little in such situations but protect the man from hurting himself and causing undue alarm to others while waiting for the desensitization to run its course. Even though tranquilizers might reduce somewhat the soldier's anxiety, one would not want to remove totally the preoccupation. To do so would be to deprive the man of the opportunity to adjust to the traumas he has suffered.

Similarly, following a death the mourners may talk at length about the loved one, and various possessions of the departed person may now become treasured mementos. They not only provide a symbolic link with the departed person but can serve as a focus for desensitizing preoccupations and discussions. For the purpose of this discussion, I will use the term grief to refer to this desensitizing process. Once grieving is accomplished the person is then free to become involved in new relationships. If grieving does not occur, the person may not adjust adequately to the loss, and various kinds of psychological abnormalities may also result.

Helping children grieve. Although children of divorce do not actually lose a parent, they may never again live with the departed parent and are likely to react to the separation by grieving. In fact, considering the healthy purposes of the grief reaction, I would consider it unhealthy if a child old enough to appreciate what was happening did not react with grief. (In those rare situations where the child actually welcomes the separation because it promises a cessation of misery, of course, the failure to have a grief reaction is not a sign of a psychological problem.) Parents who inhibit their children from expressing their feelings will generally squelch their natural expression of grief. Parents who will not cry and express other emotions of remorse and regret in front of the children—in the misguided belief that it is best to protect them from such displays—serve as poor models for their children's expressing their grief. Parents who show little tolerance for their children's repetitious questioning may deprive them of the repeated discussion and preoccupation that are crucial for psychological relief. And, of course, parents who provide little or no information about the separation further impede their children's adjustment. Such information gives the children specific things to think about and particular concerns over which they can have emotional reactions. Without such data there is less chance children will grieve. In addition to the value of the specific information gained, the *process of seeking and receiving the information* in itself enables the children to reassure themselves of parental interest and involvement.

Although children of divorce may not need mementos of the departed parent (the real person is usually still available), they should have the opportunity for frequent contact with the person who has left the home, either personally or by telephone. Parents should also recognize that withdrawal into fantasy during this period need not represent an impending psychiatric deterioration; rather, it can serve as part of the grieving process and enable the child to work though reactions to the separation. Play fantasy may serve similar purposes. For example, a little girl may reenact with her dolls the various events surrounding the separation. Each time she does this the pain becomes a little more bearable. Or she may play that she is visiting her father in his new home and thereby lessen the sadness of her separation. Or a child may become preoccupied with a storybook that depicts either directly or symbolically events related to the separation. Often a child selects a story with a happy ending, one in which the parent returns. Obviously, the selection relates to the story's wish-fulfillment potential for the child. Parents should not discourage children from indulging themselves in these preoccupations to some degree. Only if children become so preoccupied that they seriously neglect important areas of their lives such as school and peer play should such withdrawal be discouraged. When the fantasies have served their purpose, and if the child has generally adjusted well to the separation, the time devoted to fantasies will gradually diminish.

Differences between grief following divorce and grief following death. An identifiable grieving reaction is less frequently seen following divorce than following the death of a parent. This is partly due to the fact that there is less of a loss. A parent's living elsewhere (even at a greater distance) is a very different thing from a parent's being dead. Also, death is a sudden event, no matter how long anticipated. Separation, in contrast, is the next step in a series of events that have slowly led up to it. It is rarely as shocking as death, and so less grieving is required to deal with it. When one adds to these factors the child's tendency to deny, as well as parental grief-suppressing influences, it is not surprising that so few children grieve overtly at the time of the separation. In spite of its infrequency, however, grieving does occur, and I believe that it is preferable that it should, because failure to grieve may result in the child's developing disturbed responses to the separation. There is no single type of unhealthy reaction exhibited by the child who has not had a grief reaction. Rather there are a variety of problems that result from such suppression. Many of the symptoms described in the remainder of this chapter result from the failure of children to express their thoughts and feelings about the separation.

SADNESS AND DEPRESSION

Unless the children react with relief to the separation because it brings about a cessation of parental strife (the rare situation), the children are bound to be sad over the departure of one of their parents. I will use the term *sadness* to refer to the state of unhappiness with which many children may respond to the separation and the term *depression* to refer to a deeper and more painful state of sorrow. Sadness is the more common and predictable state. Depression, however, generally suggests that psychological problems are present in the child, in the parent(s), and in their relationships with one another. Because normal sadness may evolve into depression, there may be times when it is hard to differentiate between the two. Nevertheless the distinction may be useful. Sadness usually subsides with time and is generally of short duration. Depression may last for a considerable period, and because psychological problems are usually contributing, additional symptoms are generally present and treatment may be necessary.

Sadness. Probably the main manifestation of sadness in children whose parents have separated is diminished capacity for pleasure. These children may no longer be able to derive pleasure from play or from watching their favorite television programs. When they do play, they may become preoccupied with themes involving a search for a lost loved one or the magic reappearance of someone who has disappeared. Or they may not be able to enjoy spending time with peers and may withdraw from them. They may walk around in a forlorn state and resort to daydreams as their primary source of gratification. Some may try to escape from their feelings of sadness by compulsive involvement in physical activities or academic pursuits. Some do all right in school, where they can become distracted from their unhappiness, but when home alone they become absorbed in their unhappy preoccupations. Some try to deny their sadness with comments such as "It doesn't bother me." But the stiff-upper-lip front usually doesn't hold up too long, and a child may burst out in tears, only to resume the facade. The sadness of many such children may be deepened by their feelings that they have been abandoned because they are not worthy of affection.

For most children there is gradual improvement in the unhappy state. They adjust to the loss, involve themselves once again in their previous activities and sources of pleasure, and give up their unhappy preoccupations. The most important determinant as to whether such sadness will be short-lived is the rapidity with which children become reassured that the absent parent is still involved. In addition, if the parents are able to avoid power struggles, the sadness is likely to go away even more rapidly. If, however, sad children do not have these healthy experiences, it is possible that the sadness will continue and turn into depression.

Depression. A state of depression in children is usually characterized by loss of appetite, diminished interest in and concentration on studies, general apathy, loss of enjoyment from play and peer relationships, helplessness, hopelessness, irritability, obsessive self-criticism, and withdrawal. In addition, some children exhibit feelings of impotence and vulnerability, extreme boredom, inability to complete projects and assignments, poor motivation, low frustration tolerance, and inability to use play to work out their reactions to the separation. In severe cases depressed children may become preoccupied with self-destructive fantasies, may become accident-prone and unconcerned for their personal safety, and may exhibit suicidal gestures and even attempts. The full-blown picture, of course, does not have to exist to justify using the term—there are varying intensities of depression that would warrant the label.

In recent years many mental health professionals, especially psychiatrists, have come to view depression as primarily or even exclusively produced by a biological (metabolically determined) disorder. Many clinicians tend to dismiss environmental, especially family, factors that may have contributed psychologically to the depression. But unlike many of my psychiatric colleagues, I believe that the vast majority of depressions are psychologically caused. I am not talking here about the disorder known as bipolar depression, formerly referred to as manic-depressive psychosis, but about the more common types of depression. Although I consider there to be a genetically determined predisposition to the development of depression, I believe that the environmental and psychological factors are the most important. Therefore, although many of my colleagues are prone to treat depressions almost exclusively with medication, I emphasize psychotherapy, although I do use antidepressants to help alleviate depression in selected cases. My position on this point is even stronger for children. My experience has been that manifestations of bipolar depression in children are even more rare than in adults and that therefore medication is even more seldom warranted. My comments here, then are based on this view of depression. I may be in the minority among psychiatrists on this point; however, my opinions are certainly shared by many psychotherapists who are not psychiatrists.

Because of their natural lightheartedness (as well as the ease with which they can utilize primitive denial mechanisms) children tend not to become depressed as readily as adults. Nevertheless, parental separation is a depressing event, and children do become depressed in response. That is natural. If few or no additional factors contribute to or entrench the depression, it should lift within a few weeks or, at the most, months. The healthy human being is quite resilient—and children are especially so. If the depression persists, it is likely that other factors are contributing.

In children who have not gone through a healthy grieving experience, pent-up feelings may contribute to a general feeling of discontent. Emotional expression is followed by feelings of psychological cleansing and even elation; whereas suppressed feelings continually press for release. The internal psychological conflict produced between the feelings that press for release and the forces that repress them is emotionally draining and anxiety provoking. Such states rob one of the capacity for enjoyment and contribute to depression. Accordingly, parents of children who have not had a grief reaction ought to attempt to help them have a mourning experience—even though belated. They should encourage the children to talk, should point out the value of crying and releasing one's feelings, and should serve as models for such release themselves.

Parental depression, especially in the parent with whom the child lives, may also contribute to children's being depressed. If the custodial parent sees the separation as an opportunity for a better life, it is likely that the children will come to take a positive attitude as well. If, however, the custodial parent becomes distraught and depressed, the children are likely to react similarly.

If a child has been overdependent on the absent parent, the loss is felt much more sharply and depression may become severe. The feelings of helplessness may become profound, as such children may fear that they cannot survive. Sometimes these children have been overprotected by the departed parent and made to feel that their very existence depends upon the maintenance of a close tie with the parent. Such children must be helped to understand *and* experience that they have the capacity to function without the absent parent and that survival does not depend upon his or her continuous presence.

Depression sometimes develops in children who interpret a parent's leaving as a rejection and abandonment of themselves rather than of the remaining parent. Such children may consider the parent's leaving to be a statement not only that they are not loved, but also that they are not lovable. A girl whose father has left the home (however benevolently) may reason: "If he loved me, he would stay. His leaving means that he doesn't love me. If he doesn't love me no one can love me. I am unlovable!" The resultant feelings of self-loathing contribute to the child's depressive reaction. In working with such a child I try to help her recognize that her father still loves her, even though he no longer loves her mother; and that her mother still loves her, even though she no longer loves her father.

In situations in which there is indeed some deficiency in the absent parent's affection, I try to help children understand that the deficiency lies in the unloving parent, not in themselves. If I can get such children successfully to gain affection from substitutes, this message is more likely to be incorporated as the child has living experiences that verify it. Although these children may be justified in feeling angry that they got short shrift "when God gave out fathers (mothers)," I try to engender in them a sense of pity for parents who go through life without ever knowing the joys and gratifications of contributing actively to the growth and development of their own children. I also try to help the children direct their anger into constructive channels.

Pent-up anger can contribute to depression. Anger at the time of parental separation is not surprising, when one considers that children of divorcing parents are losing one of their most treasured possessions—a parent. Some children are very inhibited in expressing their anger. Often they grew up in households where they were made to feel guilty about angry feelings—especially those felt toward their parents. But even without an inhibiting family environment, children of divorce are in a particularly difficult position with their anger. They may fear expressing anger toward the departed parent, lest they see even less of him or her; and they may fear directing it toward the custodial parent, lest he or she too will abandon them. Many psychological symptoms can arise from pent-up anger. The guilt children feel over releasing their anger and/or the punishments they anticipate for such expression prevent them from revealing it. They may, however, direct it against themselves. The target is a safe one and can be relied upon not to retaliate. The most common manifestation of self-directed anger is obsessive self-criticism. These children may berate themselves mercilessly with comments such as "I'm no good," "I'm terrible," "I can't do anything right," and "I'm worthless." And this self-criticism contributes to the child's depression. Such self-berating may seem puzzling, because nothing the child is doing or saying seems to warrant such severe self-loathing. The comments become readily understandable, however, when one replaces the name of the child with the name of the actual person at whom the child is angry (generally one or both of the parents). "I'm no good" then becomes "He (or she) is no good." "I'm terrible" becomes "He (or she) is terrible." When such children can be helped to express more guiltlessly the anger they really feel they will have less need to direct their anger against themselves and hence will be less depressed.

Some children exhibit their depressive tendencies via self-destructive preoccupations, accident proneness, and even suicidal tendencies. Although suicide is rare among children below the age of twelve, it certainly does happen. A significant percentage of bona fide suicide attempts by children in this age group occur among those from broken homes. (In this young age group it is often difficult to differentiate bona fide suicides from death resulting from feigned attempts in which the child's poor judgment resulted in accidental death.) Despair and loneliness associated with feelings of being unloved and unwanted may be too much for such children to bear. A revenge element is often present. A boy, for example, may have the fantasy that his parents, whom he sees as rejecting, will be painfully guilty over the way they have maltreated him. He may fantasize being buried while his guilty parents cry out remorsefully how bad they feel about their neglect of him and how they wish that they could once again have the chance to show their affection. But it is too late; they must live with their guilt. Sometimes the suicide attempt is associated with a desire for death and rebirth into a happier life with truly loving parents—parents who never divorce. Some children feel so insecure and inadequate that they do not feel that they can survive without the loving care of both parents, so they kill themselves rather than suffer a slow, torturous death.

George, a nine-year-old boy who was referred to me for treatment, demonstrated well the relationship between denial, repressed anger, and depression. George's father was a heavy drinker who could not keep a job because of his alcoholism. His mother, a masochistic woman, not only supported her husband but meekly submitted to his verbal and physical abuse. George too was beaten frequently by his father, even as early as the age of nine months. Finally, when George was three, his mother left her husband and returned to the home of her mother. During the following year George saw his father on two occasions. Once the father took him to the movies and once he was taken along while the father visited with drinking friends. After the age of three George never saw his father again, and at the time of referral the father's whereabouts were unknown.

George came to treatment because of depression. Few activities gave him pleasure. Although a good student, he got little enjoyment from his academic accomplishments. He had little interest in being with friends because he got so little pleasure from playing with them. He criticized himself mercilessly over the most minor mistakes and indiscretions. When asked about his father, he spoke of him in the most glowing terms. He described three or four years of frequent visits during which they enjoyed together only the most pleasurable activities. When confronted with his mother's version of what had happened, he claimed that his mother's memory was at fault. About his stepfather, who was also cruel to George at times (but nowhere nearly as cruel as his father had been), George stated: "He's almost as good as my father was to me." It was quite clear that George had to deny his father's rejection as well as the anger he felt over it. The repressed anger was contributing to his depression and self-deprecation. Even the anger George felt toward his stepfather could not be expressed and was contributing to his depressed feelings.

Low self-esteem is intimately associated with depression. Often, the self-loathing of depressed people reaches preposterous levels in which there is massive denial that they could have any qualities worthy of the interest and/or affection of anyone. However, the feelings of low self-worth are usually not entirely delusional. The depressed individual is often doing things that contribute to the development and perpetuation of feelings of low self-esteem. In my therapeutic work with such patients, I look into how they may be contributing to this aspect of their problem. Engaging in activities that are generally considered unacceptable produces feelings of low self-esteem. Exaggerated or inappropriate guilt is intrinsically associated with self-loathing. People who do not express or assert themselves properly are left with churning resentment and frustration that cause self-loathing. Although these and other sources of low self-esteem are best explored by trained therapists, parents should be alerted to these factors and do whatever they can to alleviate them in their children.

I wish to emphasize that I have only touched upon some factors that may contribute to depression. A child who is moderately to severely depressed generally has significant psychiatric difficulties—difficulties of which the complex origins are beyond the scope of this book and beyond the capacity of parents themselves to alleviate. Accordingly, I cannot recommend strongly enough that parents whose children are depressed seek psychiatric treatment for them. The treatment of such children is vital because depressed children are likely to become depressed adults, and suicidal children (if they survive) are likely to become suicidal adults. And the broken home, in which children have been exposed to significant strife and deprivation, appears to be a most important contributing factor to the development of adult depression and suicide.

FEAR OF ABANDONMENT

Children of divorce will often consider the departing parent to be abandoning them. Although continually reassured that this is not the case—that they are still loved very much—they tend to hold on to this concept of what is going on. Their world becomes a shaky place indeed. If one parent can leave the home, what is to prevent the remaining parent from doing so as well? Children living in an intact, relatively stable home are not concerned to a significant degree with a breakup of the home. For children of divorce such an event is part of the scheme of things. They may come to view all human relationships as potentially unstable. It is almost as if no one can be trusted. The resulting insecurity and instability can be frightening.

The parent's preoccupation with their conflicts prior to the separation and with the various legal and other details associated with the separation may allow little time for emotional investment in the children. Although both parents may still be in the house, the children already feel abandoned. And the new obligations that the custodial parent usually has to assume may result in the children's having even less time with the remaining parent than they had before.

A mother may have initiated the divorce proceedings because of certain activities of the father that she found objectionable. From the children's point of view, the father has been forced to leave the house because he has been "bad." What is to stop their mother from similarly forcing them to leave the house when they are bad? They may come to feel that no matter how much love their mother may have for them, they have now become an added burden for her. And indeed, the pressures of time, work, and money a divorced mother must bear on her children's behalf are often formidable. Her awareness that having children lessens her chances for remarriage must, at times, be painful. Thoughts about how much easier her life would be without the children are inevitable. These thoughts may even be verbalized by the mother; but even if not, the children sense them and react with fears that their mother may abandon them in order to lessen her burden. Commonly, such a mother displaces onto the children the resentment she feels over her situation, and this further intensifies their fears of rejection and abandonment.

Some children may react with panic states in which there may be sweating, palpitations, trembling, agitation, and an assortment of fears. There may be fear of their getting sick with no one to care for them, and there may be associated fears of dying. I am not referring here to the kind of panic states, much more frequently seen in adults, in which there is no known external cause. Such states may very well be related to biological abnormalities, and medication is clearly the primary treatment. Rather, I am referring here to panic states in children that have their onset following the parents' separation and that are much more likely to be the result of psychological factors.

Other children may not exhibit these panic states but become generally tense over their fears of abandonment. Such tension may reveal itself by generalized irritability, low frustration tolerance, difficulty falling asleep, trouble concentrating in school, and tics (especially of the face). Difficulty concentrating on television is a very sensitive indicator of tension in a child. Although the abandonment fear may contribute to such states of tension, other factors often contribute. A boy, for example, may harbor intense hostility toward one or both of his parents and may feel very guilty over his anger. He may become anxious when his rage builds up to the point where it can no longer be contained. In order to protect himself from the terrible consequences he anticipates from the expression of his anger, he may continue to squelch his hostility. And his fears that his anger will be exposed can contribute to his tension. Not only does such a child need reassurances (and living experience to corroborate) that his fears of abandonment are unwarranted, but he also has to be helped to feel less guilty over his hostility.

Following the separation, some children (especially very young ones) may wander around the house looking for the departed parent even though repeatedly told that the parent will no longer be living in the home. The child may search the closets and under the beds or may stand pathetically at the door awaiting the parent's return. Some children will express fears that the departed parent will find substitutes for themselves elsewhere. One little girl roamed around the house crying, "I'll need a new father." In response to their abandonment fears many children will reach out to strangers, seeking affection. Often children's play will serve to lessen abandonment fears. For example, they may create stories in which all the homes are intact and the children receive an abundance of love and care. Or, more symbolically, the play fantasies may include animals whose caretakers provide them with dedicated protection and affection. The animals, of course, represent the children themselves. It is as if each time the children bestow favors on the animals they provide themselves with similar gratifications. Some children will deal with their abandonment fears by endless conversations with the departed parent on a toy telephone.

A child may become overly dependent upon and cling excessively to the custodial parent. Separation anxieties may develop, and the child may refuse to visit friends or go to school. When the school becomes the special focus of such fears, the term "school phobia" is often used. The label is a poor one because it implies that the child is afraid of the school; usually the child is afraid to part with the parent at home, and if that parent were permitted to stay with the child in the classroom, there would generally be no fear. Many factors contribute to such separation anxieties. For example, the custodial parent may become overprotective in order to compensate the child for the loss of the other parent or to lessen guilt over the separation, and overprotection entrenches the child's overdependency and fear of separation. In a more complex way, the child may be very angry at the parent (for having instigated the separation, for example) and fear that the hostile wishes will be realized by harm befalling the parent or by the parent's dying. By clinging to the parent and keeping him or her ever in sight the child is reassured that the hostile wishes have not caused the parent any harm.

Some children will try to lessen their feelings of abandonment by provoking punishment from one or both parents. They are willing to suffer the pain that such punishment entails for the reassurance that the parent is still very much there. What better way is there to confirm a parent's existence than to be struck or maltreated by him or her? Other factors, of course, may be contributing to such behavior. For example, the provocative behavior may serve as an outlet for hostility. Or the child may feel guilty over his or her anger, and receiving punishment may serve to reduce this guilt. All children want controls and will test parents with various provocations in order to learn from experience what is acceptable behavior and what is not. The child living with only one parent will have to use that parent more frequently for this purpose and so will appear, from that parent's vantage point, to be more provocative than previously.

Some children, in an attempt to lessen abandonment fears, will involve themselves in various maneuvers designed to increase their parents' affection for them. For example, when with his father, a boy will side with him against the mother, refrain from saying positive things about her, and confine himself to criticisms that he knows his father wishes to hear. And he will involve himself similarly with his mother. In this way the child attempts to ensure that he is in the good graces of both parents. When parents realize what is going on, they do well to communicate to their children that such games cause them to lose, not gain, affection. The children should be helped to appreciate that parents can only resent being taken in, and that the children risk experiencing more rejection than they might have otherwise. In addition, the children should be helped to appreciate that they cannot feel good about themselves lying in this way, and that feelings of unworthiness are adding unnecessarily to their difficulties. In short, children must be helped to appreciate that no one likes liars: neither the people they lie to nor the liars themselves.

For a child to tell each parent what the child believes that parent wants to hear is so common it is almost predictable in the vast majority of children of divorce. Unfortunately, there are parents who may be so blinded by rage that they relish every criticism of the other parent, no matter how preposterous. This serves only to polarize the parents even further and can thus contribute to a perpetuation of difficulties for both the parents and children.

When a mother moves back with her own parents following the separation the children are less likely to suffer with abandonment fears. Although they no longer live with their father, their two grandparents may make them feel that the trade wasn't really so bad. However, the situation usually isn't so simple. The grandparents often resent their new obligations, and the grandparents' resentment may cause the children to suffer further feelings of rejection and fears of abandonment. Also, observing their mother's dependent relationship with her parents cannot but weaken children's respect for and feelings of security with their mother. The situation may produce even greater feelings of insecurity in the children.

Many abandonment fears diminish with time, as the children have the living experience that their fears are unwarranted, that they still have good relationships with both parents, that the parents are still available to them in spite of the separation. Distortions of and misconceptions about reality often contribute to children's abandonment fears. And it behooves parents to help their children correct such distortions. Children must be helped to appreciate that they still have *two* parents and that if something happens to the custodial parent they can still live with the noncustodial. There are children of divorce who will say, "My father divorced *us*" or even "My father divorced *me*." Obviously, the child must be led to understand that the father has divorced only the mother, not the children.

In addition, the parents should discuss with the children exactly which friends and relatives would be available to take care of them in the event that both parents could not. (All children should be told, at the proper time, who will be caring for them if their parents die or become so incapacitated that they cannot care for them. For the children of divorce such information is even more important.) In situations in which there are few, if any, friends or relatives who could care for the children if something were to happen to both parents, then boarding schools and foster homes should be discussed. The children's gaining the feeling that no matter what happens, there will be someone to take care of them is crucial to the alleviation of abandonment fears. It can also be useful to impress upon children the fact that as they get older they will become increasingly independent and less at the mercy of adults who might reject them. Older children may see the importance of applying themselves to educational and career pursuits so that they will be less beholden to others and less impotent to deal with rejections.

ACTUAL ABANDONMENT

As mentioned, most children feel abandoned by the parent who leaves the home. In most cases this perception is false and the departing parent maintains an active interest in the children. However, there are situations in which the term abandonment is appropriate. Some parents cut themselves off from the children entirely, or the contacts are so infrequent and/or made with so little conviction that the children are essentially deprived of a real relationship with the absent parent. It is to this problem of truly abandoned children (abandoned either in fact or psychologically) that I direct my comments here.

Total abandonment. I believe that in psychologically healthy individuals maternal and paternal instincts are inborn and strong. Nevertheless, there are parents who take the position that it's best for the children that they have no contact with them following the separation. "It's best that I make a clean break of it," such a parent may proclaim, or, "Rather than see them once in a while, and raise their hopes and then disappoint them, it'll be better for them if I never see them at all." An extreme form of rationalization for rejecting children goes like this: "When one divorces, it's best for the departed parent and children to consider one another *dead*. Each must pick up the pieces and start life anew, without in any way impeding one another." Although it is obvious how the children can be seen as interfering with the adult's remaking his or her life, no explanation is given regarding how the children's continuing contact with the adult hinders *their* growth and healthy development.

There are also parents who, somewhat rejecting of their children before the separation, become so much more so afterward that they can justifiably be placed in the category of abandoning parents. A father may suddenly become so swept up in his "freedom" that he completely neglects his children. A mother may become so burdened by her new responsibilities that she will have little time and strength for affectionate involvement with her children; or the resentments she now harbors may compromise significantly her maternal expression.

"Always reassure the children that the absent parent still loves them." When abandonment occurs, it is common for the remaining parent to protect the children from the perceived harmful effects of the truth. Statements frequently utilized in the service of this protective goal include: "He loves you inside; he just can't show it." "She doesn't want to be mean; she can't help it." "I guess he forgot to come to see you. His memory was never very good." Parents who protect their children in this way are generally well meaning. Often they are supported by professional authorities who hold the view that the children's learning that a parent doesn't love them will cause psychological damage. "Always reassure the children," they advise, "that the absent parent still loves them."

Unfortunately, both the parents and professionals here are misguided. The explanations provided the child can only be confusing. "What can this thing called love be all about," the child will wonder, "if someone can love you and never (or rarely ever) show it?" I do not claim to have a firm definition of the word love; but the word does not apply to a situation in which the so-called lover has practically no interest at all in being with the alleged loved one. Such children are likely to grow up with distortions about love that will interfere with their forming successful relations with others in the future. In addition, they will often sense, at some level, the parent's lack of conviction in what he or she tells them. Accordingly, cover-ups breed distrust of the remaining parent. Children have had enough distrust produced already with the departure of one parent; they certainly don't need to develop distrust of the remaining parent.

In a situation of abandonment, children should be told the

truth as realistically as possible. If the absent parent's interest amounts to one visit or greeting card a year, then the children should be told that the parent has little love for them but does think enough of them to extend him- or herself to that degree. If there is no contact at all, then the fact that the parent does not love them should be allowed—gently—to emerge. Once again, however, I would try to instill the notion that something is seriously wrong with parents who cannot love their own children. To be angry at the abandoning parent is reasonable; but pity is also appropriate.

The children have to be helped to become comfortable with their angry reactions to the abandonment and not to feel guilty over their resentful feelings. They should be helped to appreciate that angry thoughts and feelings (including profanities and death wishes) are natural and inevitable in such situations. However, mere expression of the anger accomplishes little more than providing temporary release. The children should also be helped to use their anger constructively to try to build a relationship with the absent or deficient parent. If these efforts fail (and they most often do), the children should be helped to understand that the angry feelings will best be dispelled by their gaining substitute satisfactions from others.

And the child should try to feel pity for the parent, because the latter is missing out on one of the most enriching experiences of life, namely, loving and rearing one's own child. If the children show signs of trying to gain the affection of a parent who has proved him- or herself incapable of providing love, they should be discouraged from this futile pursuit. (Telling the children that an unloving parent really loves them can contribute to these futile endeavors—another reason for not providing the children with protective explanations.) In addition, I try to help children appreciate that just because their own parent does not love them does not mean that they are unlovable. It behooves them to seek other living relationships in compensation for the loss of the parent. Such children, however, will believe that they can indeed gain affection from others only when they have *living experiences* that this is true. Only after the children have enjoyed such substitute relationships will they really be convinced that the defect does not lie within themselves.

Partial abandonment. Only in extreme cases is there total separation between the child and the parent. The more common situation is the one in which the rejecting parent has varying degrees of contact with and interest in the children. Here again, the custodial parent should help the children see as clearly as possible the reality of their situation. The children should be discouraged from trying to extract more affection than the absent parent is capable of or willing to provide; for example, two postcards a year, one visit a year, one Christmas present a year. They should be helped to recognize that some degree of rejection is not the same as total abandonment. The children of such a parent can try first to gain more attention from the parent by expressing their grievances. Also, they should try to determine if they may be contributing to the parent's alienation and attempt to alter any behavior patterns that may be causing some of the parent's withdrawal. Once these efforts have been made (such contributions by the children usually play a minor role in parental withdrawal), the children do well to accept what the parent has to give, however limited, and not strive to acquire what is impossible to obtain.

Children who decide to have nothing to do with such parents because they have so little to offer (and this decision is more common among adolescents than among younger children) may be depriving themselves of valuable gratifications from the relationship. And custodial parents who actively try to prevent minimal and unpredictable contact are doing their children a disservice. (Sometimes such parents may even try to prevent legally the deficient parent's infrequent and unreliable involvements.) They may justify their intervention with the argument that such sporadic involvement and its attendant frustration does the children more harm than good. I believe that unpredictable involvement, even with its frustrations for the children, is generally better for children than no contact at all. The children of a deficient parent have to be helped not to place themselves in positions where their hopes are going to be unnecessarily raised and then dashed. They have to be helped to resign themselves to what they can realistically expect to gain from the deficient parent. We all have to learn how to make such compromises in life in our relationships with others, and accomplishing this in childhood can be a useful preparation for similar experiences in later life.

If both the deficient parent and the children still wish to have contact with one another, in spite of the parent's defects, this should be respected by the custodial parent—except, of course, in situations where the children are exposed to physical brutality or other obviously damaging behavior by the rejecting parent. Often the custodial parent who tries to sever the relationship with the deficient parent does so not so much from a concern for the child's best interests as from a desire to wreak vengeance. The absent parent's deficiencies serve as the excuse for such action. By depriving the absent parent of any contact with the children, the custodial parent attempts to gain the maximum in retribution. Of course, the children's needs here are being ignored in the service of vengeful gratification.

Furthermore, if the custodial parent is successful in restricting or even prohibiting (with court support) visitation with the neglectful parent, the latter is provided with an excellent weapon against the former. For example, a mother may decide that the father's infrequency and unpredictability of visitation is bad for the children and thereby justifies a total cessation of visitation. She may even obtain a court order to "protect" the children from the frustrations they suffer in their relationship with their father. In response the father is likely to say, "I would visit you much more often because I love you so much. However, your mother has stopped me from visiting you, and she even got the judge to agree with her. There is nothing I can do about it now." Her action not only provides the father with a rationalization that the children are likely to believe but gives him a weapon to use against her. The children may then blame the mother for the cessation of visitation rather than recognize their father's defects. It would have been far better for the children to have had living experiences in which they gained an accurate picture of the father's negligence on their own.

How children can determine the degree of affection of the absent parent.

Whether the absent parent is deeply loving, moderately affectionate, partially abandoning, or totally abandoning, the children are generally confused about his or her degree of love for them. Often these children have similar questions about the custodial parent's affection as well. Such children can be encouraged to look for behavioral patterns that can provide useful information about the parent's degree of affection.

I realize that criteria for parental affection cannot be measured precisely and that there is the distinct possibility that children (especially younger ones) will have difficulty utilizing them accurately. For example, a five-year-old girl may consider her father's three visits per week to be deficient and conclude that he has little affection for her. It behooves both parents to help children correct this kind of inaccurate interpretation, because misunderstandings like this can cause children unnecessary worry and feelings of deprivation. Even so, most parents, I believe, will agree that there are valid criteria by which to judge parental affection. Children should not be deprived of their benefits because of their occasional misapplication.

One measure is the frequency with which the parent wishes to be with the children. Parents do have other duties and obligations than spending time with their children; however, in spite of these, loving parents will want to spend significant amounts of time with their children and will manage to do so. The parents who frequently find excuses for not having such contacts (visitation limitations notwithstanding) may very well be defective in the depth of their feelings for their children.

Another criterion is the parents' willingness to inconvenience themselves in order to be of help to the children—especially when the children are sick, injured, or having other difficulties. I encourage children to observe how much pride parents appear to have in their accomplishments. And I suggest that children try to determine how often a parent speaks favorably about them to others. I also encourage children to determine how often the parent enjoys *doing* mutually pleasurable things with them. If this rarely occurs it may suggest some deficiency.

Children should be encouraged to ascertain the amount of physical contact the parent desires to have with them. Parents who are somewhat compromised in their affection for their children have little desire to have such contact. The younger the children the greater the likelihood that such physical contact will involve snuggling and gentle roughhousing, cuddling, tucking them in, and allowing the children to come into the parent's bed on holiday and weekend mornings.

Children should be helped to appreciate that it is normal and expected that a parent will occasionally get angry at them; even a few times a day is within the normal range. However, if a parent is consistently grumpy and irritable, then there is probably a problem.

Although these criteria for parental affection may be difficult to apply, I have found them extremely useful in my therapeutic work with children of divorce. When properly utilized by parents who are willing to discuss them openly and honestly with their children, these criteria can provide valuable information that may help the children avert, as well as deal with, many of the psychological disturbances that may result when parents divorce. The criteria are particularly useful for children who feel that they have been abandoned. If this has indeed been the case (either actually or psychologically), then their suspicions will be confirmed and they will be in a better position to resign themselves to their misfortune and take those steps necessary to deal with the situation. And if the criteria demonstrate that the children's fears of abandonment were not warranted, they can provide invaluable reassurance and lessen an unnecessary burden that such children may have been taking on.

RUNNING AWAY FROM HOME

Although not common, running away from home is one of the ways some children react to parental separation. There is generally no one single reason for a given child's flight from the home; one or more factors may contribute in varying combinations.

Common reasons for children's fleeing the home.

First, a child's disappearing from the home is an act that is predictably going to attract the attention and involvement of the parents. In fact, of all the things a child can do to attract attention and concern, running away is one of the most powerful. And parental concern may reassure runaway children that they are still wanted—that they have not been totally rejected and abandoned. Fears of being abandoned are thereby reduced. These reassurances are especially enjoyed at the time when runaway children finally return home. The parents may have spent hours, days, weeks, or longer distraught with guilt and worry. They may have enlisted the aid of the police and even the public media. When the runaway finally makes a grand reappearance or is dramatically discovered (often with the child's conscious or unconscious assistance), there are parental sighs of relief, thanking God that the child is all right, and so on. All this serves to reassure runaways that they are loved and wanted. Even if they are punished after this initial period of parental elation and joyful reunion, the attention-getting purpose has been served.

Running away from home can lessen rejection and abandonment fears in another way. By running away, it is as if children say to themselves: "It is not we who have been abandoned. We are the abandoners. We decide if separation of parents from children is to take place. We decide how and when it will occur." A face-saving element is also present here. The reasoning is similar to that of the jilted boy who claims that it was he who rejected his girlfriend and not vice versa. By considering himself to have initiated the rejection he gains a sense of power and control over the event and protects himself from the humiliation of being rejected.

Or fleeing from the home may serve as a cry for help from outside sources. In the inevitable discussions that take place after these children return, the assistance of people such as ministers, relatives, and therapists may be enlisted. As a result of the involvement of these parties runaway children may gain help for themselves. Sometimes the children will ask the counselor to encourage the parents to reconcile. But as I have said before, it would be unwise, if not intrusive, for such a counselor to intervene and encourage the parents to stay together. If one does this, one allows oneself to be used as a tool in the children's manipulations and only encourages them to run away again for this purpose or to utilize similar forms of manipulative behavior.

A common fantasy among runaway children (and probably among many adults) is that of grief and regret being suffered by those who have maltreated the child. As in the typical suicide fantasy, the contrite parties weep at the memory of the maltreated one, regretting the neglect, cruelty, and insensitivity that they exhibited in their relations with the departed. So powerful is this fantasy that there are some for whom it plays a significant role in suicidal acts. (Of course, many suicidal people appear to lose sight of the fact that even though suicide may indeed provoke such displays, they will not be there to observe the displays and gloat.) Runaway children often entertain similar images, fantasies that afford not only attention and affection but vengeful gratifications as well. Such children may derive immense satisfaction from envisioning the pain and grief their families suffer. A child might ruminate while away: "My father has hurt me by leaving the home; I'll hurt him in the same way. Just as I was sad when he left, now he'll be sad that I'm gone."

There is a more complex way in which running away relates to children's anger. Anger over which a person feels guilt may be projected onto someone else. These people deny that they harbor any anger within themselves and assume that it resides in others. Children who are guilty over their angry feelings may project them onto their parents and then expect that their parents will act out such anger by various forms of punishment. And they may flee from their homes in the hope of avoiding the cruel treatment they anticipate.

Other factors, as well, may contribute to children's fleeing the home. Some children consider the separation to have been the result of their having been "bad," and they may run away in order to avoid causing even worse trouble in the home. Some children may believe that the guilt that their running away will produce in their parents will be so great that the parents will change their minds and stay together in order to avoid further flights from the home. In these instances the flight is a guilt-provoking device designed to manipulate the parents into staying together. Fleeing the home can also serve the forces of denial. If runaways are not home to observe a parent's absence, they can more easily believe that the parent is still there. Some children may flee the general atmosphere of loneliness and depression that has prevailed in the home since the separation. Some run away in search of a parent who has truly abandoned the family and whose exact whereabouts are unknown. They hope to find the parent and live with him or her or convince the parent to return. Sometimes the more complex mechanism of identification with the departed parent may contribute to the child's flight. When a parent dies, some children (sometimes almost overnight) take on personality qualities of the deceased parent; and as I've mentioned, children of a parent who has left the home may act similarly. This identification is an attempt to reunite with the absent parent. Similarly, by imitating the absent parent's behavior (in this case, departing from the home), such children act as if they have a piece of that parent within themselves and so gain a feeling of closeness and lessen their sense of loss.

Dealing with children who run away from home.
Parents should try to surmise exactly which factors are operating when a child runs away. If a child announces plans (or threatens) to run away, the parent generally should discour-

age the child, take reasonable precautions, and impose practical restraints. The parent who responds to the running-away threat by packing the child's belongings and accompanying him or her to the door is only deepening the child's problems. A child who makes this threat is often asking for more attention and affection; inviting the child to leave cannot but produce even more feelings of rejection. After all, a parent who accompanies the child to the door is conveying the message that the parent wants the child out of the house. Parents may do this because they recognize the threat as manipulative and do not wish to allow themselves to be coerced. But one need not go so far to avoid manipulation. One can still refuse to comply with children's inappropriate demands *within the house*. Accompanying the children outside, rising to the dare, only increases their sense of rejection and adds further humiliation. Telling the children that running away is not allowed, that under no circumstances will they be permitted to do so, that they are still loved, and that their absence would cause terrible pain for the parents, will often prevent them from doing what they really don't want to do anyway. Letting them go so that they will have the living experience of how terrible it can be outside the home causes children to feel rejected and thereby compounds their problems.

Most children who leave the home usually go to a place where they will easily be found. Their fear of the unknown and their appreciation that they do not have the wherewithal to fend successfully for themselves causes them to stay close to home. Often they will hide in a nearby park or in a friend's house. When they feel that they have gotten enough mileage from their absence, they will allow themselves to be discovered. Or they may return home with some feeble excuse—for example, they really wanted to stay away but had to return home because they weren't sure the cat would be fed or because they had forgotten to take a toothbrush.

On occasion, a child will stay at the home of a friend whose parents don't know what is going on. When the friend's parents find out, they generally insist that the youngster return home and usually inform the child's parent of his or her whereabouts. However, there are neighbors who take pride in protecting children from the indignities they describe themselves to be suffering at the hands of their parents. Such neighbors may basically feel insecure about their own parental capacities and therefore revel in the praises bestowed upon them by the runaway. Or they may be rivalrous with and antagonistic to the runaway youngster's parents and gain hostile gratification from harboring the child. But these "good Samaritans" are not helping anyone. Instead of encouraging runaway youngsters to go back and try to work out the problems with their parents, they only widen the gap between them. Parents should inform such neighbors that they wish their child home immediately. If there is resistance, they should not hesitate to include in their ensuing comments such words as "illegal," "police," and "kidnapping." Generally, this will result in the protectors' reconsidering their position. Even on those rare occasions when the youngster is fleeing from real abuses, friends or neighbors should not take it upon themselves to provide protection. Community agencies should be brought to intervene in such cases.

I believe that the best attitude for parents to take when runaway children do come home is to express gratitude that they are safe, but also to express the anger that has been felt toward them for having caused the parents such grief. In order to let them know that they are still loved and missed, such children should be embraced. In response to the cruelty of their act—for having caused the parents to go through such an ordeal—they should be appropriately punished. This does not, of course, mean physical punishment. One could argue that punishing runaways on their return only increases the sense of rejection that contributed to their running away in the first place. I do not deny this possible negative effect of punishment. However, I believe that it is more than outweighed by the beneficial effect—namely, to deter the child from running away again.

IMMATURITY

In response to a trauma or to any situation in which children's usual satisfactions are not adequately provided, it is common for them to go back to earlier developmental levels in the hope of regaining gratifications enjoyed previously. Or such children may fail to advance beyond the developmental level they have reached in order to avoid taking on the newer demands of higher levels of maturation.

Regressive manifestations. Parental separation is the kind of trauma that may result in this kind of regression or fixation. For example, following the separation some children may start sucking their thumbs again, using baby talk, and becoming more infantile and demanding. They may ask to be fed or may want to go back to the bottle. Fully toilet-trained children may start soiling again or may ask the parent to wipe them when they go to the bathroom. Bed-wetting may be resumed. The child may feign illness (stomachaches, headaches, nausea, etc.) in order to have an excuse to avoid the demands of school and to remain home and be put to bed and pampered. Temper tantrums, irritability, and low frustration tolerance may become more frequent. Some children may respond to the new responsibilities of living in a one-parent home by whining and complaining that they just cannot do the things asked of them. They may refuse to go out and play or visit friends, when they had previously done so without difficulty. Clinging behavior (to the mother and/or teacher), rocking, or resumption of the need for a security blanket (or toy, doll, etc.) may also appear. The child may take longer to go to sleep and resume an earlier habit of making endless excuses to get the parent to return to the bedroom ("I want a glass of water," "I have to go to the bathroom," etc.). Or the child may want to sleep in the parent's bed. Masturbatory play may appear or, if previously present, may increase.

Some children exhibit fears of separation (after having reached the age where such fears are minimal) and may ask the parents to help them perform tasks they have previously proved themselves competent of accomplishing. Some children "parentify" an older sibling to provide dependency gratifications beyond what the parent(s) can offer. In school such children may work well only with individual attention by the teacher, whereas previously they could work well independently. In their fantasy play they may become preoccupied with such themes as feeding, cuddling, and protecting.

These types of regressive behavior are generally more common in younger children, as they are closer to the infantile state and are less likely than older children to have "forgotten" immature patterns. The presence of younger children in the household, too, will often provide a model for regressive manifestations and makes their appearance more likely.

Parental contributions to children's immaturity.

Generally, such fixations and regressions are transient and clear up within a few weeks or months following the separation. When they persist, other factors are usually contributing, the most common of which are parental overprotection and other forms of encouragement of the immature behavior.

Divorced parents are likely to provide such encouragement as a result of the guilt they may feel over the split in the family. Overindulging a child is one of the most common ways to reduce guilt. Visiting fathers, especially, as the "abandoners," often feel guilty and so are likely to try to provide their children with continual fun, games, and freedom from discipline during their visitation time. Because noncustodial fathers generally see the children when they are not working, they have the time for these indulgences. The custodial mother cannot so readily provide such gratifications for her children if she is to run her household effectively. Yet she may try to do so as well, her time limitations notwithstanding.

A mother left with the children may try to lessen her feelings of abandonment and loneliness by keeping them in an excessively dependent state. She may have had past insecurities about relating to adults, and the failure of her marriage may intensify these. Fearing further failures and rejections from adults (especially men), she may become excessively involved with her children—captive companions who have already proved their deep affection for her. Such a mother may find excuses for the children's not playing in the street, visiting friends, or taking other steps toward independence. Under the guise of concern for their welfare, she provides herself with companionship and makes herself feel more useful. In the extreme, such children may develop inhibitions in school and social relationships because such involvements and successes, as steps toward independence, create feelings of disloyalty toward their mother. They may even remain in their homes as adults, never leaving the mother who "needs them so much."

Either parent may consider the separation a threat to feelings of adequacy as a parent. The parent may therefore overindulge the child, hoping to prove parental competence. Or the parents may compete with one another over who can be the better parent, measuring their competence by the degree to which each can keep the children happy. Each parent may overindulge the children in an effort to win their affection away from the other or to gain an ally in the parental conflict. Such children are being used as vehicles to express parental hostility and are being bribed to serve as pawns in the parents' battle.

A woman may try to use a male child as a substitute for her lost husband. (It is less common for a husband to do this with a daughter, because his opportunities to find another woman are greater than his wife's chances to find another man—especially when she has custody of the children.) Such a mother may become seductive with her son, make comments about how he is now to be "the man of the house," and make the boy her adviser and confidant.

A parent may overindulge children as a way of combating basic inner feelings of hostility toward them. Such a parent may resent the obligations, frustrations, and restrictions of parenthood but be too guilty over such feelings to allow them to come into conscious awareness. Overprotection serves to deny and repress these hostilities. This mechanism reveals itself most clearly in the parent who frequently anticipates harm befalling the children—even when the situation does not warrant such concern and when other parents do not envision danger in the same situation. The basic hostile wish is revealed and released through the fantasy of harm befalling the child. Guilt over such fantasies is assuaged when the unconscious wish is turned into a fear; the parent can say, "It's not that I want anything to happen to my children, it's just that I worry about them." Overprotectiveness, then, serves simultaneously to gratify hostile wishes and to assuage the guilt that accompanies them. Of course, the separated parent may have special hostilities to deal with. For both parents, the children cannot but place restrictions on their lives that they could very well do without. The children's very existence requires both parents to maintain a relationship with one another that they most often would have liked to sever completely. Children may also make each parent somewhat less attractive to others as a possible mate. These additional sources of potential resentment are likely to intensify the parental overprotectiveness that is used to deny hostility.

Overindulgence of children can be used in the service of vicariously gratifying parental dependencies. That is, parents, by projecting themselves onto the child, can satisfy their own desire to be indulged. It is as if each time the child is ministered to, the parent is ministering to the fantasized projected self. And the greater the child's gratification from such indulgence, the greater the parent's. A divorced parent may experience an intensification of such dependencies after the separation. This is especially true of a parent who has been abandoned. The separation situation thus increases the tendency for susceptible parents to use this mechanism for vicariously gratifying their own frustrated dependency needs.

Masochistic parents—who get morbid gratification from pain (more commonly psychological than physical)—may find opportunities for suffering in making painful sacrifices for the child. And they may use overindulgence as a way of making such sacrifices. Another aspect of masochism pertinent here is the feeling among masochists that they are not basically of much use or value to others and that if they ask anything of others they will be rejected and abandoned. They believe that they will be accepted by others only if they relate on their terms. More specifically, they see themselves as capable of attracting only sadistic people—those who measure the affection of others by how much pain they are willing to suffer for them. Accordingly masochists operate on the principle that "The more pain I suffer on behalf of the one I love, the more I prove my affection." They allow themselves to be maltreated—to be used as scapegoats, as targets for the release of others' hostility. Allowing oneself to be taken advantage of can provide masochistic gratifications, and sacrificially giving to an overdemanding regressed child can provide a masochistic parent with continued opportunities for feeling put upon and exploited. The masochistically inclined parent who gets divorced may react to the separation by an intensification of the need for masochistic gratification. For example, the wife married to a sadistic husband may have to find new person to torture her after he leaves. A child may be the most convenient person to serve as a substitute, and sacrificial giving (and its attendant overprotection) may be selected as the mode of gratifying this need.

A divorced parent may try to compensate for feelings of inadequacy and lowered self-esteem by trying to produce and rear a perfect child. Oversolicitous attitudes may develop in the service of this cause. Working on the premise that a perfect child is one who is always happy, the parent may comply with the child's every demand. Such overprotection, as a method of compensating for lowered feelings of self-worth, may contribute to children's regression or fixation.

Parents may overindulge a child in order to obtain vicarious gratifications. Parents who raise their children in accordance with the principle "I want to give them everything I didn't have" can gain through the children some compensation for the disillusionment and disappointments of their own lives. Overprotection can enable such parents to live through the children and compensate for their own past privations—and for present and even anticipated privations too. The effort to make the child into everything such parents *wished to be but weren't and will never be* can provide such parents with solace. We all do this to some extent, and it is healthy to a degree, because it serves to provide children with parental encouragement. However, when a parent's view of the ideal existence for children is that they always get what they want when they want it, then parental overindulgence occurs and the children are likely to become overdependent. The divorced parent may have an even greater need than the parent in a relatively stable marriage to utilize this compensatory mechanism. Again, fixations and regression in the children are thereby encouraged.

There are parents who overindulge a child because they cannot tolerate anger—regardless of the age of the person who exhibits it and regardless of its appropriateness. The best way to avoid the anger of others is to prevent them from being frustrated; that is, to do everything they want. When this principle is applied to a child, the child becomes overindulged and pampered. Since the children of divorce are likely to be angry and even excessively demanding (at least around the time of separation), the likelihood of their being overindulged by such a parent becomes greater.

Parents may keep a child at an immature level in order to protect themselves against the lowered feelings of self-worth that would result if the child became their equal. The divorced parent is especially prone to feel insecure and may therefore be more likely to use this form of overprotection. Such insecure parents are essentially in competition with their children. They keep them down in order to maintain a false sense of superiority. They frequently communicate to their children such messages as "You're not old enough to do this" and "You're not mature enough to handle that" in areas where the parents of their children's peers see no difficulties.

Helping the immature child. Parents should appreciate that children's regressive behavior following separation is common and normal. Parents do well to allow intermittent gratification of regressive cravings, especially in the period immediately following the separation. The failure to allow limited gratification of regressive tendencies during this period may result in inordinate craving for regressive gratification, and this in turn can contribute to the formation of various kinds of psychological disturbance. However, these indulgences should be gradually reduced, lest they become entrenched.

Although some indulgence of immature behavior is warranted, parents should refrain from providing regressive gratifications for behavior that is suggestive of a specific psychological disorder. To do so may result in the child's developing the particular disturbance when it could have been prevented. For example, parents should not comply with a child's request to stay home from school because of minor physical symptoms. Rather they should keep a child home from school only when there is bona fide evidence of physical disease. It is better to err on the side of sending a slightly unwell child to school than to risk the development of a psychological disorder in which the child uses the most minor, and often imagined, physical complaints as an excuse to void separation from parents or the minor discomforts and frustrations that may be experienced in school and elsewhere. Parents of such children must appreciate that the risk to their children's physical health is so negligible that for all practical purposes it is nonexistent. Only in extremely rare diseases will a child's health be jeopardized by such an experience.

By the same token, the child who starts to wet should be asked to assist in the changing and washing of the sheets. Children who soil should also assist (to the degree appropriate to their age) in cleaning themselves and their underwear. Beyond the early postseparation period, a parent should not yield to infantile demands more than if the separation had not occurred. The child should not be allowed to manipulate his parents with temper tantrums. Rather, the parents must have thick skins and endure the tantrums. To indulge tantrums is to encourage their perpetuation. Having the stamina not to indulge them will generally result in their petering out.

Baby talk should be discouraged; the parents should simply not respond to communications made with infantile intonation. Children who have previously eaten on their own but now want to be fed should not be, even at the risk of their not eating. Some parents become so fearful of the child's developing severe nutritional deficiencies that they readily comply with such children's demands. But in the vast majority of children the likelihood of this happening is practically nonexistent. Practically all will begin to eat on their own when they become hungry enough. The child's request to have the bottle again might be complied with to a limited degree (allowing for some indulgence of the regressive pattern). And appropriate disciplinary measures should be imposed on the child who shirks from his usual (and now new) responsibilities.

If parents help a child understand the socially alienating effects of regressive behaviors, the child may make an effort to gain conscious control over exhibiting a symptom. Such suppression does not get to the underlying causes of a problem, but it does play a role in its alleviation. Confrontations must be benevolent, however, if they are to have any chance of being effective. For example, one can say to children who suck their thumbs: "If you knew how you looked when you put your thumb in your mouth, I don't think you'd do that in front of others."

The primary approach to the alleviation of regressive symptoms should be directed toward reducing the underlying contributing factors, not merely trying to suppress and discourage the symptom. In each child different underlying factors are operating. For example, a common cause of regressing is the belief that the separation will deprive the child entirely of the absent parent. Such children must be reassured and must have *living experiences* demonstrating that this will not be the case (except, of course, in the rare situation when it is). These children must be helped to acquire substitute gratifications and to discover that separation need not result in terrible deprivations. To this end, more fulfilling relationships with peers and other adults should be encouraged. Again, it is only when these are actually accomplished that children will be able to lessen their needs for regressive responses to the separation.

HYPERMATURITY

When parents separate, their children are generally required to assume additional responsibilities and obligations. Some children regress in response to the new demands. Others rise to the challenge and attain a new and healthy maturity. There are others, however, whose new maturity may look good on the surface but is actually a form of poor adjustment to the separation. It has an exaggerated or inappropriate quality. It is to this unhealthy form of maturity, this hypermaturity, that I direct my attention here.

Some children may manifest hypermaturity by becoming caricatures of adults. They may take on adult mannerisms, speech intonations, and affectations and use large words and adult terminology at every opportunity. They may try to relate to other children as if they were parents and treat them in a condescending manner (much to the other children's alienation). Scolding, reprimanding, disciplining, and lecturing younger children may become quite common. At school such children may become teacher's helpers (sometimes invited, sometimes not). The naive teacher may welcome the help and be delighted with such a child; the classmates, however, may call the child a "goody-goody" or "teacher's pet."

A number of factors, singly and in combination, may produce such behavior. At times there is parental encouragement for the exaggerated maturity. The parents may be impressed with such children's adultlike behavior and even show them off to friends—thereby providing significant reinforcement of the pattern. A parent may use the child as a confidant, which encourages premature acquisition of adult behavioral patterns. Seductive behavior and utilization of the child as a substitute for the absent parent can also contribute to a hypermaturity adaptation. The dependent parent may try to get the child to replace the absent parent, who served as a protector and adviser, and may pressure the child into assuming the parental role.

Even without parental encouragement, some children

appear to become hypermature on their own. Some children, by becoming hypermature, can symbolically regain the lost parent. As when a parent has died, by identifying with the lost parent and becoming like him or her, such children retain the parental image within themselves and thereby can vaguely believe that there really wasn't a loss. Or the adaptation may be a way of compensating for a sense of helplessness. Children are weak and helpless; they have no choice but to bear the rejections, abandonments, and other maltreatment they may suffer at the hands of adults. By assuming adult status the child gains a delusional protection from such indignities. Boys, especially, may acquire a new toughness in order to defend themselves against the sense of impotence that the separation causes. Children may also view the separation as proof of the unreliability of adults; by becoming adult themselves they reduce such anxieties.

In another way, the hypermaturity may be an attempt to regain the parent who has left the home. A girl may have learned that Dad left Mom because she wasn't a good wife. Accordingly, she may try to surpass Mom as a wife in order to attract Daddy back to the household. Similarly a boy, learning that Dad was asked to leave because he wasn't a good husband, may become hypermature in the attempt to attract his mother. The children may believe that the separation took place because one, or both, of the parents was "bad." Accordingly, they may try to be very "good" in order to protect themselves from being similarly ejected. Assuming an adult role, in which the child behaves in an exemplary fashion, can provide protection against this eventuality.

BLAME

Long before the parents make the decision to separate, their children are exposed to the concept of *blame*.

In their fighting the parents usually blame each other for the difficulties between then, so it is only natural that when the separation does take place the child tends to think along the lines of who was at fault. In years past, this problem was further compounded by the traditional legal system, which would grant a divorce only if one of the parties could demonstrate that he or she had been wronged by the other (through such reprehensible behavior as adultery, mental cruelty, addiction, or desertion). Although no-fault divorce laws have evolved from the recognition that both parties have usually contributed to the deterioration of the marital relationship, the spouses themselves usually have strong opinions as to who was at fault. And when the couple needs to resort to adversary proceedings, the lawyers can be relied upon to intensify the problem of faultfinding. Last, the children are likely to consider the parent who has initiated the separation to be the one who was at fault. They often do not fully appreciate that the party who first decides on separation may have done so only after years of tolerating terrible humiliations and indignities and may be in reality the less culpable of the two partners.

Even apart from parental influence, the idea that there is one party who is to blame is the most likely conclusion that children will come to. Children tend to think in the most simplistic terms, and the younger they are, the less likely they are to appreciate the subtleties of joint contribution to the parental difficulties. In addition, in their own conflicts, those below seven or eight tend to consider one person (usually the other guy) to be at fault. It is rare for a young child to say, "I started it."

Parents should try to impress upon the children the concept of joint contribution to many, if not most, conflicts between people. To make the explanation clearer, they should describe specific examples from their own conflicts. Such discussions, of course, are much more effective if the parents have provided the children with the basic reasons for the separation. Parents do well to try to help their children see that people have varying degrees of control over their own alienating behavior. Some acts a parent can control (such as striking another person); some cannot be controlled or can be controlled only with great difficulty (such as alcoholism). In addition, the children should be helped to differentiate between parental behavior that causes children pain as the result of misguidance and mistakes (such as marrying the wrong person) and parental behavior that purposely causes children pain (such as cruel punishments). Such discussions should help the children become more sympathetic to their parents' difficulties and less prone to blame either one of them.

If the children's need to see one of their parents as perfect contributes to the problem, they must be helped to recognize the universality of human imperfection. Growing up thinking a parent is perfect will not only contribute to the children's becoming perfectionistic themselves but will tend to make them intolerant of all others.

Of course, there are situations in which one of the parents has indeed been primarily responsible for the deterioration of the marriage. In such cases, the children are entitled to be made aware of this parent's responsibility. And in conclusion, children must always be helped to appreciate that blame preoccupations are generally unproductive and that their time and energies are better directed into constructive ways of handling their reactions to the separation.

GUILT

Guilt reactions are common among children of divorce.

I use the word guilt to refer to the feelings of low self-worth people experience in association with ideas (whether valid or not) that they have done something wrong. Whereas in blame one accuses another of wrongdoing, in guilt one accuses oneself. When people harbor thoughts or desires that are considered reprehensible by the significant figures in their lives they are likely to feel guilty over them. And if these are acted out, the person is likely to feel more guilty. In fact, the failure to experience any guilt would be a sign of trouble. If individuals felt no guilt about indulging themselves in every act, no matter how much harm it caused others, we would live in a world of fear and chaos. By producing guilt in children during their formative years, society can relax its vigilance somewhat and rely on most (though certainly not all) adults not to indulge themselves in acts that do violence to other people.

Associated with the ideas of wrongdoing that are central to guilt are feelings of worthlessness. It is as if the individual were saying: "How terrible a person I am for what I have done." Generally, there is also an anticipation of punishment in the guilt reaction, although this may not be clearly realized. In some situations, of course, the particular consequences are well known. But there is often a vague feeling that something unpleasant or painful is going to happen because of the transgression, whereas the individual may not be able to pinpoint exactly what.

The guilt reaction is inappropriate when it is exaggerated, when the consensus of the group within which the individual lives is that the act is not blameworthy, and when the individual fancies responsibility for events for which there was none. It is these inappropriate guilt reactions that can be a problem for children when their parents divorce.

Children to whom guilt is communicated. There are situations in which the child, in a sense, has played a role in the parental conflict. Children who learn that their conception was planned in an attempt to improve a faltering marriage and that the "marital therapy" didn't work are likely to consider the separation to be their fault and believe that another child might have been more successful in keeping the parents together. Children who learn that their birth was unplanned and that the burden of their upbringing contributed to the marital discord are also likely to feel guilty about the separation. If the parents separate soon after the child is born, because of unwillingness on the part of a parent to assume parental responsibility, that child when older may conclude that his or her birth contributed to the breakup.

A parent may be unable to tolerate the demands and burdens of raising a handicapped child and wish to get out of the marriage in order to avoid such responsibilities. The parent may state this overtly or may provide other reasons for the withdrawal—excuses that serve to cover up the true motives. The child of such a parent is likely to appreciate (even if not directly told) that the handicap was a major contributing factor in the parent's abandonment (a word that has more applicability to this situation than to other types of parental departure from the home). Accordingly, the child will feel guilty and is likely to say: "If I wasn't so sick, my father (mother) wouldn't have left." Such children must be helped to appreciate that the real fault lies with the rejecting parent rather than with themselves. Such children inevitably feel angry over their parents' rejection of them; yet they may become inhibited about expressing their anger lest they suffer even further abandonment. They need to be encouraged to vent their anger; however, they must also be helped to resign themselves to the rejection and obtain substitute gratifications so that there will be less anger generated. Encouraging in such children a "he's more to be pitied than scorned" attitude toward the rejecting parent can reduce anger and lessen their loss of self-esteem.

There are people who are not and may never be ready for parenthood, and yet they have children. These parents may have completely healthy children and yet may not be willing or able to take care of them. Such a parent's leaving is, in a sense the child's fault—because had the child not been born, the marriage might have remained intact. And the child is bound to recognize this and feel guilty. It is often helpful to approach this child in a manner similar to that described for the handicapped child.

There are situations where parental differences over the raising of the children are a significant source of marital discord, and this can result in their children's feeling that the separation was their fault. When a father complains bitterly that he is overwhelmed by the financial burdens of the household, then leaves and fails to fulfill his financial commitments to the family, the child is also likely to feel guilty.

In all these situations the separation has indeed taken place, at least in part, because in some way the existence of the child is linked to the causes of the marital breakup. And most often this is communicated to the child, either overtly or covertly. Sometimes parents attempt to lessen children's guilty reactions by trying to convince them that the separation was not their fault. While it is the children's "fault" in the sense that had they not been born the marriage might still be intact, such children must be helped to appreciate that the real fault lies with deficiencies not in themselves but in the parent. In addition, anger and self-esteem problems should be dealt with as I have described.

Guilt as a way of gaining control over the uncontrollable.

A far more common situation, especially around the time of separation, is that children feel they were somehow the cause of their parents' difficulties when there is absolutely no evidence that this was the case.

Some children decide that their having been "bad" was the cause of the separation, and they may promise their parents repeatedly that they will forever be "good." They may seize upon any indiscretion or transgression, no matter how slight, as the cause of the separation, and the preoccupation may reach obsessive proportions. Children may even quote comments made by the parents to justify their conclusion that the separation was their fault. For example, a boy may interpret the father's saying to his mother, "I can't stand being in this house any longer," to mean that *he* is the objectionable one, rather than his mother. Some children may repeat the "bad" behavior they think caused the separation in order to strengthen their notion that it was a causative factor. Such children may even *start* doing bad things in order to maintain this notion. On occasion children may begin to exhibit antisocial behavior *after* the separation and then claim that the parents separated because of their bad behavior.

Many factors may underlie the development of this delusion of guilt, but the one that is most significant and frequent is the need to control the uncontrollable. Implicit in the statement "It's my fault" is the notion of control. Such children feel helpless to change their parents' decision regarding the divorce. If, however, they can convince themselves that they were the cause—that something *they* did brought about the decision to separate—it follows that there is something they can do to bring about a reversal of the decision. Logically, if their being bad caused the parents to separate, then all they need to do is be good and the parents will reconcile. A typical plea goes like this: "Please, Daddy, don't leave. I know you're going because I've been bad. I promise I'll never be bad again. I promise I'll never fight with my sister again, or do any other bad things. From now on I'm only going to be good. I'll take out the garbage every day, walk the dog. . . ."

Although this type of guilt delusion most often arises without direct influence from the parents or others, there are times when there may be an active parental contribution. For example, the family atmosphere may be one in which personal responsibility is always invoked to explain any incident, especially an unfortunate one. No matter how capricious the event and no matter how innocent the family members may have been, somehow someone is considered to have caused it. This tradition of finding out who was at fault can lead the children to look to themselves when parental separation occurs.

The parent who consults a child about the divorce decision, even to the point of asking the child's permission, may unintentionally contribute to the child's developing this form of guilt. Sometimes the parent isn't really seeking the child's permission; rather, the parent hopes that the child will approve so the parent can feel less guilty. In other instances, the parents may take the child's view into serious consideration and may even stay together because of the child's disapproval—so great is the parental guilt and fear of angering the child. In such cases the children's feelings of control are not delusional; they are *told* they have control and *in some cases may actually have it*. (Children who do indeed have the power to keep their parents together may develop a different kind of guilt over keeping parents together in a state of misery.)

Reassuring children that the divorce was in no way their fault is usually futile. Parents may become quite frustrated because their repeated reassurances that the separation was not the children's fault are to no avail. But these children's failure to respond to reassurances is understandable. Because the guilt provides these children with the illusion of being able to control and even reverse the calamity of parental separation, they do not give it up easily. To do so would result in their having to accept their impotence—something most people do not willingly do. It is the impotence-potency issue that must be addressed if this problem is to be reduced.

Parents do well here to help the child appreciate that there are certain things in life that one *can* control, and others that one *cannot*. For example, one *can* control whether one throws a ball, does one's homework, eats a piece of candy, or hits one's brother. One *cannot* control such things as rain, snow, lightning, or the movement of the sun. And the latter category must include, for the child, parental divorce. Children must be helped to resign themselves to this reality. However, it is important not to stop on that defeatist and depressing note. Children need to learn that they *do* have it within their power to do certain things that can help them lessen the pain of separation. They have it within their power to gain substitute gratifications to compensate for the loss of the parent by involving themselves with others, both peer and adult. When they are able to accomplish this goal, a contributing element to the delusion will have been removed. And when they have real experiences in which they learn to differentiate the controllable from the uncontrollable, to change what they can, and not futilely to try changing what they cannot, then another element in this type of guilt reaction will have been reduced.

Guilt over disloyalty. Most children with separated or divorced parents have loyalty conflicts. Most youngsters grow up with a deep sense of commitment to the members of their family, especially their parents. All children are supposed to love and respect their parents and may even learn to feign or profess such attitudes if they do not in fact exist. Even when the marriage is faltering, each parent may continue to attempt to foster in the children (though often without conviction) these attitudes toward the spouse. But when the separation occurs, children may find themselves in a situation where their loyalty is openly tested, where they are required to make choices and take actions that reveal their preferences. At such times children's feelings of guilt may be profound—even to the point of paralyzing them from taking action or making decisions.

Some children take the side of whichever parent they are with at the time in order to avoid alienating that parent, but at the same time they will feel guilty over their disloyalty toward the absent parent. Generally, children must be helped to avoid taking sides, even to the point of risking the alienation of a parent. Younger children find it more difficult to avoid getting drawn into taking sides or professing agreement without conviction. Older children become freer to extract themselves, and it is common for adolescents to take the position "I wash my hands of both of them." To be sure, some parents' behavior is so alienating and reprehensible (to the spouse and/or the children) that it spares the children guilt over their disloyalty. The children's rejection of such a parent becomes justifiable, and there is little guilt, only relief.

Some children will feel guilty for having a better time with their fathers on visiting days than with their mothers at home. It is helpful to point out to them that this is a natural reaction—many children have better times on visiting days, because there are fewer restrictions being placed upon them. Mother has to make them get up early, go to school, do chores and homework. Father, however, may not have to do such dirty work and often comes off as the good guy. Noncustodial parents can reduce children's guilt by providing more realistic visitation experiences. Involving the children in continual fun and games (often to assuage parental guilt) is not in their best interests. A more balanced experience—one that includes usual routines and occasional, inevitable, but not contrived frustration—is healthier and avoids the development of this type of guilt.

Visitation schedules may be rigidly defined in the separation agreement and divorce decree. If so, a child's need for a visit of specific length at a particular time may not match what the parents have legally agreed upon. A child may feel guilty and disloyal for not wishing to visit with a parent at a particular time, or for wishing to have a visit shorter than the allotted period. In such situations the parents do well to inquire whether reasonable visitation experiences are being provided. If the answer is no, they should try to rectify the situation. But even when this is accomplished, the child may prefer an alternative arrangement—perhaps a shorter visit, bringing along a friend, or even a skipped visit (with advance notice to both parents, of course). And children must be helped to appreciate that such change in the visitations need not reflect disloyalty on their part.

The situation most likely to produce disloyalty guilt in children of divorce is custody litigation in which the children are asked to state which parent they wish to live with. Recognizing this, the parties involved in custody litigation may hesitate to ask the children to express their preferences. However, to refrain from doing so may deprive the decision makers of valuable information. When I conducted custody evaluations I tried to avoid asking children direct questions about parental preference. Rather, I tried to deduce from a child's comments, play fantasies, dreams, and so on which parent he or she would prefer to live with. I took this indirect information into consideration with other data when making my recommendation. It was only near the end of the evaluation, after I had established a good relationship with the child, that I *might* introduce directly the question of preference as to custody. But I generally did not need a direct statement; the indirect information I received was usually enough. My reasoning on this point is that children will feel less guilty if the judge orders them to live with the parent whom they basically prefer than if they must overtly make the choice themselves. They can then take the position to the rejected parent that "It wasn't me who rejected you, the judge has ordered me to live with Mommy (Daddy)." Placing the decision in the judge's hands not only lessens children's fears of retaliation by the rejected parent but reduces disloyalty guilt as well, as children can convince themselves that they played no part in making the choice.

Guilt over hostility. A child's self-blame may relate to guilt over expressing the hostility toward one or both parents that is generally produced by the divorce. Except in those relatively uncommon situations in which the child welcomes the parents' separation, the parent who leaves the home is viewed by children as an abandoner and this cannot help but make them angry. But children of divorce may fear expressing anger toward the parent who has left the home, lest they see even less of that parent. They may also fear expressing anger toward the parent with whom they live, lest that parent leave too. If parents convey the message that a child's anger at them is inappropriate, "wrong," or "bad," then the child is likely to become even more inhibited. For example, parents may actively tell children how terrible they are for having hostile thoughts or feelings and that "good" children never entertain such terrible ideas. Or they may be the kinds of people who never (or rarely ever) express their anger and thereby serve as models for the children's not expressing theirs either.

A more subtle way in which parents may inhibit a child's anger is demonstrated by Marc's situation. Marc's parents separated when he was four and his father left the home. Marc spent much time with his maternal grandparents, who visited him frequently. On one occasion Marc said to his grandfather: "I'm not the kind of boy who would think mean things about his daddy." The grandfather responded: "Of course not. We know that you're not that kind of boy. We know that you'd *never* think anything mean about your own father." The grandfather related the conversation to Marc's mother, who related it to his father. During the ensuing weeks, every time Marc asked his parents or grandparents whether they considered him to be the kind of boy who thought mean things about his father he was reassured that "no one, even for one minute, thought that Marc would ever be that kind of boy and think such terrible things." And the more Marc was reassured, the more reassurance he asked for. What was happening was that the family members, under the guise of reducing Marc's guilt over his hostility, were actually increasing it. Their "reassurances" were actually confirming to him that a boy who has such thoughts is indeed loathsome. Because Marc was inevitably having such thoughts (as all children of divorce, at some level, must)—and his statement that he was *not* the kind of boy who has such thoughts is proof that he was having them—he could only conclude that he was loathsome as well.

All concerned would have done better to have made comments along these lines: "All boys and girls have mean thoughts about their parents at times. When a parent does something that a child doesn't like, the child is bound to have mean thoughts and feelings. There's nothing wrong with you for having them. The best thing you can do with these feelings is let them out—talk about them—so we can find out what to do about the things that are making you angry." When Marc's parents and grandparents switched their tactic and provided comments along the lines described above, there was a disappearance of Marc's preoccupations and questions. As a bonus, Marc's expression of his angry feelings resulted in his father's visiting more often.

Observing the parents' altercations and the destructive effects of their anger on one another can so frighten children that they may become inhibited in expressing their anger. The anticipation of punishment (which may or may not be clearly realized) is a common concomitant to guilt about hostility. Punishment (even self-denigration and social alienation) can reduce guilt. Such children may try to lessen their guilt by courting punishment. They may overtly or covertly encourage scapegoatism. They may become accident-prone. Or they may become disruptive and do just those "bad" things that will predictably get them punished. Clearly, such methods for reducing guilt are self-destructive and only worsen the child's condition. One must help such children feel less guilty over their hostility (in a manner appropriate to each kind of guilt-inducing situation) if one is to reduce their need to lessen guilt with self-destructive maneuvers.

Self-blame as a denial of parental blame. Some children will place the blame for the divorce on themselves in order to deny parental participation and fallibility. It makes many children feel more secure to view their parents as perfect. And if the parents have the need to present themselves as perfect (by never admitting defects, for example), then such tendencies on the children's part may be enhanced. A separation is a clear statement of deficiency in at least one parent (and sometimes both). Children with an exaggerated need to maintain images of parental perfection may consider the personality defects that led to the separation to have been theirs rather than their parents' and may create a host of deficiencies to confirm this notion. Generally, the fantasized defects are similar in kind to those utilized to gain a sense of control over the uncontrollable ("I was bad," "My allowance is too big," "I fight too much with my sister"); here, however, they serve to maintain the delusion of parental infallibility.

Parents who need to present themselves as perfect must appreciate that they are doing their children a disservice. They must recognize that maintaining a facade of perfection is a sign of weakness, and that the stronger and more mature person is willing to admit faults. They should appreciate that their children will ultimately realize that they are covering up their deficiencies and will lose even more respect for them. Healthy parents have enough confidence to appreciate that any revelation of occasional liabilities will be more than counterbalanced by the children's appreciation of the parental assets. And whatever loss of respect a parent suffers from revealing deficiencies is generally small compared to the loss incurred when children realize that their parents lack the courage to reveal occasional defects.

It is to the parents' advantage, therefore, to let children know that they are not perfect. This should be done naturally, as situations arise (and they inevitably do in the course of living). And the divorce situation is one that can allow for such appropriate disclosures. Parents should recognize as well that children's viewing their parents as perfect will produce inevitable disappointment and disillusionment with all others they may encounter. In fact, this very factor could even contribute to dissatisfaction in and even dissolution of the children's own marriages. In addition, such an image of their parents may result in the children's setting perfectionistic standards for themselves. And this may result in continual self-dissatisfaction, as they can never live up to the impossibly high standards.

Some children's need to see their parents as perfect may also stem from lack of confidence in their own abilities to cope with situations that they in fact are quite capable of handling. When we try to help such children give up the delusion of parental perfection, it is important also to try to build self-confidence and a sense of competence. Later in this chapter I will introduce some approaches to help enhance a child's self-esteem.

RECONCILIATION PREOCCUPATIONS

The reaction of most children to the announcement of their parents' separation is to plead that they not separate. Except in the rare situation in which children have been so traumatized by the departing spouse that they welcome the separation, children would generally prefer to live with the pains, frustrations, and discomforts of their parents' conflict than to be deprived of one of them. Often, it is the parents who are suffering much more than the children. Children by nature are, like all of us, very self-absorbed and are not generally affected by arguments that Mommy or Daddy cannot stand the pain any more and will be happier living out of the home. Nor is it easy for children to project themselves into the future and believe that they may be better off after their parents separate.

The children's pleas that the parents not split up can be one of the most guilt-provoking experiences a divorcing parent may have to suffer. Separating parents must appreciate that their guilt is healthy and predictable and an inevitable part of their decision. Parents should also realize that the children's pleas that the parent(s) reconsider the decision are proof of their affection. After all, if children were not preoccupied with reconciliation it would reflect a deficiency in their relationship with the departing parent.

Beyond simple pleas to the parents that they reunite and fantasies that they will, children's reconciliation preoccupations can take many forms. For example, some children will make threats, often pathetic and impotent, to the absent parent: "If you don't come back home I'll tell everyone you're mean" or "If you don't come back, I'll tell Grandma." Some try to bribe: "I'll give you all the money in my piggy bank," "I'll paint a beautiful picture of you and we'll hang it up in the living room," "I'll never be bad again." Some try to use money as a manipulative tool: "I'll steal all his money and then he'll have to come back home" or "We'll spend so much money that he won't be able to afford to stay divorced." Some may use depressive symptoms ("Look how miserable you've made me") and even suicidal gestures ("Without you life isn't worth living") in order to produce so much guilt in departed parents that they will return. And others attempt to use force: They hope to make absent parents so miserable by their incessant tantrums, outbursts, and tirades that they will finally submit and return.

George, who was eight years old when I first saw him in treatment, is a good example of how children exhibit reconciliation obsessions. George's parents had divorced a few years before, and his father was living abroad. The father frequently wrote letters describing in great detail his intense love for George. Sometimes the letters promised that the father would be visiting the United States very soon and would then spend much time with George. Exact plans were always to come in the next letter. However, each succeeding letter brought only excuses and procrastinations. Other letters would promise airplane tickets so that George could visit his father. Again, these were always to be sent in the next letter; and needless to say, they were never forthcoming. George felt like a yo-yo, his hopes ever being raised and then dashed.

In an early session George drew a picture of a boy on a beach chasing a butterfly. The butterfly was described as very beautiful. However, each time the boy was about to catch the butterfly, it managed to escape—just as he was about to grab it. And the story ended with the boy's never catching the butterfly. A clearer statement of George's predicament could not be asked for.

Normally reconciliation preoccupations diminish with time as the children become used to their new life-style and become resigned to the fact of the divorce. However, there are children who persist for many months, even years, in trying to get their parents to reconcile—even though they have been told repeatedly that there is no chance whatsoever of the parents' remarrying. There are children who will entertain fantasies of their parents' reuniting even after one or both have remarried. When such preoccupations persist beyond the usual time for their disappearance, other factors are usually operative— factors that go beyond the mere fact of divorce and the natural desire to resume what the child considers to have been a happier state of affairs.

Malevolent ties between the parents as a cause of children's reconciliation preoccupations. I believe that the most common reason for the persistence of reconciliation preoccupations in children is the failure of the parents to become *psychologically* divorced. Although they may be *legally* divorced, and even remarried to others, they may still maintain a psychological tie that can be quite strong. The persistence of such ties (even though subtle and disguised) is the most powerful contributing factor to continuing reconciliation fantasies in children.

The most common manifestation of this kind of parental tie is the maintenance of hostilities. Arguments over alimony, support, visitation, and so forth can persist for years. And lawyers and the courts can be relied upon to contribute to this prolongation. Although a hostile relationship might seem to offer the child little hope for reconciliation, it actually provides much more hope than a parental relationship in which matters have been settled and there is little, if any, residual hostility. Children appreciate, either consciously or unconsciously, that a hostile relationship between their parents is a much deeper one than little if any involvement at all. In the malevolent relationship the ex-spouses expend significant time and energy on one another (either directly or through their lawyers). When the separated parents fight, mental images of the parents' involvement with one another are produced in the children's minds. And such imagery contributes to the children's reconciliation obsessions. In contrast, when the parents have essentially settled their differences, such fantasies of togetherness are less likely to occur. The children of the hostile parents appreciate—sometimes clearly, sometimes vaguely—that their parents still need one another—even if the need is for a kind of sadomasochistic gratification (and divorce provides ample opportunity for such gratification for those with the propensity). Sensing their continuing needs for one another cannot but produce hopes in the children that their parents will once again live together.

Some children may actually foment difficulties between the parents and help perpetuate their fighting from the sense that any contact between the parents is more likely to bring about a reconciliation than no contact at all. And the parents' need to continue their hostilities may make them easy prey to their children's schemes to bring about these involvements. Each may be selectively gullible to the children's provocative comments about the other, whereas on any other topic they would be cautious about taking what the children say at face value.

An even more subtle form of interaction may contribute to the perpetuation of children's reconciliation fantasies. The parents may decide that any type of friendly and civil involvement on their part could produce reconciliation fantasies in the children. Accordingly they may strictly refrain from any contact in front of their children and may reduce their other communications to an absolute minimum (even less than would be naturally indicated and desired). In most cases, such an arrangement is only apparently made for the benefit of the children. Sometimes it is a rationalization for the parents to protect themselves from acting out on or giving in to their residual attraction for one another. The facade of coolness and aloofness protects them from expressing their strong desire for involvement. As is often the case, malevolence is used as a device to protect the individual from benevolence. In such a situation, people expend more energy in maintaining "distance" than if there were the usual and necessary contacts—and the amount of mental imagery involving the ex-spouse is greater than in those with more relaxed attitudes. As is often the case, the mental life of the parent becomes the mental life of the children. They too become involved in the strict adherence to the rules and regulations of the distance-keeping operations, and they too get involved in this tie, which only looks like a nontie.

Benevolent ties between the parents as a cause of children's reconciliation preoccupations.

It is hard to determine how many separated or divorced people maintain benevolent ties with one another. Not only does embarrassment often lead such individuals to hide their involvements, but legal factors may play a significant role. For example, many states will not recognize a period of separation to be valid if there has been sexual contact during the period, and the couple may have to start counting the days of separation all over again if they wish to qualify for a divorce. Even among those who definitely plan to divorce, intermittent sexual contact is not uncommon. Although the children are generally not exposed to sexual involvement, they are generally aware of the continued benevolent involvement out of which sexual contacts take place. Seeing their parents still occasionally getting along well together cannot but stimulate fantasies of reconciliation in them.

With greater social receptivity to varying life-styles, the "on the fence" situation is becoming more widespread. People go on for years without making a final decision. One father, for example, may spend two or three nights a week at home. Another stays for a few days or weeks, departs, only to return again for another stint. In these circumstances the children cannot help but have persistent reconciliation fantasies. The children may add to the frequency of the visits and contacts by structuring situations that encourage or provide the parents with excuses for involvements. They may, for example, insist that both parents be present at every possible school function, birthday party, and so on. They may even enlist the aid of grandparents and other relatives who support a reconciliation.

Just as the children may try to find excuses to promote their parents' contact with one another, the parents themselves may use similar tactics. Mom may call Dad for advice on inconsequential matters or to tell him about something cute the child did that day. Dad too may find justification for contacting Mom about trivial things that pertain to the children. Each parent here is using concern for the children as a rationalization for involvement with the spouse. And such involvements perpetuate reconciliation fantasies in the children.

Sometimes, too, there may be false friendliness used to hide hostility, just as artificial aloofness may be used to disguise deep attraction. The parents may present facades of friendliness, believing that it is bad for the children for them to show their deep rage. When they do come together their words and gestures are ever so polite. Generally, the children are not fooled. They appreciate (even if only vaguely) that there is still a lot going on between their parents. Again, the basic continuation of the hostilities contributes to the perpetuation of reconciliation fantasies.

Another common parental contribution to reconciliation preoccupations in a child is similar fantasies on the part of a parent. For example, when a mother persists in her hopes that she may ultimately be reunited with her husband, it is extremely difficult if not impossible for her children to resign themselves to his departure. Even if she refrains from verbalizing her hopes, the children sense them. Her statements that the father is never returning are unconvincing, because she conveys a feeling of longing when she speaks of her husband. Her taking every opportunity to resume contact will also reveal her true feelings. Similarly, a father who persists in trying to convince his rejecting wife to reconsider her decision will strengthen his children's reconciliation fantasies regardless of the firmness of their mother's refusals.

Factors within the child as a cause of reconciliation obsessions. The preceding discussion has already touched on several aspects of the child's postseparation experience that may foster reconciliation fantasies. For example, when the departed parent offers the child much more gratification than does the custodial parent, reconciliation preoccupations are likely to persist. There was a time, not too long ago, when the court was required to give a mother custody unless gross and extreme negligence could be definitely established. Accordingly, many children were forced to remain with mothers who were far less equipped to take care of them than were their fathers. This contributing factor to reconciliation preoccupations is now becoming less common, however. Living with the preferred and more suitable parent lets a child be less obsessed with the return of the absent parent.

Children who are excessively guilty over conscious or unconscious hostility toward the departed parent may become obsessed with the parents' returning to the home. They may be preoccupied with the latter's welfare, fear frequently that the parent is sick or injured, and seek the continual reassurance of the parent's well-being that his or her return to the home would provide. There may also be separation anxieties that make the termination of each visitation especially difficult. Reconciliation obsessions provide hope for the reduction and even cessation of such separation anxieties.

Jealous rivalry problems may contribute to a child's obsession with parental reconciliation. A boy, for example, living with a dating mother may find the flow of men in and out of his mother's life an unbearable burden. He had enough trouble dealing with the jealousy he felt toward his father for the intimacies he shared with his mother. He may fix on his mother's remarrying his father as his only way of stemming the tide of these unwanted strangers. Similarly a girl, even if living with her mother, may learn of her father's dating and develop similar reactions. Toward the parent of the same sex as well, a child may develop jealousies over dating and see reconciliation as the only hope for reducing such feelings of rivalry. For example, a girl may be jealous over the attentions her mother is receiving and long for the time when there was only one man in her mother's life.

Children whose guilt over their parents' separation is an outgrowth of the need to control an uncontrollable situation may also become preoccupied with their parents' reuniting. Typically, they are preoccupied with ideas that the divorce took place because they were "bad" and conversely, that the parents will reconcile if they are "good." In their eyes, only if their parents reunite can they hope to reduce their guilt and feel better about themselves.

There are also areas (increasingly rare) where divorce is very uncommon or where the child of divorce is stigmatized. Such children may try to hide the fact that their parents are separated, and in the service of avoiding disclosure they may become preoccupied with reconciliation.

I can best introduce my next point anecdotally. There are well-known psychological experiments in which a hungry rat in a cage is taught to press a bar in order to obtain a pellet of food. Psychologists differentiate between the strength of learning when the pellets are given *periodically* and when they are given *aperiodically*. In what is referred to as *periodic reinforcement* the rat is rewarded (reinforced) with a pellet in accordance with a fixed relationship between bar presses and pellet release. That is, the rat receives a pellet with every press, or every second press, or every fifth press, and so on, depending upon the plan of the experiment. When the rat appears to have learned to press the bar in order to obtain pellets, the rat is said to be *conditioned*. In *aperiodic reinforcement* there is a random and ever-varying relationship between bar presses and pellet release. Sometimes the rat may receive a pellet immediately after a bar press; then the rat may not get one until it has pressed the bar ten, twenty, thirty, or even more times; and then it may get two, three, or more pellets in succession.

Now imagine an experiment in which three rats in three separate cages each receive a total of 100 pellets in the conditioning process. The first is given a pellet after *each* press of the bar. Then no further pellets are given. Let us say that after x number of presses the rat returns to the random frequency of bar presses present before the reinforcement program was instituted. In other words, the rat, no longer gaining pellets, stops pressing the bar more than it normally would in chance encounters with it as the rat roams the cage. The conditioning is now said to have been *extinguished*. If the second rat is also conditioned with a total of 100 pellets, but each one is given only after *five* bar presses, it may take $5x$, $10x$, $15x$, or even more bar presses before the rat returns to the previously random frequency of bar presses. Having expected unrewarded presses, the rat has become accustomed to them and expects most presses to be unrewarded. Accordingly, it takes a much longer time to become deconditioned. Let us now consider the third rat, who is rewarded aperiodically. Sometimes the rat receives two pellets in a row, or three pellets out of five presses, and at other times there may be fifty or a hundred presses before a reward. Such a rat's tolerance for unrewarded presses is far greater than that of the other two rats, and the extinction of conditioning may take significantly longer. In fact, $100x$ or $200x$ or even more presses may be required before this rat returns to random frequency. In some cases, the rat never gives up and continues pressing until dropping from exhaustion—so powerful is the aperiodically conditioned response.

I believe that parents who provide their children with little affection, but who still give some in an unpredictable way, are likely to foster the kind of response exhibited by the third rat. And children of such parents may become obsessed with parental reunion in the hope of gaining affection from the lost parent. They just never seem to give up trying to extract affection from a parent who appears to have little (but not *no*) capacity to provide it. While others can only wonder why they never give up, never seem able to see the obvious, these children may spend their whole lives in this futile quest.

Another behavioral pattern observed in lower animals that may also exist in humans and play a role in children's reconciliation preoccupations is called *imprinting*. If one takes the fertilized egg of a duck, removes it from the mother, and allows it to hatch in a cage in which there is a moving mechanical toy (not necessarily resembling a duck), the newborn duckling will develop a strong attachment to the toy similar to that it would have developed with its natural mother. More specifically, if during the first thirty-six hours of the duckling's life it has absolutely no contact with any other moving objects, it will follow the toy wherever it goes in a manner similar to the way it would have with its natural mother. The following attachment response is said to have become *imprinted*. So powerful is such imprinting that the duckling will follow the mechanical device even when its natural mother appears, and the preference for the toy will persist throughout the duckling's life.

It appears that for many lower animals there is the capacity to form a deep bond with the *first moving object* with which the animal has physical contact. The most important determinant is that the contact take place during the earliest hours after birth, generally referred to as the *critical period*. For example if a duckling spends the first thirty-six hours with its natural mother, it will no longer be possible to get the bird to form a following attachment with another adult duck or a mechanical toy. And if an animal is totally isolated from moving objects or animals during the critical period it will exhibit significant impairment in forming attachment bonds throughout its life.

So strong is the imprinted bond that the animal forms with the first moving object that the bond may persist even when the original object becomes a source of pain and even when pleasure-giving substitutes are present. In fact, if the first moving object provides the animal with pain during the critical period (in the form of mild electric shocks, for example), the attachment may become even stronger. Also, in what is referred to as the "law of effort," the bond appears to be strengthened if the animal has to make greater than normal efforts in order to have contact with the first moving object. For example, if the duckling has to walk up an inclined plane each time it wishes to have contact with the object, it forms a stronger attachment bond than if the object were more easily accessible.

Such inborn reaction patterns are more readily studied and

demonstrated in lower animals than in human beings, although they have been well demonstrated in animals close to us on the evolutionary scale. There is good reason to believe that humans have similar inborn reaction patterns, but we are less compelled to respond to them in an uncontrollable and reflex way. It appears, for example, that the migration of birds to warmer climates in winter is a manifestation of an inborn reaction pattern. It is likely that the bird has little if any control over such behavior. Humans obviously have much more control over their movement to a more comfortable environment. In lower animals mating behavior appears to be reflex. Humans have far more control over their behavior when sexually stimulated.

In spite of our greater control over such genetically programmed patterns, however, it does appear that they do exist in modified form in humans. It is probable that the attachments that a child makes to its mother and father in the earliest months of life may become so deeply embedded in the child's psychological structure that the child is compelled to attach himself or herself to the parents no matter how rejecting one or both parents may be. It is even possible that the parent who provides pain or is emotionally remote may be harder to give up than the one who has been more benevolent. Children sometimes run away from residential treatment centers in order to return to parents who have subjected them to the most cruel treatment. The treatment centers' staff members, who have made every attempt to treat the children with love and care, are perplexed as to why such children are so compelled to return. Perhaps the animal imprinting studies provide an explanation. And perhaps they explain, as well, why children may become preoccupied with hopes that an absent parent will return even though that parent has treated them in the most rejecting manner.

Additional ways of helping children reduce reconciliation preoccupations. As part of the process of adjusting to parental separation, as mentioned before, children need to find substitute relationships, both adult and peer. The child who fails to do this is more likely to become preoccupied with the departed parent's returning. Of course, reconciliation obsessions themselves can interfere with the development of such relationships, and a vicious cycle can develop. Accordingly, parents should do their best to promote such substitute relationships as soon after the separation as possible.

The parental factors in children's reconciliation obsessions may be formidable. Many parents, once they understand the kinds of contributing factors that I have described, may be able to alter their behavior and so reduce their children's reconciliation preoccupations. But some may require personal counseling before they can accomplish this. In many cases the only hope for the children's giving up the obsession is joint counseling of the parents. Such counseling presents special problems. First, the parents' participation may in itself foster the very symptom it is designed to alleviate. That is, the fact that the parents are cooperating in an activity may well increase the children's hopes for reconciliation. This drawback, however, is often far outweighed by the advantages of joint counseling. In addition, separated and divorced parents generally prefer to have as little to do with one another as possible. Accordingly, they are generally unreceptive to joint counseling, even for the benefit of their children.

Some parents may agree to counseling but use it as a platform for perpetuating their conflict rather than cooperatively trying to reduce the hostilities. And when lawyers are still on the scene, such counseling may make a mockery of the therapy as the parents withhold that which might compromise their legal positions. For these reasons I have had little successful experience with joint counseling of separated or divorced parents whose maintenance of hostilities has been the primary factor in their children's reconciliation obsessions or other difficulties. Working with one of the parents is more common; the other parent may or may not see another therapist. When treating children I have on several occasions had the experience that the malevolent interaction between the parents has been so deep and fierce that I have had to inform them that I am working against insurmountable odds—that it is unlikely, if not impossible, for me to help the child as long as the parental hostilities are maintained at such a pitch. And the therapy has failed because they have been unable to extract themselves from their continual conflict.

Children whose social stigmatization contributes to their reconciliation fantasies must be helped to appreciate that the problem lies with those who stigmatize rather than with them. And those who try to hide the fact of divorce must be helped to see that they are giving themselves new and unnecessary burdens to bear.

Although true psychological divorce is far more important than legal divorce in reducing reconciliation obsessions, informing the children when the divorce has been finalized can still be of value. I generally suggest that parents actually show the children the divorce decree. Of course, the younger the child, the less significance such a document can have. Older children might be shown significant clauses that clearly state that the marriage has terminated. Printed words have a certain power, and children are especially subject to their influence. And when remarriage takes place, a further reduction in reconciliation obsessions may occur. However—and I cannot emphasize this point too strongly—even after the remarriage of both parents, if they are still psychologically involved with one another, their children are likely to be given hope for reconciliation, no matter how vigorously the parents deny the possibility.

SEXUAL AND IDENTIFICATION PROBLEMS

Growing up in a household with only one parent is likely to deprive the child of the psychological benefits to be derived from the two-parent household. The boy's relationship with his mother and the girl's with her father serve as models for their future relationships with the opposite sex. In addition, the same-sexed parent serves as the most important model for the child's own sex role. And living with someone in the same home is very different from visitation—despite the absent parent's best efforts to provide love, interest, proper guidance, and so on. In this section I will focus on two possible sources of difficulty that may arise in the divorce situation, namely, sexual and identification problems.

Sexual problems. Some parents deal with the frustrations they experience over the loss of a spouse by attempting to get their child to serve as a substitute. A mother, for example, may tell her son, "You're the man of the house now that Daddy's gone." Although a boy may find the comment anxiety-provoking because he does not feel equipped to assume the awesome responsibilities of such a position, he may also find it gratifying because it suggests that he can satisfy cravings for fuller possession of his mother. Growing up independently, and subsequently developing relationships with other females, thereby becomes more difficult. Normal maturation becomes even more difficult if the boy has a prolonged experience of being the mother's confidant and assuming many responsibilities that his father ordinarily would have. A girl, similarly, may be encouraged to take her mother's place by the father—with similar repercussions.

When the parent becomes sexually seductive with the child, the chances of psychological problems arising become even greater. I am not referring necessarily to overt sexual experiences with the children but to such common forms of stimulation and subtle seductivity as undressing in front of older children, titillating embracing and stroking, and frequent talk about sex and nudity. The parent's seductive behavior may provide an outlet for sexual cravings. For example, the mother, having failed in a marriage (even if the father's difficulties actually brought about the separation), may be insecure with other men, and this may contribute to her choosing her son—someone who is captive prey and has already proved his loyalty and affection. And similar considerations hold for fathers and their daughters.

A good example of the way in which a divorced mother's seductivity can affect a boy is provided by Jim, who was referred to me at age eight because of facial tics and tension.

Jim's father had divorced his mother two years previously because he considered his wife to be "neither a good wife nor a good mother." He complained that his wife was more interested in nightclubbing, socializing, and vacationing than in staying home being a wife to him and a mother to Jim and his younger brother. Jim's mother felt that her husband was boring and never wanted to have fun; she was receptive to his request for a divorce. Although Jim's father considered his wife to be somewhat deficient as a mother, his lawyer discouraged him from trying to win custody of the children, claiming that the court was most unlikely to consider her defects as a mother so severe that it would deprive her of custody. In addition, Jim's father was ambivalent about fighting for custody because he was not ready to assume the extra burdens that custody would have entailed. Accordingly, following the separation Jim and his brother lived with their mother.

Jim's mother considered herself to be "modern and liberal" about undressing in front of her children—that is, she freely did so, and in a way in which it was clear that she flaunted her nakedness. She never closed her bathroom or bedroom door, often slept in the nude, and claimed that this would help her boys grow up uninhibited. Jim and his brother were discouraged from ever closing their bathroom and bedroom doors. Every night, before going to sleep, the boys gave their mother a back rub; then she would give each boy one in return. She was one of the first to go braless when the style came into vogue and often wore low-cut dresses and blouses. She complained that she was always being propositioned by men, even at social gatherings where her husband was present, and claimed not to understand why. (She invariably reported such overtures to her husband.) Similarly, she wondered why wives often seemed to be cool or even antagonistic to her. In spite of all this seductivity she had had only one short-lived affair during her marriage and got little pleasure from sex.

Jim's main presenting complaints were marked tension and severe tics of the face, neck, and shoulders. Although present about three years, the tics had increased during the two years since his father had left the home. As I talked with Jim it became apparent that he was being sexually excited by his mother and that his tension resulted from his pent-up sexual urges. In addition, the anger he felt toward his mother for so titillating him was also repressed and contributed to his tension.

I knew from the outset that my chances helping Jim were not good. My experiences with reducing the seductivity of such mothers had been poor. The attentions, positive feedback, and other gratifications that such women gain from their seductive behavior are so great that they generally have little or no motivation to reduce it, let alone give it up. And in women like Jim's mother the seductivity had become deeply ingrained—they hardly know how to act any other way. Their gait, gestures, and vocal intonations are sexualized, even when they are serious or sad. If these women enter therapy with complaints unrelated to their sexual exhibitionism, the therapist will generally have to wait until a good relationship has been established (and this can take months or years) before dealing with the sexual problem. And even then the therapists' chances for success may be small. Since Jim's mother had no therapeutic relationship with me and had anticipated that my treatment would focus on Jim alone, she was unreceptive to any comments of mine directed toward changing her behavior—whether or not they were related to her seductivity.

Accordingly, it was no surprise when she denied that she was being seductive with Jim. Nudity was just being "modern," back rubs had nothing to do with sex, bralessness was just a style, sleeping naked was healthy, and so forth. My inquiries only made her suspect that even though I was a psychiatrist, I probably had a dirty mind, like most men. In spite of her resistance to my explanation that Jim's tics were related to her seductivity, she agreed to follow some of my advice. She promised to stop undressing in front of Jim and to cut down on the back rubs. However, she would not promise to give them up completely, because "they felt so good." At the same time I advised Jim to refrain from undressing in front of his mother and to discontinue the nightly back-rubbing ritual.

During the next few weeks Jim's mother reported that she was trying hard to follow my advice but that every once in a while she "made a mistake" and would leave a door open when undressing or going to the bathroom. An incident that she described three weeks after I had given my advice convinced me of how futile my attempts were. She had taken a shower and had "forgotten" to bring a towel into the bathroom. "Fortunately" she had not closed the door, so she called out to Jim and asked him to bring her a towel. However, in accordance with my suggestion that he not view her naked, she asked him to cover his eyes with his hand as he came into the bathroom and to be sure not to peek through the slits between his fingers. I asked her what she thought he might be thinking as he inched his way toward her with the towel. As I expected, she denied that he might be visualizing her nakedness. When Jim sheepishly admitted that that was exactly what he was thinking, she expressed surprise and disbelief.

At the beginning of a subsequent session I came into the waiting room, where Jim and his mother were sitting together looking at a magazine. As I approached them I heard Jim's mother say, "Do you think they have nude swimming there?" When they came into my office I asked Jim's mother what had prompted her question. She told me that they were looking at an advertisement inviting tourists to New Zealand. The advertisement depicted a beach scene. Yes, the bathers were all clothed, and Jim's mother was just wondering aloud if they had nude bathing in New Zealand. No, she did not think that her question conjured up visions of naked people in Jim's mind. She was again amazed when he hesitantly admitted that it had.

I made very little progress with Jim. His mother was compelled to be seductive to him, managed to circumvent every suggestion I made to her to reduce her seductivity, and had practically no insight into her behavior. It was no surprise that she discontinued Jim's therapy after a few months. Her conclusion was that all my talk about sex was making her son worse.

A parent may be seductive with the opposite-sexed child not so much for sexual release but as a manifestation of rivalry with the absent spouse. The seduction is part of a broader campaign to win the child away from the spouse. It becomes a vengeful and hostile maneuver. Such parents, feeling insecure as marital partners, may try to prove themselves extremely effective as parents. And seduction may be utilized to enhance the child's affection—and thereby the parent's self-esteem.

The seductive parent builds up the child's hopes for more intense gratifications—which are generally not forthcoming. The frustrations and resentments so produced in the child may result in distrust toward all members of the opposite sex and can contribute to numerous difficulties in future relationships.

One form of seductive behavior is for a parent to flaunt his or her sexual partners. And a father's parade of dates can contribute to a girl's sexual problems, as is well demonstrated by Carol. Carol's parents divorced when she was thirteen. Her father had had numerous affairs and often made no secret of them to his wife and children. When Carol's mother could no longer tolerate her husband's infidelity and saw no reason to believe it would stop, she divorced him. After the separation he was compulsively on the make, never remaining involved with one woman for more than a few months. In addition, he seemed to have a strong need to have Carol meet every girlfriend during her visits with him, no matter how transient the relationship. Even when picking Carol up at his former home, he would often have a woman friend in the car.

When I first saw Carol, she was sixteen but could have passed for twenty-three. Well dressed and well groomed, she had taken great pains to be attractive. When I spoke with her, I felt as if I were not with a teenager but with a sophisticated (or at least pseudosophisticated) young woman. She denied having any problems but claimed that her mother wanted her to see a psychiatrist because of Carol's refusal to date boys her own age or a little older. She insisted that she found high school and college boys "immature" and felt much more comfortable with men in their thirties. The event that caused Carol's visit to me was her mother's finding in Carol's drawer a photo of her at a nightclub with a man who was at least forty and probably closer to fifty. Carol discussed how she found her schoolwork "boring" and was planning to quit school and become a receptionist in a large New York firm. There she felt she would be in the best position to meet men who were "interesting and mature." She had been having sexual relations since age fourteen, did not particularly enjoy it, but found that if she submitted it prevented many hassles with men and kept them interested in her longer. She did not concern herself with whether the men she dated were married. "It's none of my business," she said, and besides she often found married men "exciting." Carol insisted that she did not need therapy but was willing to come this one time in order to get her mother "off her back."

During the two years after her parents' separation, Carol had visited her father practically every weekend, and on most of those occasions some time was spent with one of his dates. On a few weekends she accompanied her father and a girlfriend to resorts. During the year prior to Carol's consultation with me, visits to her father had tapered off as she became more interested in her own dating. Near the end of the interview, Carol stated: "I know you think that I'm jealous of my father's dating all these women and that I'd really like him to be dating me. I think that's a lot of psychological crap. I know you probably think that I'm going out with all these older men because I want to sleep with my father. I know you think I probably have an Oedipus complex or something. Well, I think that's a lot of crap too."

Carol refused another interview and never returned. About five years later, I learned from the person who had referred her to me that she had indeed quit school and become a receptionist. She was then living with a man in his middle forties, but was firm in her decision that she would not marry him.

If deprived of a father, the child of divorce is likely to develop abnormally strong dependencies on the mother, the only remaining parent. A boy, for example, may remain excessively involved with his mother, become a "momma's boy," and in extreme cases never marry. Those who do marry may still be so involved with their mothers that marital problems arise. Such dependencies may (though not necessarily) be associated with homosexual problems, overt or latent. In other words, not all momma's boys are homosexuals and not all male homosexuals are momma's boys, but there seems to be some relationship between the two. A girl, too, may develop such dependencies and may never marry, using as her excuse her "loyalty" to her mother.

The female needs a male in her home in order to learn how to relate to men, both actively and passively. She has to learn what men are all about as well as learn about herself—especially about the kind of woman she is—via male comments and feedback. A girl growing up without a father is likely to be deprived of these important experiences. Girls who have been brought up without fathers sometimes look upon men as strange. They do not know about men: what to like and what to dislike; what to do and what not to do. They may find quite early that making themselves sexually available is likely to result in attentions that they might not otherwise have enjoyed, and this may become their primary way of involving themselves. Such behavior may be intensified by an intense longing for male affection that may have existed for years. Whereas as a child such a girl may have been unable to attract male surrogates for her father, she now finds that—almost like magic—she has a way of gaining their enthusiastic interest. And when she can gain sexual pleasure herself in the process, it may be hard for her to understand the dangers of making herself freely available to a large number of men. The absence of a father may interfere with a girl's development of internalized self-inhibiting mechanisms (commonly referred to as conscience) and make such a lack of inhibition in sexual expression even more likely.

Having been rejected by her father, a girl may develop a strong dislike for and distrust of all men, and these attitudes may interfere significantly with her ability to enter into rewarding relationships with them. Sometimes her own hostility will be projected onto the men she meets, and this will add to her fear of them and anticipation of rejection by them. Such girls may never marry; if they do, marital problems are likely.

As described earlier, the intermittently rejecting father may induce in his children an exaggeratedly strong craving for his affection. Like the aperiodically reinforced rats, the children never give up trying to gain affection from him. The daughter of such a father may become most attracted to men who only rarely provide her with gratification. She may be willing to suffer many humiliations in the hope of receiving the rare satisfaction; and the pattern may become so deeply embedded that she will spurn those who consistently treat her well. It seems as if being badly treated by a man is the kind of experience she is most familiar with and willing to involve herself in. She may basically distrust any other kind—even though she may claim that she constantly seeks men who will treat her well but has the misfortune of their always turning out otherwise. In addition, such women may have so deeply associated love with pain that they cannot imagine one without the other.

In order to help children avoid the problems with sexual development that may result when a parent is absent or deficient, parents in single-parent homes should make every reasonable attempt to provide surrogates for the absent parent. I am not suggesting here that the single parent rush into marriage with a new partner for this purpose; remarriage should be embarked on primarily for the parent's own needs, with derivative benefits for the children. Rather, the children should be helped to find substitute relationships that compensate for the loss of a parent. For example, when the father is absent from the home (the most common situation), the mother should try to involve the children with male teachers, scout leaders, clergymen, uncles, grandfathers, and other males. Similarly, a father who lives alone with his children should help them get to know women in these and similar categories.

Identification problems. Children of divorce are, in my experience, at heightened risk for gender identification problems. Let me explain some of my basic views on gender identification; I will then discuss the implications of these ideas for the identification problems that children of divorce may suffer.

To begin, there are obvious differences between the sexes that are undeniable. Let us refer to these, for the sake of this discussion, as the *primary sexual functions:* the functions that are unique to each sex. In women these functions are child-bearing and breastfeeding, because a woman cannot turn these activities over to a man. The man's primary sexual function is that of fertilization; he cannot transfer this function to a woman.

So much for the obvious and irrefutable.

In addition to the primary sexual function, each sex, I believe, has the inborn capacity and the desire to function in the other's primary area. For the sake of this discussion, I will call these the *secondary sexual functions*. These, I believe, have both genetic *and* environmental components. For example, the woman has the desire to involve herself in traditionally masculine activities and to enjoy the many satisfactions they can offer. The man likewise has deep-seated instinctive urges to involve himself in his child's care.

A central problem of gender identification in our society, I believe, has been that *each sex has been denied the opportunity to obtain gratifications in this area of secondary sexual functioning*. The examples of subjugation of women are well known. Men, too, have been subjected to prejudice; they have been enslaved by the tradition (more of their own making than of women's) that it is unmasculine to involve oneself in the particulars of child rearing. Hugging and cuddling one's baby, feeding it, cleaning it when it wets and soils, dressing it, and so on, are activities that men have been led to believe are unmanly. The goal we should strive toward (and we have made some headway in recent years) is that both men and women be enabled to gain gratifications in their areas of secondary sexual functioning. This will necessitate not only great flexibility by social institutions to accommodate women in their childbearing and child-rearing years, but also an alteration of social attitudes regarding the male's involvement with his children. The ideal is not, I believe, a fifty-fifty split—half the time the mother is with the children and half the time the father. Rather, I believe that when the children are in their earliest years they do best with the greatest amount of time being given by the mother. This is not to say that the father should not actively participate in the rearing of the infant. Every encouragement and every opportunity should be given him to satisfy his paternal needs without the fear that he will compromise his masculinity.

In line with this view, I do not agree with efforts to minimize gender differences in children in order to prepare them for a future world that will allegedly not recognize such differences. I do not believe that boys and girls in childhood should be dressed identically or given only identical toys. In the traditional game of "house," the girl will still generally want to play the role of mother and the boy that of father. However, I would also encourage the "father" to share the child care and housework while mother studies or works at something she is interested in. These are the kinds of identifications that I believe are healthiest for parents to foster.

Divorce can interfere with the smooth development of gender identification in several ways. First, the child of divorce has limited contacts with the parent who lives away from the home. If this parent is of the same sex, the child will be deprived of opportunities for identification. For example, one of the ways in which all children strengthen their identifications with their parents is through play and play fantasy. Even in the intact home, when a father is away at work, his son may play that he is doing his father's work in order to entrench his masculine identity. But if the father leaves, it becomes progressively harder for the child to continue the make-believe. In addition, the custodial parent's dislike of the absent parent can make it more difficult for the children to identify with him or her. For example, it is hard for a boy to identify with a person whom his mother (his first and most important love object) intensely dislikes: "If she says he's no good, how worthwhile can he be?" In addition, it is difficult for a boy to model himself after someone who is hostile to his mother.

Another issue is the *quality* of contacts. A same-sexed parent living in the home may be a *poorer* model for identification than one who lives elsewhere. The identification process, however, takes place primarily during the first three to four years of life. If the separation takes place after the child has reached this age, then the child may not suffer significant problems related to gender identification.

A mechanism that the child of divorce may utilize to compensate for the loss of the same-sexed parent is that of accomplishing a very rapid identification with that parent, as is sometimes seen in both children and adults after the death of a parent or other loved one. In some cases it appears as if the individual were saying, "I will *be* him (her). In that way there will be no loss at all"—so complete appears to be the identification. However, since it has delusional and fantasized elements, and since it has occurred almost instantaneously, this type of identification does not have the depth of the more natural and slowly developing process. Accordingly, the behavioral patterns so acquired are less adaptive to the reality of the child's life. In addition, because there has been less discrimination in the formation of the identification (the child has incorporated the whole bag, so to speak), more maladaptive patterns are likely to be taken in.

A kind of reverse gender identification sometimes occurs following divorce. In the absence of the father a boy may take on feminine traits. (These may or may not have anything to do with a homosexual orientation. Not all effeminate boys are homosexual, and not all homosexual boys are effeminate.) Sometimes a boy may try to deny his effeminate orientation by trying to exaggerate masculine traits. The more supermale he can be, the less his need to face his basic feminine identification. As is true of most, if not all such cover-ups, the disguise does not work completely, and the underlying problem will usually reveal itself in subtle ways. That is, the basic feelings of weakness that often accompany such an adjustment are sensed by others, and the youngster does not utilize the most effective and efficient methods for dealing with life's problems. On occasion, a girl will identify with her separated (but not totally absent) father in the attempt to gain affection from a somewhat deficient custodial mother. Observing her mother yearn continually for her father, she hopes to gain her mother's affection by this identification. If such a girl's father originally wanted her to be a boy and has over the years communicated his dissatisfaction with her sex, his attitude may further promote this pattern.

INSECURITY AND LOW SELF-ESTEEM

All of us experience feelings of inadequacy at times. And when psychological problems are present, such feelings of low self-worth are even more common. Here I'll discuss the specific factors that make children of divorce especially likely to develop feelings of low self-esteem. I'll also offer ideas for lessening the chances of such feelings developing and for reducing them when they do occur.

Factors in the divorce situation that may contribute to children's low self-esteem. If parents separate soon after a child is born, the child, when he or she becomes old enough to appreciate this, may feel that "if I had not been born they might still be together. They wanted one another—that's why they got married—but they didn't want me. When I was born, they became so unhappy that they got divorced." The notion may have its roots in the need to gain control over an uncontrollable situation, as discussed earlier in this chapter, and the therapeutic approaches to this delusion have been described there. Children who learn that they were conceived in an attempt to save a faltering marriage may reason that another, better child might have been successful in accomplishing this. The sense of failure associated with these ideas cannot help but lower a child's feelings of self-worth.

If the children live in a community where there are few other children from divorced homes, they may feel very different from and less worthy than those living in intact homes. If, in addition, they are stigmatized, they may feel even less worthwhile. It is important to help such children see that the divorce situation in no way warrants a person's being laughed at and that it has nothing to do with being bad. They have had bad luck, but they have done nothing to justify their being taunted or rejected. Also, they have to understand that they are not necessarily what others say they are.

The economic hardships that a divorce often causes may play a role in diminishing children's self-esteem. This is especially true when the divorce results in a significant lowering of the family's life-style. Although material possessions do not play a significant role in determining one's self-esteem, they do have an effect. It is often more difficult for poor people to feel good about themselves than those who have a reasonable degree of material comfort.

A particularly difficult situation is the one in which a child suffers because of a parent's bad reputation. For example, the son of a notoriously misbehaving alcoholic father may be ridiculed. As difficult as it may be, parents must try to help such a child appreciate that his stigmatization is totally inappropriate and cruel. He in no way contributed to his father's behavior and therefore is in no way to blame. Those who ridicule him have distortions in their own thinking; it is *they* rather than *he* who should be ashamed of themselves.

Parental factors contributing to low self-esteem in children of divorce.

Although most divorcing parents are deeply involved with their children and regret the pain that the separation is causing, and in spite of formidable attempts to reassure children that they are loved, children are still likely to feel that they have been abandoned by the departing parent. And they often assume that they have been rejected because they are unlovable. Young children judge their self-worth by their parents' views of them. (It is only later, when they go into other homes, attend school, and broaden their experiences that they utilize other criteria—both external and internal—for determining their self-worth.) When children believe that a parent does not love them and conclude that they are unlovable, their self-esteem suffers considerably. Such children have to be helped to appreciate that they may have a "wrong idea" and that the parent did not leave because they were unlovable.

Also children who have in fact been rejected or who are receiving limited affection have to be helped to accept that reality, lest they become preoccupied with futile and esteem-lowering attempts to gain more involvement than the parent is capable of providing. When, indeed, the departing parent has no love for the children, then a more shattering blow will have been dealt to their self-esteem. Such children have to be helped to appreciate that the deficiency lies within the parent, not within themselves. They may see an absent father's failure to pay child support as a reflection of their own worthlessness: "If I was worth anything, he'd send the money. I'm not worth paying for." Again, these children have to be helped to understand the distortions that are operating here.

The separation inevitably produces feelings of insecurity in children. The realizations that important people can disappear and that home stability is fragile at best make children feel small and vulnerable. And these feelings inevitably lower a child's self-esteem.

Divorce usually places new burdens on each of the parents. For example, the custodial parent is now all alone in caring for the everyday needs of the children, and divorce can create economic, personal, and career problems for this parent. The noncustodial parent, too, may see visitations as a source of restriction. Even if the parents do not verbalize frustration or resentment, the children are likely to sense them. And feeling like a burden often adds to a child's low self-esteem.

Information from both parents helps children gain a knowledge of their assets. With one parent gone, children are deprived of one source of potentially esteem-enhancing information.

Children who take sides with one parent in the parental conflict, risk alienating the other. The loss of affection may lower feelings of self-worth. Children who believe that the "good" child is one who is loved by both parents will feel that alienation of one parent makes them "bad."

The child may identify with the rejected parent and

assume that the departed parent has little if any affection for the whole family, not just the parent who remains. In the situation, for example, in which a father has left the home, his daughter may assume that because Mommy is not acceptable to Daddy, she and the other children are not acceptable to him either. Such a child has to be helped to differentiate clearly between herself and her mother and to understand clearly what traits the father claims are the sources of his alienation. If these traits do exist in the mother, the child has to be helped to determine whether she shares them—and if so (and this is unusual) to change them. If and when such clarification can be accomplished, it can help the child avoid self-esteem problems. The same considerations hold for the situation in which the mother rejects the father. The children, by identification, may assume they are similarly rejectable.

The child may be used as a scapegoat. Each parent, for example, may take out on the child the resentments felt toward the other. Being used as the target of hostility cannot but make the child feel loathsome.

Earlier in this chapter I discussed some of the elements in the divorce situation that may contribute to a parent's becoming overprotective. Children of such a parent are likely to become immature and regressed. Whatever gratifications these children may derive from regression, they are also likely to feel shame and to become fearful that peers will learn of the childish behavior. Shame and fear compromise feelings of self-worth.

A parent who attempts to use a child as a substitute for the spouse who is no longer available produces ego-debasing anxieties and frustrations in the child. Similarly, to use a child as a confidant and advisor in matters on which the child is totally ill equipped to provide advice is to produce feelings of inadequacy.

Factors in the child that contribute to low self-esteem. Many of the inappropriate ways in which children react to parental separation are designed to enhance self-worth, or at least to prevent a lowering of self-worth. But such attempts usually result in further lowering of self-esteem. Let us take, for example, the boy who is guilty over hostility he feels toward his father for leaving the household. An intrinsic part of guilt is a lowered sense of self-worth: "How terrible I am for what I have thought (done)." Although spared the guilt and the anticipated consequences of expressing his anger, the boy suffers depression and associated self-hate resulting in an even greater loss of self-esteem. Or a girl may spare herself guilty feelings over her hostility to a parent by projecting her anger onto others: "It is not I who am angry, it is he (she)." She may thereby protect herself from the lowered self-esteem associated with awareness of her hostility, but she will suffer with esteem-lowering fears of those upon whom she has projected her hostility. Any child who holds in and suppresses resentment of the separation, who does not deal with anger-provoking situations, suffers with the self-dissatisfaction inevitably associated with pent-up resentments.

Children who try to hide the separation from their friends may protect themselves from anticipated ridicule; but they usually suffer lowered self-worth associated with inner shame and fears of disclosure. And when the secret is inevitably revealed, they suffer even more shame and social alienation (for being a liar) than if they had disclosed the separation in the first place.

The child who plays one parent against the other in an attempt to win favor may suffer guilt and feelings of disloyalty over the dishonesty—and these feelings, too, will generally lower feelings of self-worth. Furthermore, the child who does not report back to one parent information about the other when requested to do so, may also feel disloyal and unworthy.

Additional ways of helping children of divorce deal with self-esteem problems. Because psychological problems are so closely associated with misguided attempts to enhance a lagging self-esteem, anything parents can do genuinely to increase children's sense of self-worth can be beneficial. In fact, one can consider the *genuine* enhancement of self-esteem to be the universal antidote to most psychological symptoms.

I emphasize the word *genuine* here because it is common for people to try to raise children's self-esteem by bestowing undeserved praise, flattery, patronizing compliments, and pretended affection. Compliments not actually associated with specific accomplishments can be ego-debasing rather than ego-enhancing. To say to a child, "Aren't you a nice girl" or "What a fine boy you are" makes most children squirm. They sense that these particular comments are being resorted to because the praiser cannot think of more specific and honest ones, that is, praises based on actual accomplishments. To say, however, "Boy, this cake you baked is really good!" or "You play the piano beautifully" or "What a swat! You hit the ball right over the fence" makes a child stand a few inches taller.

Of all the approaches to enhancing self-esteem there is none so important as the gaining of competence. One cannot feel good about oneself if one cannot focus on specific talents, skills, knowledge, and so on that one possesses. Accordingly, to raise children with a strong sense of self-worth, and to help them avoid using misguided and futile methods for compensating for feelings of low self-esteem, parents must enable their children to gain competence in important areas of living. They must help their children learn how to handle themselves in their daily activities. They must help them learn to relate satisfactorily and gratifyingly to others, so that they can gain the self-confidence and ego-enhancing pleasure that comes with successful involvements with others. They must help them become aware of areas in which they tend to act inappropriately, and teach them by word and experience how to avoid repetition of self-defeating behavior. Unless one has something specific and concrete about which to feel good, self-esteem is fantasied and cannot really produce a feeling of stability. Misguided and predictably futile esteem-enhancing maneuvers (such as lying about accomplishments, empty boasting, and inability or refusal to admit defects) only create more problems.

Children must have the feeling that there is some appreciation of their accomplishments by their parents and other significant individuals. We cannot enjoy competence in a vacuum. The proud bicycle rider who yells, "Look, Ma, no hands" gains additional ego-enhancement from the mother's admiration. At the same time, children should be helped to appreciate that the most important esteem building comes from a worthwhile endeavor. External praise should not be the primary reason for such pursuits but an enjoyable, esteem-enhancing fringe benefit.

Feeling genuinely needed by at least one or two people is also crucial to self-respect. One of the important considerations I use for determining if depressed people are suicidal is whether they believe that no one in the whole world would miss them if they were dead. Although children are dependent on their parents, children must still feel that their loss would be painful to their parents if they are to have a healthy sense of self-worth. Recognizing that they have the power to make their parents laugh, to give them warm inner feelings, and to contribute to their pleasure in having a *family* contributes to children's feelings of self-worth.

Children of divorce are bound to question the need their parents have for them. Rightly or wrongly, children may feel that they are a burden rather than a help to their divorced parents. Parents, therefore, should communicate to their children how much they need them. But words alone are generally not enough. Children must have the living experience (that important term again) that the parents enjoy being with them and are genuinely interested in the things they do. It is as if the child says: "I have the capacity to give them pleasure. With me they can have fun. I am therefore a worthwhile person." To provide this living experience, parents should try to find activities that are enjoyable to both the children and themselves and to refrain from activities that they find boring.

A common source of lowered self-respect in children, especially those with psychological problems, is the notion that they are the only ones in the world who have the "terrible" thoughts and feelings that they harbor within themselves. Parents often corroborate this notion and thus deepen children's self-hatred. It is important for divorcing parents to reassure their children that most, if not all, people have angry thoughts and feelings. When appropriate, parents should tell children that they themselves have (or have had) similar emotional reactions. Such comments can help children feel less loathsome as they come to appreciate that they are not so unique. In addition, the parents' revealing (when appropriate) deficiencies of their own can help children feel better about their own defects.

When patients tell me, "I feel terrible. I'm no good," I will often ask if they are doing something that may contribute to such feelings. Often, after some thought, I get an affirmative answer (admittedly, more commonly from an adult than from a child). The child may be cheating, stealing, or lying. The child of divorce may be spying on one parent or playing one parent against the other. In such situations I generally tell the child: "As long as you continue doing that, you're going to feel lousy about yourself. I think that when you stop doing that, you'll see that you'll feel much better about yourself."

The divorce situation can provide children with esteem-enhancing experiences if they can rise to the occasion. The extra responsibilities that children of divorce are often asked to assume can provide them with an increased sense of competence. In addition, I urge many parents to join community organizations for divorced people. (The best known of these family-oriented organizations is Parents Without Partners.) There are many potential esteem-enhancing benefits to be derived for children from such membership. These organizations provide children with opportunities to be with many other children of divorce, thereby lessening their feelings of being different. Through these organizations children can form relationships with substitute parents of the same sex as the one who has departed from the household. For older children, discussion groups can be beneficial. The sense of belonging to a special club, the feeling of communality, and the recreational activities can all increase children's sense of self-worth.

ANGER

Anger, I believe, arises primarily from frustration. (Although one can make minor distinctions between the terms *hostility* and *anger*, for the purposes of this discussion I will use the words synonymously.) Anger has survival value, because the purpose of the anger response is to enhance our efficiency in fighting threats to our well-being. But frustration occurs whenever we are thwarted (or believe we are being thwarted) from obtaining something we desire, regardless of whether it is vital to our survival. And since life inevitably produces frustrations within us, anger is predictably going to arise in us from time to time.

Sources of anger in children of divorce. Children of divorce have usually been exposed to many frustrating experiences. The constant conflict between their parents before the separation deprives them of a calm and loving environment. Following the separation they usually feel abandoned. Children may also resent being different from their peers; others have two parents at home, they have only one. The divorce generally causes each parent new frustrations and resentments, and the children may become targets for parental hostility. But children are too small to fight back and too dependent to run. Being captive prey is likely to produce retaliatory hostility in them. Also, a custodial mother may have to take a job (something she may have never done before), and her absence from the home may be a source of resentment in her children. In addition, social tradition—often incorporated into the legal system—may require the mother to assume custody when the father would have been the preferable parent. Such a mother's resentment adds to her deficiencies as a parent and causes the children even greater frustration. Their inability to live with the preferable parent provides them with yet another reason to be angry.

Of course, there are other things that can occur in the divorce situation that may make children resentful. The mother and father may be perpetuating their hostilities, and so the expected termination of the terrible conflict never seems to come. Mom may prevent the children from seeing Dad because he has been remiss on support payments. Dad may be unreliable about visitation, frequently being late or not showing up at all. Unwelcome strangers, like men and women friends of the parents, may appear on the scene. The children may have to accommodate the offspring of these new strangers, who may even become their relatives. The separation may require various material privations or a move to a new and less desirable home. In fact, there is hardly a section of this book that does not make reference to some situation that is an actual or potential source of resentment to children of divorce. Accordingly, it is not surprising that problems related to anger are, in my experience, the most common problems with which children of divorce (and their therapists) have to deal.

Problems caused by anger inhibition. Mental health professionals use the words *repression* and *suppression* to refer to psychological processes that remove unacceptable thoughts and feelings from awareness and relegate them to unconsciousness. Strictly used, the term *suppression* refers to a conscious process: The individual does not wish to think about something and decides to ignore and to try to forget it. In *repression* the process is unconscious. But often both processes operate simultaneously, and for the purposes of this book I do not think the distinction between them is crucial. Accordingly, I will use the terms synonymously, not only for the sake of simplicity but because there are many times when the distinction blurs.

Problems may result from the suppression and/or repression of the anger that children of divorce often experience. Rather than release their anger in healthy ways, they bottle it up. Pent-up anger then contributes to the formation of various symptoms that serve to repress or disguise the anger. But these methods of dealing with repressed anger are poor solutions to the problem.

Generally, the kinds of problems caused by repressed

anger result from the child's being guilty over or fearful of expressing anger. Such children may have grown up in a home where they were taught that expression of anger toward a parent is a terrible thing to do. Sometimes parents directly tell their youngsters that good and acceptable children are never hostile toward their parents and do not even have angry thoughts about them. Other parents may serve as models for anger suppression; they may never fight, and thereby produce more anger suppression in their children than they would have if they openly criticized hostile expression. (The situation is analogous to that of the sexually inhibited woman who complains: "I can't understand why I can't be freer sexually. My parents never told me it was sinful or bad. In fact, they never even spoke about sex!" For the silent parent, sex is unmentionable. And unmentionable things produce far more guilt and fear than the mentionable.) Or observing the devastating effects of the expression of anger on each of the parents may inhibit the children from expressing hostility. Or, as mentioned, by its very nature the divorce situation may cause children to suppress their anger. One parent has already left; expressing resentment might result in their seeing even less of that parent. And they may fear exhibiting hostility toward the remaining parent, lest he or she leave as well.

One of the most common ways in which children may deal with their anger over the separation is to *deny* it. Most often this denial is unconscious—they are really not aware that they are angry. Through denial a child deals with an anger (in this case an inner one, the child's own anger and its threatened eruption into conscious awareness) by simply making believe it doesn't exist. When asked how they feel about some of the obviously anger-provoking situations associated with the separation, such children may respond with a host of rationalizations designed to protect them from awareness of their anger. One patient, when I asked about her feelings about her father's limited involvement since leaving the home, stated, "It doesn't bother me. I know he has to spend so much time working to send us money that he hasn't time to see us or call us." A son of a physician stated, "My father can't come and see me because he'd have to leave his patients and some of them might die."

A related method by which some children may at the same time deny and express their anger is excessive concern for the safety of the parent(s). As I have described, fearing that harm will befall a parent can allow for a release, through fantasy, of hostile wishes. However, there is little if any guilt, because the child experiences the dreaded event only as a fear. The child may become oversolicitous in response to such fantasies, may become profuse in praising the parent(s), and may even buy gifts for frivolous reasons.

Some basic principles of anger psychology. The situation that is most likely to cause anger is one in which the individual experiences frustration over an inability to remove an irritant. Anger's purpose is to enhance our efficiency in removing the source of irritation. As long as the painful stimulus is present, anger will be provoked and increased, resulting in more and more intense emotional reactions such as rage and fury. It is useful to view anger as the first and mildest of these three states. Anger does not preclude rational thought and action. But when the anger does not work, when the source of irritation remains, the individual may enter into a state of rage. Whereas in anger one can still focus on the irritating stimulus, in rage the anger is much greater, rationality is reduced, and wilder and more generalized actions occur.

For example, a woman's husband has a drinking problem. When drunk he has often forced himself upon her sexually. At such times she has found him detestable. One night, her husband comes home from the bar and starts the usual routine. She angrily says, "Now you just stay away from me. When you're this way you're disgusting!" Her angry tone of voice communicates to her husband that she means what she says, and her anger increases her physical capacity to protect herself.

Now let us assume that her husband, unaffected by her comments, starts chasing her and traps her in a corner. She now enters into a state of rage. She kicks wildly, screams, claws, and thrashes. Her words and actions, although generally directed toward driving off her husband, are less specifically focused on him. They are wild and chaotic.

Let us say that this woman, even in the state of rage, would not murder her husband, even if a weapon were available. If the rage built up further, however, she might enter into a state of fury in which she became capable of killing him. The term fury would also refer to a state of insane rage in which the woman might go berserk and begin attacking innocent parties.

Following any step in this encounter it would be reasonable for this woman to tell her husband that she wants a divorce. Such a statement would be best made in a state of angry irritation, however, without rage or fury. She would then be using her anger in a healthy and effective way—to remove the noxious stimulus (in this case her inebriated, abusive, assaultive husband).

In a world where there are always things to frustrate us, we do well to deal with such irritants at the earliest possible time, using our anger at the earliest moment, when it is at its mildest level and when we can more rationally focus on the irritant and remove it. The longer we take to do this, the longer our anger builds up, the more likely our anger will turn to rage and even fury, and the less likely we are to deal rationally with the situation. This principle is fundamental to this discussion of helping children of divorce deal with their anger and the situations that provoke it.

The survival of civilized society depends on a significant degree of anger inhibition. Long ago it was recognized that inducing guilt is a very useful way of restraining individuals from acting out their angry impulses. In fact, it has been one of the most widely used methods, because it has the advantage of individuals' deterring themselves, from fear of *internal* rather than *external* forces, from performing hostile acts. Parental teaching, educational systems, religious training, legends, and myths have all played their role in producing such guilt.

However helpful the guilt deterrent has been, it has often been misused. Since anger can lead to rage, then fury, many social institutions have prohibited and discouraged expression of the milder forms of anger as a safety measure against the expression of the violent forms. This is like banning totally the use of fire because it can be so destructive. We must not allow unbridled expression of anger if society is to survive. Yet we must not deprive individuals of anger's value as a tool of survival. Such repression also contributes to the kinds of psychological problems I describe in this section. Anger must be harnessed and used to help with life's frustrations.

Like other people, children must not be filled with guilt over the inevitable angry feelings they have. Yet they must not be allowed to vent their anger whenever and wherever they wish. Children are continually bombarded with "Don't do this" and "Don't do that." It is no surprise, then, that they suffer many frustrations and resentments. But children can neither flee from nor fight their parents' prohibitions, and so they utilize various mechanisms to deal with their anger. They may deny and repress it; they may release it symbolically through games; they may release it by identifying with and observing others who are releasing theirs (via watching sporting events or television violence); they may project it out onto others; or they may release it symbolically through dreams and fantasies. We know relatively little about the reasons why a child chooses a particular mechanism to deal with anger. Why does one child project it and another repress it? Why does one child deny it and another direct it toward him- or herself? No doubt social influences and parental models play a role; but even in the same family one can observe different ways of dealing with anger.

In spite of our ignorance there is much that we have learned about the causes and the alleviation of anger inhibition problems. Here I will focus on things parents can do to help their children avoid and alleviate such problems.

As repressed anger strives for release, an internal psychological conflict may be set up. This may produce a *state of tension*, the causes of which are generally unknown to the child who just feels tense and doesn't know why. And the tension may manifest itself in a number of ways. The child may become hyperirritable, cry easily, and react in an exaggerated fashion to the most minor disturbances and irritations. Some children develop tics. Most commonly these are of the eyes (blinking) and the mouth (grimacing and puckering movements). In more severe tics, the head and shoulders may become involved, and various vocal tics (grunting noises, frequent throat clearing) may appear. It appears that every individual has one or more points or organs of weakness that are commonly the first areas to exhibit difficulty when there is tension. Sometimes a physical illness that leaves residual changes may predispose a certain area to respond to stress. For example, some people react to tension with spasm of the muscles of the scalp, and they get tension headaches. In some, the muscles of the lower back become tight and rigid, and a low back pain syndrome results. Some experience contraction of the muscles of the gastrointestinal tract with resulting vomiting or diarrhea. In others the heart beats more rapidly and palpitations result. Or the respiratory rate may increase, with associated shortness of breath.

All children experience occasional *nightmares*. Nightmares are, more than anything else, the result of repressed hostility. Since all children have to learn to repress their hostility if they are to get along with others (and if civilized society is to survive), all children, at times, have nightmares. And since children of divorce are more likely to be angry, they are more likely to have nightmares than the child living in an intact, relatively serene home. In the typical nightmare, the child is fearful that a horrible and dangerous figure will enter, or has already entered the child's room. Usually the intruder comes in from a window or closet or from under the bed. I believe that the interloper is the fantasized symbol of the child's unacceptable angry impulses, which have been relegated to the unconscious. Daytime activities such as sports, sibling fights, and television, which have provided some release of hostility, are no longer available. At night, leftover hostility from unresolved daytime frustrations presses for release. In the nightmare, the symbolic derivatives of the child's anger (the horrible creature) press for expression into the child's conscious awareness (symbolized by the child's room). The greater the child's guilt over his or her anger, the more it will be repressed. The urgency for release becomes correspondingly greater, as does fear of the anger symbols when they threaten to erupt into conscious awareness. Up to a point the more guilt-ridden the child and the greater the anger the more frightening the nightmare. When the guilt is extremely great, however, even symbols of the anger will be repressed and no dream will be experienced. The child will be "protected" from nightmares—and this vehicle for release of anger will not be available.

The evil figures can also represent the child's own hostility projected outward (they are outside his room); or they can symbolize hostile elements within significant figures (such as his parents). When the frightening figure threatens to abduct the child, the dream may reflect separation anxieties—the child's fear that with diminished parental protection, he or she will be at the mercy of those who might prey on children. The nightmare, like all dreams, is rich in meaning. The many elements that may contribute to its formulation are beyond the scope of this book to discuss in detail. Central to nightmares, however, are children's *own* repressed hostilities; and the fears experienced during the dream are most commonly of their *own* anger. It is for these reasons, I believe, that the child of divorce is likely to experience an increase in the frequency of nightmares, especially around the time of the separation.

(The nightmares just described should be differentiated from the frightening dreams children often have after watching scary and/or violent movies or television shows. These nightmares are in an entirely different category. They generally portray the same material to which the child has been exposed, whereas the repressed-hostility nightmares are much more idiosyncratic. Movie- or television-program dreams are best understood as desensitization phenomena. Watching the show has been psychologically traumatic, and the fears engendered may have been formidable. By reliving the experience in dreams, children gradually recover from the trauma.)

The development of *compulsions* is another way in which

children of divorce may deal with anger. In the handwashing compulsion, for example, patients may consider their hands to be the potential tools for acting out unconscious, unacceptable (generally hostile or sexual) thoughts and feelings. By compulsively cleaning them, a child symbolically "keeps them clean"—that is, innocent of committed crimes.

The term *compulsion* refers to an act that an individual is compelled to perform even though it may appear senseless. Trying to restrain oneself from performing the act produces ever-mounting tension, which can be reduced only by giving in and engaging in the compulsive behavior. Most often such sufferers do not really know *why* they have to perform the act, although they may at times provide weak rationalizations to justify it. No one knows with certainty the cause(s) of compulsions. It is probable that there is a high genetic biological loading. Some psychiatrists consider compulsions to be entirely biological. My own opinion is that the biological-genetic loading is probably strong and that some individuals are thus much more likely to develop compulsions than others. However, I believe that there is a psychological component as well, and it is psychological factors that concern us here.

A ten-year-old boy I once treated presented symptoms that demonstrate quite well the relationship between compulsions and repressed hostility. Although his parents were not separated, they were highly intellectual people and very inhibited in expressing affection, and so were psychologically separated from one another and from him. The boy feared that if he knocked against an article of furniture (even accidentally) there would be the most terrible consequences—the worst of which was that God would punish him by striking him dead with lightening. He especially feared hitting his foot against something, because the possible punishments for that seemed to be worse than if his hand or torso hit the furniture. Although he was cautious, he somehow would slip up at least a few times a day and "accidentally" bump into or even kick some household articles. He would then become very anxious, examine the furniture very carefully, and run his finger over it to be certain that it wasn't scratched or marred. Gradually the examination process developed into a specific ritual in which he had to rub his finger over the area exactly three times, after which he experienced some alleviation of his anxiety. In addition, he would look up toward heaven and pray to God not to punish him for the terrible thing he had done. Finally his pleadings too became formulated into ritualistic prayers that would reduce his anxiety if stated in a particular way.

I considered the furniture to represent the patient's parents and his bumping into (and even worse, kicking) them a symbolic expression of hostility toward them. It was as if each time he hit the furniture he released symbolically the anger he felt toward his parents. The ritualized inspection for damages and scratches served to assuage the boys's guilt—to reassure him that he had not in fact harmed his parents. God, of course, represented the parents (especially the father, whom the boy saw as more punitive). Again, ritualizing the prayer served to diminish the anxiety and provided a predictable (although magical) way of reducing it. Generally, children with such compulsive rituals require psychiatric treatment. In this boy's case, a central focus in his therapy was the reduction of guilt over and fear of expressing his anger. However, mere expression of hostility was not enough; other issues related to his anger and appropriate release of it also had to be dealt with. It was only then that his symptoms were alleviated.

Phobic reactions regarding a parent (especially the absent one) may also occur. The less direct contact we have with a person, the greater the likelihood that we will harbor distortions about that person. When parents separate, the child is likely to develop distortions about the absent parent that would not otherwise have arisen; for instance, the child is likely to see such a parent as unduly punitive. The child's image of the absent parent as hostile may be further intensified by the projection (caused by guilt) of the child's own hostility: "It is not I who have these horrible hostile thoughts, it is he (she)." The absent parent may then be seen as so hostile that the child expects to be injured or severely maltreated in other ways. With such anticipations the child may dread contact with the parent, even to the point of becoming phobic, that is the child may fear any contact at all with the parent.

Or the child may become excessively fearful that the parent may become sick or injured. Such concerns are reactions to the basic unconscious wish that harm befall the parent. The basic hostile wish is expressed as a fantasy in which the parent is harmed. The child assuages the guilt associated with such fantasy by turning the wish into a fear. It is not that the child *wants* harm to befall the parent; it is that the child *fears* the calamity. In this way the hostility is released through fantasy and the guilt assuaged by transformation into a fear. Another notion that may contribute to a phobia is the child's belief that hostile thoughts per se have the power to harm. Such a child may become overwhelmingly solicitous and may need frequent proof that the parent is well in order to be assured that the basic hostile wishes have not been realized.

And separation anxieties may develop in the service of keeping the parent ever at the child's side, thereby providing the child with the reassurance that the parent has not been harmed. In the extreme the child may develop what is often referred to as a "school phobia." Nowadays this problem is often seen as one type of separation anxiety disorder. Although many factors contribute to this disorder, one factor is the child's need to be constantly at the side of the parent in order to be reassured that conscious and unconscious hostile wishes have not caused the parent harm. Sometimes the fear of harm from, or fear of harm befalling, a parent is displaced onto an object or an animal. A child may become morbidly frightened of dogs, certain figures on television, or other selected phobic objects.

Children's repressing their hostility and directing it toward themselves can also contribute to their becoming *depressed*. When self-recriminations are present this mechanism becomes even more obvious. We can best understand such criticisms as being displaced from a significant figure onto the children themselves. For the child of divorce the significant individuals are generally one or both parents. If we follow the formula "substitute the word *father* or *mother* whenever the child's name appears in a self-disparaging statement," we generally get a clearer understanding of what is going on in the child.

Changes parents can effect within themselves that may help their children's anger inhibition problems.

As I've often mentioned, some parents have very rigid standards about anger expression, and they may have overtly or covertly induced guilt in their children for any expression of anger. Such parents should try to see that these standards, although they have a long tradition, are not consistent with our present knowledge of what is best psychologically for children. Anger is a normal reaction to frustrations. In my discussions with parents, some fear that I am encouraging them to let their children run wild and turn into little savages. I try to reassure them that this is definitely not my goal—that this would be substituting one disease for another. Rather, my hope is that their children will find a healthy balance between too much and too little repression of anger.

I try, too, to help parents differentiate between angry thoughts, feelings, and actions. Parents do best for their children by attempting to lessen guilt over angry thoughts and feelings (which we have little power to control) and angry deeds (which we generally have the capacity to suppress). For instance, a mother can say, "We see how angry you are about Daddy leaving. You can be as angry as you want, but you can't go around the house breaking things."

The question of children's cursing at parents often comes up. I generally advise parents to reassure their children that they accept the fact that the children's anger at them may cause curse words to come into their minds. However, I suggest they add that at this time children's cursing at parents is unacceptable behavior, and that if the children are angry at them they should use more polite words than those that come into their minds. I also advise parents to try to reduce guilt by telling their children that such words do have a use, because they allow for a release of anger in a way that does not cause anyone physical harm. For example, a parent might say, "I can understand how angry you are that Mommy has to work; but I won't let you go around using such language to me. That kind of language may be okay with your friends out on the street. What we have to do is figure out ways for you to be less angry about my working."

Parents do well to appreciate that angry outbursts are especially common around the time of the separation, and their tolerance for them has to be particularly high during this period. I do not suggest that *no* disciplinary measures at all be taken; rather, that they be used more sparingly during this period.

If divorcing parents can reduce their warfare, this contributing element to their children's hostility and guilt may be reduced. Children who frequently observe their parents treating one another in a cruel and inhumane fashion may become fearful of expressing their anger lest they cause similar suffering to others.

There are parents who cannot tolerate a child's anger because they feel that "If someone is angry at me, regardless of the age of the person and the reasons for the anger, I must be at fault. It cannot be his (or her) problem, distortion, or inappropriate reaction to me. I must be abominable." Accordingly, they may do everything to squelch their children's anger. Their children may come to feel very guilty about their anger because of the devastating effect it has on the parent. Such a parent generally needs to be loved by everybody, and sometimes therapy may be necessary to help the parent alter this view.

Parents who consider themselves perfect, or at least attempt to present such a view of themselves to their children, may consider their children's anger to be a sign of a defect within themselves. So they strongly discourage the children's expression of anger in order to maintain the image of perfection. As explained before, however, such parents are doing their children a disservice. Parents should appreciate that revealing deficiencies in natural and uncontrived ways (as long as they are not extensive and frequently exhibited) will result in the children's *gaining* respect for the parent, as they come to appreciate that it is the strong rather than the weak person who has the courage to admit defects. If such parents can allow their children to express anger over defects in themselves, one of the elements contributing to the child's guilt will be reduced.

In the 1970s we experienced the popularization of what I consider a misguided application of psychological principles. Unfortunately, this approach continues to be popular among many mental health workers. The idea is to encourage children openly to express their resentment. Some practitioners consider such expression the primary aim of therapy as well as one of the most valuable ways of helping children avoid the development of psychological disturbance. "Once the hateful feelings are let out," we are told, "the loving feelings are then free to express themselves." And the method used to facilitate the release of the angry feelings is *labeling* them. Accordingly, the little girl whose divorced father is late for his visit is told, "It must make you feel very angry that Daddy is late again." If the child agrees and expresses her resentment, the method is deemed successful. Guilt has been reduced by the parent's speaking the unspeakable, and the child's expressing her anger presumably drains the pool of repressed feelings that have caused her discomfort and even psychological problems.

I believe that a child who was comfortable expressing her anger would respond indignantly to such a comment with a response such as: "Of course I am. Wouldn't you be?" She would recognize the absurdity of the statement and its implicit condescension. But if she were not consciously aware of her anger, "labeling" would not serve well to bring her in touch with it. Such an approach may be a good first step for many children. It may lessen some guilt via the parent's mentioning the unmentionable. The method's main fault lies in its incompleteness. It does not give proper attention to the primary purpose of anger: to *remove* a source of irritation and frustration. It may allow for temporary release of anger and alleviation of some tension, but it does nothing to bring about a change in the situation that caused the anger in the first place. Accordingly, the anger is likely to be continually generated. The child must also be encouraged to direct angry feelings toward specific goals in order to accomplish something more than emotional release. For example, the little girl might be asked: "Have you told your father how angry it makes you when he's late?" or "What do you think you can do while you wait for him so you won't be thinking all the time about when he's going to come?" Helping the child to use her anger constructively is more likely to solve the anger problem than mere encouragement of anger expression.

Helping children with their anger inhibition problems. If parents are to help their children express their pent-up resentments, they must serve as models for such expression themselves. Like cigarette-smoking parents who warn their children against the pitfalls of smoking, parents who do not practice what they preach are not going to be taken very seriously by their children.

In accordance with what we know about the various stages of anger release, children should be encouraged to express their resentments at the earliest possible stage so that their anger does not get suppressed, repressed, and built up internally. They should learn to become sensitive to angry thoughts when they first arise, and they should be made aware of any tendency to make excuses that justify their not utilizing their anger appropriately. They should learn to recognize the physical sensations they experience when they first become angry. And they should be encouraged to express their resentments at the earliest possible time in an effort to alter the situation that is causing the resentments in the first place.

Children should also learn not to pursue lost causes. I often quote what I call Fields's Rule (after W. C. Fields, the comedian, who allegedly first stated it): "If at first you don't succeed, try, try again. If, after that, you still don't succeed, forget it! Don't make a big fool of yourself." To encourage children to persist in trying to achieve a goal that appears hopeless can be psychologically harmful and even cruel. Rather, they should be encouraged to resign themselves to certain failures and to redirect their attention to alternative pursuits that have a greater likelihood of success. If, after reasonable efforts, a father proves incapable of affection for his son, the youngster should be helped to gain affection from others who are capable of providing it. The concept of substitute gratification is important in helping children resign themselves to a failure. It is much easier to concede defeat in one area if there is reasonable hope of success in another.

One way for a child to reduce anger is to appreciate that the thing he or she may want may not be a reasonable thing to desire. If the child can stop craving that thing, the child is less likely to be frustrated and hence angry. In my work with children I often refer to this principle as "changing your mind about the thing you want." A girl, for example, who wants her mother to discontinue dating is going to be continually frustrated and angry as long as she persists in hoping that her mother will stop. If, however, she can be helped to appreciate that her mother has the right to recreation and is usually in better spirits upon her return, then the girl may give up or reduce her demands and thereby become less angry.

A related alteration of thinking that I often suggest for children with anger inhibition problems is what I call "changing your mind about the person you're angry at." The most common example is the child who has been brainwashed by one parent into believing that the other parent is the incarnation of all the evil that ever existed in the world. If one can help such children correct some of these distortions, they will less likely to be angry.

As I work with children who are guilty over their anger, I always try to help them differentiate between angry thoughts, angry feelings, and angry deeds. I try to help them recognize that angry thoughts and feelings are inevitable and that all people experience them. In addition, I try to convince them that all people, at times, have the desire to perform angry acts and that most *do* act these out to a limited extent when the damage done will be minimal; but that most *do not* when the inflicted damage would be great. My emphasis is on the fact that these are the reactions and experiences of *most* people. This helps children feel less guilty about their own anger reactions as they come to appreciate that they are not different from others regarding their angry thoughts and feelings.

Magical thinking is especially prevalent in three- to five-year-olds, and many people carry remnants of such primitive thinking into adulthood. One form of magical thinking is the idea that thoughts in themselves have the power to bring about real events. Children who believe that their angry thoughts can actually harm the object of their hostility may become very frightened of expressing them. In attempting to help a child correct this distortion I may tell a story such as: "The dog was really angry at the cat, so angry that he wished that she would be killed. One night he wished *very hard* that the cat would be run over by a car. The next morning he went to see what had happened to the cat. But she was still alive! The next night he wished *even harder* that the cat would die. But still the cat stayed alive. And night after night and day after day—no matter how hard he wished the cat to die—she stayed alive. No matter how hard he wished the cat to be dead, she still stayed alive. His thoughts just couldn't harm her!"

Some children are so repressed about anger expression that they have little if any conscious awareness of angry thoughts and/or feelings. For example, one mother reported that her daughter waited three hours for her father to show up on visitation day and he never appeared. When I asked the child how she felt about her father's not showing up she replied, without any show of emotion, "He must have forgotten. Sometimes his memory isn't very good." The child was obviously guilty about expressing the angry feelings I knew she harbored within her and justified her father's behavior with the explanation that he had some kind of inborn deficiency in his memory that caused him to forget. One cannot get angry at a person with such an unfortunate handicap.

It would have been useless to have tried to introduce this child to the psychoanalytic theory of forgetting, which holds most forgetting (in people without physical disease) to be unconsciously motivated. In this father's case, the forgetting was a manifestation of his basic lack of interest in seeing his daughter. But to accept this fact might have resulted in her becoming angry at him—something she was morbidly afraid to do. "He's just that way," she rationalized. "He often does that. I'm used to it; it doesn't make me angry." At this point I replied, "I cannot imagine that in all that time—in the three hours that you waited—that you didn't once, somewhere in the corner of your mind, have at least *one* angry thought about him. Some little angry feeling. I can't imagine someone in that situation not getting at least a little angry. I know that I myself would have been furious." My hope was that I would make the admission of an angry reaction acceptable.

Although the child responded with further denials during that interchange, she subsequently allowed that she did occasionally get angry under similar circumstances. My approach was based on the assumption that even in the most severely repressed people, with enough prompting some of the anger does manage to erupt into conscious awareness. The expression of this little spark of anger is strongly encouraged by the therapist and the hiding of it emphatically discouraged. Patients are thereby made to feel that expression of anger makes them like everyone else, and this can reduce fears of revealing it. Although a parent might try this approach, it is important to appreciate that it must be used with caution; too much pressure on the child to reveal the transient angry thought and/or fleeting angry feeling may produce anxiety and further repression. But used judiciously, such an approach can help some children more guiltlessly express their anger.

Acting out of anger. There are children who, instead of repressing their anger and possibly channeling it into various symptoms, release it directly. For the purposes of this discussion I will use the term *acting out* when the hostile release is antisocial and unaccompanied by significant guilt.

The relationship between breakup of the home and antisocial behavior in children has been extensively studied (especially with regard to juvenile delinquency). And most agree that children of divorce are more likely to exhibit delinquent behavior than those in an intact, relatively happy and stable home. After all such children are being deprived and frustrated, and it is reasonable to assume that some of them will act out their anger. A sibling may be a convenient and safe victim; or the parent with whom the child lives may become the focus, the absent parent not being so readily available. The parent who initiated divorce proceedings may be selected as the target, regardless of how justifiable the decision and regardless of how little was his or her contribution to the marital difficulties. From the child's point of view, *that* parent caused the separation and *that* parent should be blamed. The forms of acting-out behavior vary according to the child's age and level of sophistication. They range from primitive temper tantrums in the very young, through bullying of peers, disruptive behavior in the home and classroom, cruelty to animals, fire setting, defiance of authority, to a wide variety of other types of antisocial behavior.

Factors that may contribute to acted-out anger in children of divorce. The capacity of children to experience guilt over antisocial behavior relates to their experiences with parents (and, to a lesser extent, teachers, clergymen, and other authority figures) during the formative years. Both by instruction and imitation of the parental model, children take on the principles of behavior to which the parents adhere. The parents' dos and don'ts become the children's; the parents' rights and wrongs are accepted as valid for their children.

In the intact home, when one parent is not on the scene, the other is generally available to teach, discipline, and impart those values that contribute to the development of healthy guilt mechanisms. When one parent is absent from the home there is some reduction of the exposures that produce a strong capacity to experience guilt. Also, traditionally, the loss of the father is especially conducive to a child's failure to develop strong guilt mechanisms. Social tradition may still impart to many children that the father is the severer disciplinarian. Most teachers, for example, know that summoning a child's father to school implies that a more serious offense has been committed than when a mother is asked to come. Since the overwhelming majority of separations involve the absence of the father, the frequent development of guilt deficiencies in children of divorce is not surprising.

One of the factors that motivate children to inhibit themselves from acting out antisocial impulses is the parental affection and approbation they obtain for doing so. But a child of divorce, feeling involved and perhaps even abandoned (whether or not such feelings are justified), may reason: "What's the point of stopping myself from doing bad things? Even when I'm good no one praises me. No one even cares."

The child of divorce has often witnessed some of the most cruel behavior that one individual can inflict upon another. Parental hostilities frequently reach sadistic levels. The atmosphere often becomes one of continual distrust. The most cruel things may be said, with no holds barred on the use of profanity. Impulsive acting out of destructive behavior toward one another is common. The desire for vengeance may reach obsessive and even psychotic proportions. In such an environment it is not surprising that some children model themselves after their parents and behave similarly. In addition, parents who are obsessed with their conflict tend not to focus much attention on training and disciplining their children. Deprived of external restraints, the children are not likely to develop internal restraints to their antisocial behavior.

Bruce, a seven-year-old boy, demonstrated how a vicious parental conflict could affect a child. Bruce's parents became embroiled in a violent divorce conflict when his father learned that his mother was having an affair. Bruce's father had always had a short fuse and a violent temper. Bruce's mother also tended to resort to screaming at the slightest provocation, and the neighbors generally knew when she was disciplining the children. Following the divulgence of the mother's affair, the father made an immediate decision for divorce; he saw absolutely no hope that he could ever forget his wife's infidelity or work out the problems that might have contributed to her involvement with another man. Once the divorce process started rolling, other issues became sources of conflict: property distribution, money, visitation. The father's lawyer was determined to extract his pound of flesh, and the mother's lawyer adamantly held the position that Bruce's father was not going to keep "a penny more than he's entitled to." The father saw red every time his wife's name was mentioned; and the mother found fault with just about everything the father said or did. The most petty incidents became the foci of violent arguments, during which the parents cursed foully at one another, threw things at one another, and on occasion even came to blows. When Bruce and his sister were not direct witnesses to the parental battles, they could not avoid overhearing them.

In the classroom and at home, although a little on the edgy side and with some tendencies toward being a wise guy and a loudmouth (via identification with his father), Bruce had never had a significant behavior problem. But within a month of the onset of the parental conflict there began a steady deterioration in Bruce's behavior. He began to refuse to do his homework; when he did do it, it was messy and slipshod. He became disruptive in the classroom; he learned little, and he interfered with his classmates' learning as well. He bullied, teased, and provoked other children. When his teacher tried to discipline him, he responded with a barrage of profanities. He reacted similarly to the principal, to whose office he was frequently sent. Finally Bruce was referred to me.

When I first saw Bruce he was so tense that he could not sit still; he bounced around or rocked in his seat. His eyes blinked furiously. He bit his fingernails frequently and even, at times, his lips. Often he would nervously wet his lips with his tongue. When I asked him his age, address, and telephone number he responded with "Bug off" and "Dry up." He absolutely refused to involve himself in any therapeutic activities, and after a few sessions he refused to attend the sessions any longer. I advised the parents that I did not think that it would be a good idea to pressure Bruce into coming, because doing so might sour him even further on therapy. I told them that the best hope for alleviating Bruce's antisocial behavior was reducing their own conflict. Although they appreciated the validity of my explanation, they were so swept up in their vicious battle that they were unwilling and unable to extract themselves from it. Two years later, I learned from the referring physician that the parents' battles were still going strong (even though they were divorced) and that Bruce had been expelled from school and was attending a military academy, where he still had a severe disciplinary problem.

In Bruce's case it was clear that the anger he felt toward his parents was being displaced onto classmates, teachers, his principal, and me. His parents were serving as his models for angry acting out. Although he often vented rage against his mother, he rarely had a single complaint about his father. This related, in part, to the fact that his father had already left the home and expressing anger toward him might result in his seeing even less of his father. In addition to the acting out of his anger, then, there was still a significant degree of anger repression. And this resulted in the state of agitation and tension that was so typical of him. Bruce had been a relatively healthy boy before the onset of his parents' battling. I am convinced that if they had been able to divorce in a more civilized fashion, Bruce would not have developed the problems that not only disrupted his education at that time but may have marred the rest of his life.

Parental encouragement (either conscious or unconscious) of a child's antisocial acting out is common when a child exhibits such behavior. For example, a neighbor complains that Henry threw a rock through her window. Henry's father responds indignantly, "My Henry? Never. My Henry would never do such a thing." A shopkeeper complains that Doris has been caught stealing from his store. Doris's mother responds nonchalantly, "Doris tell the man you're sorry." In both of these cases the parent is encouraging a repetition of the child's antisocial behavior by depriving the child of any real discouragement. Moreover, Doris's mother's response is an excellent example of one of the more common ways in which some parents subtly encourage their children to act out: Their words discourage the behavior, yet their verbal intonations and gestures encourage it.

Parents are not usually able to act out their own impulses of misbehavior because of internal inhibitions or the awareness of the consequences of doing so. But children lend themselves well to the acting out of such parental impulses. Some parents identify with their children, and each time the children exhibit antisocial behavior, the parents derive the kinds of gratification they would enjoy if they themselves were performing the antisocial acts. Lacking the judgment of the adult, the child may more readily engage in behavior that the adult would be wary of. In the intact household such parentally sanctioned acting out is generally directed outside the home. In the divorce situation it is generally directed toward one parent and encouraged by the other, although its expression outside the home may also be fostered.

The divorced parent usually has less contact with the former spouse than has the visiting child. Accordingly, the child may become a readily available tool for parentally encouraged acting out. Children are used for this purpose in many ways. They may serve as informers and provide information that could be devastating when litigation is taking place. Or one parent may encourage a child not to comply with the requests of the other, even in such small matters as which foods to eat and when to go to bed. A mother may "forget" to have the children ready for the father, and they (even though old enough to appreciate the time and day) may also "forget" to remind the mother. Or Father may "forget" the time to return the children, and they too may suffer similar memory lapses. Or the children may dawdle in preparing for their father's visit; Mom's sense of urgency for getting them ready on time may leave much to be desired, and the children get the message from the mother and dawdle even more. The father may recognize that his bringing the children home early presents the mother with various restrictions and inconveniences. Their acting up may serve as an excuse for the father's early return, so they may misbehave in order to ingratiate themselves to him. Or the mother may encourage antisocial behavior in the children in order to hurt the husband by making him feel guilty: "Look at all the trouble you've caused by leaving. Look how upset they've become since you've gone."

Children of divorce almost always feel insecure, especially around the time of separation. And angry feelings, especially when acted out, can seem to offset feelings of insecurity. Although destroying furniture, for example, does not accomplish anything useful or constructive, it does provide a child with a sense of strength as well as the relief of having let out some anger. Rage reactions often frighten others, too, and this can contribute to a child's feeling of power.

The boy whose father has left the home may engage in delinquent acts in order to gain a feeling of masculinity to compensate for the loss of a male model. He may equate antisocial acting out with masculinity, a view fostered to a significant degree by the public media. Living only with his mother (and in some situations with other females as well), he may gravitate toward tough guys and delinquents and become a willing member of their gang. A mother living alone with her son may try to compensate for feelings of deficiency as a wife by becoming an outstanding mother. In the service of this goal she may try to make the boy well disciplined and well behaved. The child may react with antisocial behavior—not only from the hostility that such pressures produce in him but because acting out serves to negate the weakness and femininity the boy sees as part of the image his mother is trying to create.

A child may become delinquent in order to provoke punishment. This may be done in the service of reducing guilt. But it may also represent an attempt to gain an absent father's attention or even to make him come home. If children become so unmanageable that their mother cannot handle them, she may resort to enlisting the father's aid. Although such involvement with the father may be painful, the children appear to feel that it is worth the price. In other words, if their choice is between having no father at all and having a father who reprimands, disciplines, and punishes, they choose the latter. In addition, there are times when children want the father's help in strengthening guilt mechanisms, and provocative behavior may appear to be (or may actually be) the only way to secure such help. By their delinquent behavior they are seeking external controls for the inner ones they feel to be weakening.

Children of divorce live with the fear that the parent who has left the home may abandon them even further and that the remaining parent may also leave. One way for such children to gain reassurance is through testing the parents' tolerance for disobedient behavior. They work on the principle that the more disruptive behavior a parent will put up with, the more that parent proves affection for the child. Although the provocations may bring about punishment and various kinds of parental alienation, they do not generally result in the parents' further abandoning their children—and they are thereby reassured.

Another way of handling the anticipation of abandonment is for the children themselves to become the initiators of rejection. Their antisocial acts serve to keep people at a distance. They thereby become the ones who control the situation, not the ones who must passively suffer abandonment. In addition, such behavior protects such children from intimate relationships. They have already been burned; they wish to protect themselves from further disillusionment and disappointment in their relationships with others. And there is hardly a better way to do this than to provoke others with antisocial behavior.

Changes parents can effect within themselves that may reduce their children's angry acting out. Many of the things parents can do to reduce their children's acting out have been implicit in the discussion thus far. For example, if the parents become less angry at one another, their children will be less angry and less likely to be antisocial. If the parents reduce their hostilities, two important models for antisocial behavior will have been removed. Also, if the parents spend less time fighting and more time acting benevolently toward their children, the children will be less likely to be angry, will be less prone to act out, and will have less need to gain attention by provocative acts. Gaining more affection will make the children more secure, less impotent, and so less needful of angry demonstrations as a way of gaining a sense of strength. If the parents can achieve a more intimate relationship with the children, they will be less likely to fear intimacy and to push people away by antisocial behavior—and less needful of provocative testing to see if the parents still love them.

Parents of acting-out children should ask themselves whether they are overtly or covertly encouraging the children's delinquent behavior. If parents are using the child as an informant, if they are being duped into believing the child's criticism of one another, if they are allowing themselves to be played one against the other, they should make every attempt to bring about a cessation of such involvement with the child. Parents should realize that they can become tools of the children in their desire to act out their anger. In addition, the parents may be contributing to the child's angry acting out by not utilizing appropriate disciplinary measures.

Sometimes parental rage that is contributing to children's acting out may be so great that the advice I've given here may not be useful. A parent may appreciate intellectually, for example, that the continuation of hostilities is not only a waste of time and energy but also detrimental to the children, and yet may be helpless to refrain from perpetuating the vicious conflict. Some parents may be so obsessed with revenge that they may blind themselves to the repercussions of this obsession. In such cases therapy or counseling may be warranted.

Helping children reduce their angry acting out.

Whereas children with anger inhibition problems may be motivated to change because of the psychological pain they may be suffering, children who act out their anger generally do not have inner pain and are therefore not particularly motivated to change themselves. The main request that such children may make of others is: "Get off my back." They wish only to rid themselves entirely of teachers who bug them to finish their assignments and behave in class; parents who demand that they clean up their language and stop fighting with siblings; neighbors who complain that they bully their children; and so on.

What parents should do is try to help these children deal

with anger-provoking situations at the earliest possible time so that there will be less anger to be acted out. The approaches here are similar to those described earlier for children with anger inhibition problems. In both cases the child must learn how to avoid and reduce anger. In the inhibited there will then be less anger to channel into symptoms, and in the delinquent there will be less anger to act out.

Long lectures and explanations rarely help. Generally children get bored and tune the parent out. They may appear to be listening, but are in another world. Parental pleading is of little avail; in fact, it may increase the delinquent behavior because it proves that the acting out is hurting the parents. Trying to convince these children that they are hurting themselves more than their parents generally does not help, because their need to act out the anger is so great that they have to blind themselves to its self-destructive effects. However, the statement should be made from time to time, because it may ultimately play a role (however small) in reducing these children's tendency to act out. Structuring situations so that the child may actually suffer consequences for the delinquent behavior may be useful. Although this doesn't get to the root of the problem, it can serve to suppress the acting out. For example, if a child's antisocial behavior results in difficulties with school authorities and even the police, the parents should request that the usual consequences follow. To request leniency because the parents are divorced or because the child has emotional problems only serves to perpetuate the acting out.

Children want limits. They test in order to learn what is acceptable and what is not. When anger is acted out the youngster may be asking the parent for limits (often in a disguised way). I recall treating a very angry adolescent girl who charged out of her suburban home, claiming that she could no longer live under the intolerable conditions there. A few hours later she called her mother and told her that she was heading for the Greenwich Village district of New York, where she was going to devote herself to a life of as much sex and drugs as her heart desired, and that the only thing that would stop her would be if Dr. Gardner were to commit her to a local mental hospital. The mother called me, asking what she should do. I told her to call her daughter back immediately and tell her, quite firmly, that she had spoken to me and that I said if she wasn't home in two hours I would commit her to the local mental hospital. The girl was home before the deadline, cursing me in the most vile language.

I believe that when this girl arrived in New York she became quite frightened over the prospect of going to Greenwich Village and involving herself with drug addicts and free-sex advocates. Accordingly, she stopped off at a girl-friend's house and by calling her mother provided herself (via her mother and me) with a face-saving way of returning home. Instead of having to come home a frightened child begging for permission to return, she returned a hero. She could convince herself and her friends that she really would have gone to Greenwich Village and led the life she described, except that she was forced to change her plans by Dr. Gardner's terrible threats. She could not but be admired for her courage; she had fought hard, but had bowed only to Dr. Gardner's awful threat of incarceration in an insane asylum. Parents do well to keep their eyes and ears open to such disguised requests by their children and provide them with the limits and restrictions that they not only need but crave.

Peer pressure and encouragement often contribute to a child's antisocial acting out. The mob has a potential for violence greater than that of the sum of the individuals within it. In the gang one is surrounded by others who support delinquent behavior and encourage its acting out. In addition, the fear of punishment is lessened, as punitive authorities may be relatively impotent to deter or stop a mob, whereas they have great power against a single individual. Accordingly, parents should do everything reasonably possible to discourage acting-out children's involvement in such groups. This is not to suggest that parents should try to control the child's contacts outside the home by checking on the child's whereabouts, calling other homes, and so forth. This is not only futile but may encourage the child to seek bad-acting friends. Keeping the child indoors for days or weeks at a time may also increase the child's anger and cravings to join such groups.

Parents do better to inform the youngster that they recognize that they cannot stop involvements outside the home but that they have every right to decide who comes into the home. By not allowing gang members inside the home the parent gets across the disapproving message. In addition, such action diminishes the contact with the antisocial group to the degree that is within the parent's power. Comments such as these can be useful: "You know I don't like those kids you're hanging around with. They're a bad influence on you and they're helping you get into trouble. It hurts me to see how you're fouling yourself up by all the things you've been doing, and they're just making things worse. I know I can't stop you from seeing them outside and I know it won't do any good to keep you locked up in the house. However, I decide who comes into this house, and I forbid you to have any of them here."

Parents often try to remove antisocial children from groups that encourage their acting out by moving the child to a different school. But even when this can be done, such children generally gravitate toward the antisocial youngsters in the new school—and there is hardly a school that doesn't have its own collection. Accordingly, such transfers are often futile. The problem lies primarily within the child and only second- arily in the facilitating group.

Group therapy, rap sessions, and other forms of discus- sion groups can be useful for the adolescent who acts out antisocially. Such groups should be conducted by leaders with training in treating youngsters with emotional disorders; oth- erwise they may do more harm than good. Since therapists, like parents, are of the adult generation, they are somewhat distrusted. The views of a child's peers, however, often have greater credibility and can be more influential in inducing change than parental and other adult opinion. In addition, youngsters are exquisitely sensitive to peer opinion and slav- ishly obedient to it, their own professions to the contrary notwithstanding. Preferably, the members of the group should initially be strangers to one another. This ensures a greater degree of privacy; in addition, a youngster is more likely to be candid with a stranger whose alienation will not be a great loss than with a friend whose affection is valued. My experience has been that in a group most youngsters will espouse and adhere to (with varying degrees of conviction) more conservative and traditional social standards than they might actually practice themselves. Although they do this in part to win favor with the group leader, they are also motivated by the inner recognition of the value of such standards—but only in the protected group environment will they allow themselves to admit their basic adherence to the traditional social norms. In school and neighborhood such compliance with traditional values may be met with much social criticism.

It is important in a group that antisocial youngsters be in the minority. If they are in the majority, they may get support for their behavior from other delinquents, and even may be drawn into antisocial acting out. Identification with group leaders can play an important role in these children's acquiring internal restraints. This is likely to occur only if a trusting relationship with the leaders has been established and if there is genuine respect for them. It is only when this kind of relationship has been established that the child will take on the leaders' values and internalize their standards for socially acceptable behavior. In the groups that I conduct I try to help the youngsters acquire antidelinquent attitudes from group peers. I encourage group support of the delinquent's attempts not to succumb to peer pressure for antisocial behavior. I try to teach the youngster that it is often braver to defy dares and group pressure than to join in antisocial activities. I try to foster the notion that compliance is usually the weaker course.

It is important for parents to appreciate that sports and physical activities are an extremely common, usually harmless, and often socially constructive way for a person to express repressed hostility. Many youngsters I have seen who harbor deep-seated resentments over parental separation and divorce become very involved in sports. Not only does the competition provide a socially acceptable outlet for their anger, but the physical activity also serves this purpose. Tensions also are reduced by such activities.

Whatever drawbacks there may be to horror and violence in films (such as fostering violent solutions to all kinds of problems), they do allow for vicarious release of anger. Parents should recognize these outlets, because they may be useful for children of divorce, especially those who are prone to act out their hostile reactions. I am not, of course, recommending such fare as a primary therapeutic endeavor. All things considered, I believe video horror and violence do more harm than good. However, they are ubiquitous; it is just about impossible to remove a child entirely from exposure to this form of entertainment. Therefore, parents should recognize that a vicarious release of anger is being provided, the formidable drawbacks of the exposure notwithstanding.

Parents also ought to realize that many adolescent fads serve as outlets for hostile and rebellious urges. (They also provide a sense of separate identity, so important for adolescents to establish.) Choosing clothing or hair styles that may be particularly odious to parents may serve such purposes. Parents should express their disgust, thereby providing the youngster with the satisfaction that they are getting to the parents and causing them discomfort. But it is a mistake for parents to force a youngster to give up one of these styles. Parents should appreciate that these fads are among the most innocuous ways of releasing hostility. In fact, compared to some of the alternative modes of acting out available (drug addiction, pregnancy, various types of criminal behavior) they appear to be blessings. I sometimes think that the inventors of such styles should be considered for Nobel Peace Prizes, since they do so much to diminish violence in the world.

Many youngsters with delinquent behavior require therapy. However, we therapists cannot claim a high rate of success. Part of the problem is the fact that these youngsters are often not motivated for treatment; also, we are still searching for effective treatment techniques. In addition, we have often been working against great odds. It is very difficult to treat youngsters with social acting-out problems if they are continually being exposed to parental conflicts and deprivations. Therapists generally see a child one to three times a week (on rare occasions more frequently). It is unrealistic to expect therapy to reduce anger in antisocial children and help them use more appropriately what anger they do have, when after each session they return to situations that only generate anger all over again.

CONCLUDING COMMENTS

By now the reader will appreciate that psychological symptoms are complex and that many factors contribute to their formation and perpetuation. Accordingly, there are rarely simple ways to alleviate them. Those that develop in reaction to parental separation and divorce are not likely to disappear as long as the parental conflict persists. Those that are reactions to deprivation of parental affection are not likely to disappear unless the parent can provide more affection or the child is able to obtain it from others. Above all, parents who withhold important information about the separation deprive children of the opportunity to adjust optimally to it. Older children will generally be able to understand more about what separation entails. But even with younger children, attempts should be made to provide them with information at their levels of comprehension. Even though they may not understand completely what is going on, communication establishes a trusting relationship and prevents the kinds of problems that may result when events are shrouded in secrecy.

5

Common Parental Difficulties That Contribute to Children's Postseparation Maladjustments

No matter how "civilized" the divorce, the process is expensive and painful for the parents. The changes that come in the wake of divorce, too, require difficult adjustments. Divorce-related parental woes have, predictably, many impacts on the children.

MONEY

Money is an issue that preoccupies most divorcing parents both around the time of the separation and subsequent to it. Breaking up a marriage is an expensive proposition, and the specter of the cost of upkeep of two homes may be the major reason why there aren't more divorces than there are.

Marriage is a contract, and breaking up a marriage requires another contract. It is over financial issues more than anything else that divorcing spouses involve themselves in the most lengthy and often mind-bogglingly petty disputes. Besides the realistic reasons why money is of such concern to separated parents, there are many psychological ones as well.

Money can readily be used as a vehicle for expressing love or hostility, in accordance with whether one gives it or withholds it. As a treasured possession of each of the separated parents, it ranks with the children as an object that quickly gets embroiled in the parents' conflicts. For example, Mom complains that Dad shows a greater financial commitment to his new wife and children than to her and their children. Dad accuses Mom of using support money to buy things for herself, to the neglect of the children. Mom denounces Dad for sending support checks to the child in the child's name, thereby compromising her authority. I speak of the husband as the party making support and alimony payments, because although in recent years fathers have been increasingly gaining custody of their children, it is still rare for a mother to be providing support and alimony payments.

Overall money issues. Separating mothers are generally well aware that the amount of money they will receive for support and alimony will be determined in part by any income they may have. Accordingly, some mothers may quit or "lose" their jobs before the separation or divorce, only to gain employment again when the divorce decree is final. Others, recognizing that they will have to start working after the breakup of the marriage, hold off doing so until after the financial settlements have been signed. And the "good" lawyer will generally advise such a wife not to start working until that time. Fathers, too, have been known to reduce their incomes in order to lower the amount they will have to pay their wives. They seem to be so desirous of hurting their former spouses by creating economic hardships for them that they don't care what privations such a maneuver causes themselves and their children.

Probably one of the most common complaints made by divorced mothers is that their husbands are not sending the money provided for in the divorce decree. The percentage of husbands who consistently, over many years, live up to their alimony and support commitments is quite small. The withholding of such payments not only provides the husband with more financial flexibility but can serve as a very potent weapon against his ex-wife. Also, many courts are lax in enforcing this aspect of the divorce decree. The court's weakness stems from the fact that if it imposes either of its most common forms of punishment, fine or prison, it will make it even less likely that the wife will get what has been stipulated in the divorce decree and agreed to by both parties. If a wife resorts to a lawyer to help her acquire the payments, the legal fees may cost her more money than she gains.

Another reason why legal institutions tend to be very lax in pressuring fathers who fail to make support and alimony payments is the prohibitive expense of tracking the men down. Sometimes, the most the authorities can do is bring the man into court, where the judge warns him of the dire consequences of his not fulfilling his obligations to his ex-wife. But the man usually knows that these threats are empty. In recent years courts have become more aggressive with negligent fathers, and garnishing salaries has become quiet common. But this method is not particularly useful with men who own their own businesses. Fines are still not common, but prison sentences are becoming more common, especially weekend sentences. These have the advantage of still enabling the man to work (and thereby have money for his former wife) and yet helping "remind" the man to keep up on his payments.

Often, in jurisdictions where a man can be sent to prison for nonpayment of alimony and support, the man will pay at the time of sentencing (after months and possibly years of expensive and time-consuming litigation) and then suffer no punishment for having so long defaulted. He may thereby be encouraged to allow the process to repeat itself in the hope that this time around his former wife will give up the struggle rather than go through the whole process all over again.

Mothers should make reasonable attempts to get what they are entitled to. When this fails, they should turn their energies to more positive enterprises. They should understand that the struggle over money is a terrible emotional drain on themselves (and often the children). The conflict may last years, and even then attempts for payment may prove futile.

Even appealing for help from family members or resorting to public assistance is generally less humiliating and psychologically traumatic than endless litigation. Some mothers do not realize that psychopathological elements may be contributing to their failure to give up the struggle. For example, the mother who says, "I just can't sit and let him get the satisfaction," is using a poor reason for persisting. She would do better to say, "OK, let him have the satisfaction. It's better to admit defeat than to drain my energies fighting a battle that I'll probably never be able to win anyway."

Husbands who so renege should appreciate that the arguments they invoke to justify their not paying are usually unjustified. Basically, for extra financial security they are jeopardizing their children's psychological welfare. The mother whose husband defaults is often tempted to seek revenge and/or attempt to get him to pay by withholding the children from visitation. I strongly discourage this practice. The financial privation the children suffer because of their father's withholding payments is punishment enough. It only adds to their difficulties if they are prevented from continuing their relationship with their father. Admittedly, such a father has already proved himself to be deficient by his failure to live up to his financial commitments. However, this defect, as grave as it may be, does not make him totally worthless as a father or incapable of providing his children with some healthy experiences. Please note that I am not recommending that a mother protect the former husband from the children's knowing about his failure. The children should know; yet this flaw should be put in proper perspective with the father's other qualities.

Many women whose husbands default find themselves in the position of either suffering extreme material privation or going on public welfare. Such a step often represents the ultimate in personal humiliation. Many agencies will not even consider an application for public assistance until a woman proves that she has exhausted all legal efforts to force her husband to pay. Although I can understand the agencies' wish to establish true need, such a stipulation may force applicants to expose themselves and their children to needless psychological and material hardship. A further complication of public assistance payments is that once they are approved the defaulting husband may have even less motivation to pay. He knows that any funds he may send will reduce those provided by welfare, so that his family's situation will not improve unless he pays far more than welfare is going to. He often prefers to remain secure in the knowledge that his family is receiving basic necessities. He may not feel the need to raise his family above a marginal level of subsistence and may be unconcerned about the psychological effects on his wife and children of their being wards of the community.

Alimony. The payments that a divorced husband usually has to make to his wife are referred to as alimony. (Again, it is still extremely rare for a wife to be making such payments to a former husband.) The amount of alimony is usually determined by haggling between by the two lawyers. Their compromise is subject to approval by the judge, who actually makes the decision only in contested cases.

Most states require the husband to pay alimony. This situation stems from the past; the purpose was to protect the community from having to provide ex-wives with support. Generally the man has the obligation as long as his wife remains unmarried. Accordingly, many men have to pay alimony for the rest of their lives. In recent years, courts have tended to take women's financial situation into consideration when granting alimony. There are even those who feel that requiring a husband to pay alimony at all is unjust. They argue that such an obligation is unfair to a man, that his contributing to the support of his children is certainly reasonable, but that he should not be required to support his former wife for the rest of his life because of a marital mistake to which they probably both contributed.

Alimony payments often become a divorced man's greatest burden. The conflict over alimony payments is often extensive, lasts for years, and, like all continuing parental conflicts, may exact a psychological toll on the children. The reason is that a mere ten- or fifteen-dollar difference in a weekly or monthly payment, when multiplied over the rest of a man's life, is a formidable amount of money. Failure (in part or in full) to make such payments may bring a former husband to court and force him to engage a lawyer at great expense. Many men who do not make their alimony and support payments are constantly being harassed (often with justification).

The guideline traditionally used in setting alimony is that the man should attempt to support his former wife at the socioeconomic level she enjoyed during the marriage. However, it often turns out that both husband and wife have to live at a far lower level because, alimony payments notwithstanding, there is less money available for each. There are many men for whom alimony payments are indeed oppressive. However, many women have given up opportunities for career training and advancement in order to run their households and are therefore in a very vulnerable economic position when divorced. In addition, the wife's contributions at home have often enabled the husband to devote himself more freely to his own career; a wife certainly deserves compensation for this if divorce ensues. The divorced woman may have less opportunity to remarry than the divorced man, especially if she has custody of the children (the usual case). Because our present social structure contributes so significantly to the divorced woman's financial vulnerability, reasonable alimony payments are, in my opinion, still justifiable.

With greater appreciation of the woman's contribution to her husband's career and the acquisition of marital assets, many states have revised their divorce laws and require a more equitable division of the assets of a marriage. The general philosophy of such legislation is that because both parties have contributed their talents and efforts to the acquisition of property during the marriage, all common property and assets should be equitably (not necessarily equally) divided, regardless of who originally had legal title to them. Consideration is given to a woman's efforts as homemaker, child rearer, and contributor to her husband's career, and such efforts are viewed as positive contributions to the acquisition of marital property. Furthermore, a man cannot under these laws freeze in his own name assets to the growth of which his wife may have contributed. For example, if by virtue of a wife's work at home, her husband was free to build a business (either alone or with others) to which his wife had no legal title, the wife's contribution to the business is ascertained by the court and a reasonable sum is awarded to her. Although the husband is not actually required to give his wife a share in the business (or to make her a partner), he may be required to provide his wife with an amount of money approximating her contribution. This may be provided in one payment, or paid out over years.

In short, the trend seems to be toward doing away with a system in which the husband almost automatically makes alimony payments to his wife and substituting one in which the property is equitably divided. And theoretically, the person who has the greater economic need is given money by the party with the most assets—regardless of the sex of the giver or the recipient. Under this philosophy, fewer women should be exploited, and fewer men should be victimized by women whose financial situation did not warrant their receiving alimony.

In alimony and property conflicts, the vengeance elements often gets deeply involved. Although I believe that a moderate degree of vengeful feeling is inevitable (and probably normal) at certain times, in the divorce situation psychological problems often intensify such feelings immeasurably. The spouses become self-destructive as the time and energy expended in vengeful pursuits compromise their ability to involve themselves in healthier activities. Often a lawyer will encourage a wife to demand what even she considers unreasonably high payments. A wife may become so enraged by her ex-husband's failure to pay his full alimony that she may involve herself in costly litigation. Children, especially, get neglected in such situations. Therefore, for the benefit of all concerned, it behooves parents to reduce such sick vengeance. It is often healthier and more courageous to admit defeat. A significant fringe benefit of such resignation will be fewer bills from lawyers and therapists.

Ex-husbands ought to consider that their withholding of payments can backfire. They may be causing their children not only economic deprivation but psychological trauma through the alimony conflict. Such fathers should appreciate that the money they save on alimony may ultimately have to be spent on child therapists.

Support. Support is the term used to refer to the payments that a parent generally has to provide for the maintenance and welfare of the children. Most often the children's custody is given to the mother; and the law—I think justifiably—considers it to be the husband's obligation, under such circumstances, to support (or at least contribute to the support of) his children so that they do not become wards of the community. Often these payments cover medical care (sometimes including psychotherapy), summer camp, education, religious training, and so forth. Generally, fathers are more receptive to paying support than they are to paying alimony. Whereas a husband may have to continue alimony payments throughout life if his wife does not remarry, support payments are required only until the children reach a stipulated age, such as eighteen or twenty-one, or until the completion of their education or training.

It is common for a mother to complain to the children about the father's deficiencies in paying support. She may bitterly lament that he is not sending enough money to provide them with food, clothing, or shelter; that he is not on time with his payments; that he has been sending less than he should; that he has gotten too good a deal; or that instead of sending money for them, he is spending it on women. The father may protest that the money that he does send the mother for support is not all being used for the children, that she is squandering it frivolously, or that she is giving it to men friends.

Just as an alimony payment may occasionally be unjustified, there are situations in which a support payment may be totally unwarranted. I recall a situation in which a man reported to me that his divorce resulted when he learned that his wife was having an affair with his best friend. In the divorce decree his wife was granted custody of their daughter, and he agreed to pay for, among other things, all the child's medical expenses. Subsequently the wife married the friend. As time passed the little girl became upset and required psychiatric treatment. Although pinched financially, the man agreed to pay for his daughter's therapy. The psychiatrist then decided that family sessions would be useful, sessions that included the ex-wife, the daughter, *and the former friend*. The man felt strongly that his wife's new husband should pay one-third of the cost of the family sessions, since he was deriving benefit from them. But the court ruled that such sessions were designed to help the daughter, and that the man should therefore be required to pay the *total* fee. Soon after, the psychiatrist suggested that the friend receive individual treatment, again for the sake of the little girl. Again the court ruled that the man would have to pay fully for such treatment. When I last saw the man he had refused to comply with the court's decision, was appealing to a higher court, and proclaimed that he would rather go to jail than pay for the psychiatric treatment of a man who had been instrumental in causing him so much pain and difficulty.

Generally, the father sends the support check to the mother (either directly or through the court). Many fathers feel that this arrangement produces still more estrangement from the children, as the children come to see the mother as the sole provider. Some try to avoid this problem by writing the checks directly to the children so that they will know who is actually paying their expenses. Of course, such an arrangement is only reasonable when older children are involved, and it generally is a source of irritation to the mother, especially if the children then give her a hard time about turning over the money. I generally discourage fathers from doing this. Because it helps perpetuate conflict with their former wives, it is bound to hurt the children. Rather, they do well to inform the children at reasonable times and in a reasonable way where their support is coming from and hope that as they get older they will have a clear picture of the father's contribution to their maintenance.

If a father reneges on his support payments, his failure should not be concealed from his children. It is always better for children to have as accurate a picture as possible of each of their parents. Fathers who renege should also know that the material privations the children my suffer may be small compared to the psychological traumas arising from the knowledge that their own father has neglected them. He will lose their respect and compromise his serving as a model for their identification. This is a heavy price indeed for him and his children to pay for saving some money.

No matter how carefully planned a divorce decree may be, no matter how carefully spelled out every one of the stipulations regarding payments, the provisions seldom last long. Lives change, needs change, people relocate, the economy rises and falls, jobs terminate, people remarry, people redivorce, and it is extremely common for one or both parties to become dissatisfied with the agreement. If the parties can approach an alteration of the decree with some willingness to compromise, they may avoid the psychological toll on both themselves and their children of further conflict and litigation. Lawyers may attempt to effect such compromises in their renegotiations, but they are quick to rise to battle and thereby to reactivate hostilities. It would be far preferable if mediating and arbitrating professionals were available to help parents— people whose primary orientation and deep-seated commitment is only that of resolving differences. If such efforts fail, then the parties are always free to resort to litigation in the old tradition.

VISITATION

The separation agreement and divorce decree generally provide for the absent parent's visitation with the children. Parents do well to appreciate that stipulated visitation times often do not coincide with the needs and desires of the parties concerned. Accordingly, the more flexible the schedule, the more natural the visits will be, and the greater the likelihood the visitation experiences will be gratifying.

Visitation and divorce decree negotiations.

Flexibility about visitation requires a certain amount of trust and cooperation between the parents. Sadly, these conditions are often not present, and the more the distrust and antagonism, the lengthier and more detailed the schedules become.

Shorter, more frequent visits may be better than fewer, longer ones. One can compare visitation with the frequency of psychotherapeutic sessions. If a patient has two therapy sessions a week, evenly spaced, events and feelings between sessions are no more than three days old and are readily recalled. Accordingly, twice-a-week therapy is significantly more effective than once-a-week therapy. In the same way, more frequent visitation is often preferable.

Like any other transaction between separated parents, visitation arrangements can be used as a weapon. Often parents will demand more visitation time than they really want or can practically handle. The purpose here may be to use the demand as a bargaining tool in the conflict over alimony and support payments. Such parents know in advance that they will reduce the visitation requests if the spouse will grant concessions in the financial area. Parents often do not understand that they are causing their children psychological damage by such manipulations, so blinded are they by their anger. And many lawyers support these sick transactions with the justification that they are protecting their clients' interests. What such lawyers are generally referring to when they talk of their clients' interests is money.

A mother may be so enraged at her husband that she will actually believe that *any* contact he may have with the children will be harmful to them. As a result, the children may suffer from a loss of visitation experience. One mother, who considered herself to have had a happy marriage, learned that her husband was having an affair. In the ensuing weeks the husband tried but failed to explain to her that there were many deep-seated marital problems. The mother remained obsessed with her husband's treachery. Professional counseling was of no avail, and the marriage finally broke up at the instigation of the wife, who claimed that she had always been a perfect wife and that she would never forget this "knife in her back."

Both before and after the divorce this mother continually railed against her husband and his "whore" to their two daughters. Whereas previously the children had had a fairly good relationship with their father, the months of vilification of him gradually began to change their attitudes. They too finally began to hate him and see him as the embodiment of evil, filth, and treachery. They began refusing to go with him when he arrived for visits. Instead, they would spit, curse, and even throw things at him when he arrived. The mother actually professed encouragement of the children's visiting with the father and even made them available for the visits. But she knew that her brainwashing had been successful, and she enjoyed observing the scenes that ensued when her ex-husband would arrive. The court refused to transfer custody to the father and so the situation continued.

I advised the father to stop going to the house, because his attempts to get the children not only were unsuccessful but were being used by his former wife as opportunities for vengeful gratification, with the children as weapons. I suggested rather that he use every other type of communication available to let his daughters know that he loved them. But letters and presents were returned unopened, when he called they promptly hung up on him, and those who verbally communicated his regards and best wishes were angrily told to mind their own business. My final advice to this father was that he never stop completely from an occasional reassurance to the children that he still loved them. I explained to him that the children's anger (like his former wife's) revealed that they were still thinking about and were interested in him. To give up entirely might be considered by the children a rejection and would lessen the chances of their ever getting together again.

Mothers such as this are obviously disturbed and do not realize how much they are harming their children by their hate campaigns. In some cases, after many months and years, the relationship with the absent parent is renewed, and the children come to appreciate how falsely maligned the absent parent has been. In other cases the alienation is permanent, a sad loss for all concerned.

At times a parent may demand far more visitation than is reasonable in order to reduce his or her guilt over the separation. A father, for example, who never took particular interest in the children, suddenly becomes deeply involved with them at the time of separation. The children may see more of him after he leaves the house than they did before. Such enthusiasm is usually short-lived—based as it is on guilt rather than genuine affection. However, because it exhibits itself at the time when separation and divorce agreements are being drafted, it may result in the children's being deprived of beneficial time they could have been spending with their other parent.

Previsit games. Inappropriate use of visitation does not stop at the signing of the divorce decree. There are many ways in which a parent can use visitation to express hostility toward the ex-spouse. Obstructionistic maneuvers are among the most common. The father, for example, may be late or even "forget" to pick up the children, forcing the mother to cancel her own arrangements. Or the mother may take a very "relaxed" attitude about having the children ready or may have "forgotten" that this was the day for the father to get them, and thereby may wreck his plans. The actual appearance of the father may provide the mother with an opportunity to let off a little steam. Similarly, a visiting father may look forward to picking up his children because of the opportunity it provides him for release of pent-up hostility toward his ex-wife.

A mother may be excessively fearful of a father and inappropriately anticipate his harming the children. Such fears may be transmitted to the children, thereby reducing the pleasure they can derive from the visit. Ex-spouses tend to exaggerate the detrimental effects on the children of one another's behavior. Only in cases of extreme negligence or danger should restrictions be placed on visitation. Removing the children because of minor harmful exposures deprives them of the growth experience of dealing with the unpleasant and may rob them of the benefits to be derived from involvement with the visiting parent. If the parent and children wish to see one another, then the advantages probably outweigh the disadvantages. On occasion, as described earlier, a custodial parent may have such a distorted view of the absent parent that the term delusional becomes appropriate. Legal and mental health professionals may be impotent to effect a change in such cases, and so the children may grow up deprived of one parent. The only way to salvage such a situation is to transfer custody. But even then, adjustment may be difficult because the children have often been instilled with such fear by the delusional parent.

A custodial parent can undermine the children's desire to see the visiting parent with comments such as: "You *want* to visit your mother?" or "You don't *really* want to go visit with your father again on Sunday?" Or the parent may offer tempting alternatives to the visit that may discourage them from making plans with the noncustodial parent. Conversely, either parent may have residual or persistent affectionate feelings for the ex-spouse (either conscious or unconscious) and may secretly welcome visitation as an opportunity for further contact.

Although separation and divorce usually hurt the esteem of both parties, noncustodial parents usually suffer an additional blow to their feelings of self-worth. Most healthy fathers, for example, gain a sense of importance as head of a household. Whatever drawbacks there may be to parenthood, there is also a sense of pride and accomplishment. Being admired and emulated by the members of one's family can be a great source of ego gratification. The separated parent may feel this loss acutely and should make every attempt to compensate for this deprivation and loss of self-esteem. Three ways in which a noncustodial parent can regain a sense of self-worth in this area are: (1) spending as much time as is reasonable and possible with the children, (2) involving him-

or herself in a second family, and (3) finding other esteem-enhancing activities.

The visit. One of the common problems that custodial parents frequently complain of is the visiting parent's lateness, last-minute cancellations, or failure to show up for the visits. Visiting parents should be reliable and punctual about the visit. Divorce has undermined the children's stability already; there is no need to add to their difficulties. If a visiting parent has to miss an appointment, he or she should inform the children well in advance of the cancellation. Many visiting parents seem to be oblivious to the fact that building up the children's hopes and then disappointing them at the last minute can be devastating.

Separation and divorce decree stipulations can never take into account all the needs and desires of the mother, father, and children. Most often specific visitation times are designated. However, the parents should use these merely as guidelines. If the children do not wish to visit on a certain day, they should not be forced to (beyond the occasional prodding that most children need for their own good). Similarly, a parent who visits on a particular day primarily out of guilt or obligation would probably do better to select another day. When the parent and children get together but basically do not wish to do so at that specific time, it is likely that resentments will lessen the pleasure that they can derive from the experience.

The reason it is so important to take a flexible approach is that visitation is fraught by its very nature. For example, when a father picks up his children and they are in a good mood, he will tend to interpret this to mean that they are happy to leave their mother, who treats them badly, and come to him, where they will receive love and affection. The mother will tend to interpret the smiling faces to mean that they are looking forward to the indulgence and spoiling that the father will provide them in order to buy their love. If they are unhappy, the father understands this to be the result of the maltreatment they have received at their mother's hands. The mother considers their unhappiness to be caused by the dread they feel over the visit with the father and their anticipation of the horrible things that can happen when they are with him.

Separation and divorce decrees most often clump all the children together when defining the times of visitation. Such a practice does not take into consideration the individual differences of the children and their separate desires at a particular time. In accordance with the principle of flexibility, I believe that it can be to the children's benefit to visit separately at times. Not only does this avoid the resentment caused by forced visiting, but it allows each child more individual contact with the parent who is being visited. Some hold that such a practice can increase sibling rivalries. This has not been my experience. In fact, because it provides each child with more individual attention, there is less to be rivalrous about. Furthermore, separating children is the most foolproof way of preventing their fighting. It is only if one child is preferentially selected to visit more frequently that sibling rivalries are likely to be increased.

As every parent who spends a significant amount of time alone with the children knows (whether in the divorced or the intact family situation), things can get boring at times. Adults are adults and children are children, and there is just so much child's play and childishness that an adult can tolerate. It is a good idea for the visiting parent to allow the children occasionally to bring along friends and relatives. Such joiners take some of the pressures off the parent. The only danger of this practice is that the parent may too frequently allow the visitors to take over the obligation of being with the children.

The question is sometimes raised whether it is harmful to the children for the visiting parent to spend any (and even all) visiting time in the original home. Such visits are said to protect the child from the anxieties produced by being taken out of the home and having to adjust to a new environment. Actually, the nature of the relationships between the visiting parent and the children is far more important than the place where the visits occur. The quality of the activities that the visiting parent and the children partake in, and the enjoyment they derive from them, are what count. Another consideration, of course, is the receptivity of the custodial parent to the ex-spouse's return to the home. If an atmosphere of tension or gloom descends over the household as the visiting parent enters the home, then it is not likely that the original home is going to be a good place for the visitations. If, however, the custodial parent has no objections to leaving the home (and even welcomes the opportunity for a break) while the visiting parent stays with the children, then the arrangement may very well work out.

There are parents who not only have no discomfort when together at such time, but may even look forward to seeing one another. If such feelings occur routinely, then I would wonder about the reasons for the divorce. Most divorced people wish to see as little as possible of their former spouses. Routinely welcoming the ex-partner back in the home suggests that there is still a significant ongoing relationship beyond mere accommodation of the visiting parent so that visits can take place in a familiar atmosphere. There is not necessarily anything psychologically unhealthy about such receptivity of the divorced spouses for one another. Human relationships are complex. The *married* or *divorced* status is somewhat artificial, and there are many gradations of involvement between the two extremes, gradations that have not been given legal definition. With regard to the psychological well-being of adults, I do not view any of the intermediate stages (either before marriage or after divorce) as being necessarily preferable. With regard to children, I believe that they do best when raised with a mother and a father who are reasonably satisfied with one another. To the degree that the parents' arrangement provides this, to that degree the children are likely to grow up healthy.

One of the most common problems that arises over visitation results from the contrast between the children's experiences during the visits outside the home (usually with the father) and those they have with the parent with whom they live. For example, with Dad they have fun, play games, visit enjoyable places, and may have few obligations to assume. With Mom, in contrast, it's getting up early, going to school, and doing homework and household chores. Dad may feel guilty about having left the home and may try to lessen his guilt by continually providing the children with good times. In addition, he may hesitate to discipline properly lest the children get even angrier at him. Or sometimes the father provides endless entertainment in order to avoid more direct, natural contact with the children. The father may do this partly because of rivalrous feelings toward the mother or from the appreciation that it can serve as a way of hurting her. The children may even conclude that if they were to live with the father permanently, this would be the kind of life they would lead all the time. In such a situation the father gets to be the good guy and the mother becomes the meanie.

Fathers who behave in this fashion should appreciate how harmful it is to the children to be used as pawns in the parental conflict. The children have enough trouble already; they should not have to suffer the additional burden of divided loyalties. The best atmosphere a visiting parent can provide the children is one that most closely resembles the original home—especially with regard to the balance between pleasant and unpleasant activities. Indulgence of the children creates in them unreal expectations about life and makes it more difficult for the custodial parent, teachers, and others to help them learn the discipline that is necessary if they are to grow into self-sufficient, mature adults. Sometimes longer periods of visitation can reduce such indulgence. Endless entertainment can be exhausting and produce financial strains in all but the wealthy.

There are parents, however, who do just the opposite during visitation. They delude themselves into believing that merely being together is enough. They may drag the children along on business visits, seat them at an office desk for hours on end to amuse themselves as best they can, or prop them up in front of the television set for as long as they will tolerate it. The children may resent being so neglected but may be fearful of expressing their anger. Children should be helped to assert themselves in order to bring about a cessation of such a deplorable practice, and such parents should realize that what they are doing amounts to neglect.

Ideally, the visiting parent and the children should decide together how they will spend their time, selecting activities that will not cause excessive boredom or resentment in either the parent or the children. All concerned, however, must be willing to make certain compromises—as is true in the planning of activities in the intact home. When visiting with the noncustodial parent the children should be encouraged to do homework and chores. These real-life experiences help children adjust to a world in which there is both pleasure and pain.

On rare occasions, the noncustodial parent will decide (sometimes even with professional advice) that it will be in the children's best interests to cut off all contact with them. A father, for example, may proclaim: "The marriage is dead. The best thing for the children would be that they consider me dead as well." Generally, the father does not describe exactly *how* it can be in the children's best interests to have no further contact with a parent. Sometimes such a parent will have mixed feelings about this drastic step (there is some desire to remove themselves totally from the children, and yet there are lingering feelings of affection and guilt over the wish to sever ties completely) and may seek professional advice regarding what to do. Often, the parent will take the advice that supports the stronger motivation. Good professional advice would recommend that such parents look into the psychological problems causing rejection of their own children.

On occasion, a custodial parent may refuse to let the absent parent see the children, have them unavailable when the visiting parent arrives, and even hide them from the visiting parent. In response the absent parent may abduct the children and consider this the only way of maintaining contact. Many lawyers hold that one cannot actually "kidnap" one's own child. Accordingly, a safer term for this type of abduction is *child snatching*. Child snatching occurs for other reasons as well. Child-snatching parents may believe they are protecting the children from terrible treatment at the hands of the other parent. Or vengeful elements may contribute. What better way to wreak vengeance on a former spouse than to take away the children and not provide any information about their safety or whereabouts? Often, the children are taken a long distance so that even if their location is known, the parent with whom they originally were may find it difficult, extremely expensive, or even impossible to get them back.

I confine myself here to the psychological rather than the legal implications of such child snatching. It is probable that occasionally such an act may be warranted. The children may indeed be suffering terrible abuse at the hands of a parent, the court may have failed to provide the children with protection, and the other parent may find that abducting the children is the only course left. My experience has been that such a drastic act is rarely warranted and that often the child-snatching parent is grossly exaggerating, if not distorting completely, the children's plight. In the more common situation, I find, the abduction has no justification; the abducting parent harbors delusions about the other parent's treatment of the children and wishes as well to use the children as weapons in the parental conflict. And the upshot is that the children suffer immensely. The weeks, months, and even years of aching and longing for the other parent can cause permanent psychological damage. Like baggage, the children are carried from city to city and state to state, never establishing roots, never maintaining friendships, never remaining in one school or home long enough to gain a sense of security. They may suffer significantly from the secretive life they may lead, ever fleeing from authorities who are trying to locate them. And the parent who has been bereft of the children rarely deserves the psychological torture that the child snatching causes. In short, with extremely rare exceptions, child snatching is a sick act that is hardly ever justified.

Postvisit problems. A common complaint that mothers have is that when the children return from their visits with the father they are unmanageable and unkempt. The father may interpret the children's restlessness on returning to the mother as proof that he is the better parent and that the children are unhappy about having to live once again with their mother, the ogre. The mother considers the restlessness to be caused by the tensions created in them by the father or by his spoiling. In contrast, when the children return in a happy frame of mind, the mother tends to interpret this as a sign that they are glad to get rid of their father and return to the warmth and friendliness of her home; the father usually considers their happy mood to be thanks to him.

The natural course of visitation. As time passes, visitation by the departed parent may diminish. It is in the early phases following the divorce that the guilt is the greatest and the need to reduce it through frequent contacts with the children most strong. As years pass, the visits become more of a drain, especially if the parent feels the need to offer constant fun and games. The visits occupy considerable time and are often costly. Many noncustodial parents begin wishing to use their free time and money more for dating and other recreational purposes. And as the children grow older, they generally want to socialize with their friends—as they would in the intact household.

Remarriage of a parent can have a significant effect on visitation. For example, when a noncustodial father is single, the children may have little competition for his time. When he is remarried and has new children and/or stepchildren, he cannot provide the children from his first marriage with as much attention. The father's new wife may have expressed great interest in and affection for his children before her marriage; afterwards such feelings may diminish considerably. Sensing themselves outsiders in the new home, children may become less desirous of visiting. A remarried mother who has custody of the children may also be less desirous of her former husband's visiting the home—even simply for the purpose of picking up the children. His periodic reappearance may compromise her relationship with her new husband. When single, she had a greater need to get the children off her hands. Now that she is remarried, she may feel them less of a burden.

CUSTODY

Up until the early part of this century, fathers were generally granted custody of the children when a marriage was dissolved. This practice was part of the tradition under which one's heritage was traced along paternal lines. Children's taking the surname of their father, rather than of their mother, is a legacy of this custom. In addition, wives were often looked upon as just another form of property, certainly without the privilege to own things in their own right—especially property as valuable as children.

The beginning of the women's movement in the late nineteenth century and the Child Labor laws passed in the early part of this century led to a change in attitude toward child custody. Once children could no longer be exploited as cheap labor, fathers became more receptive to giving up their children to their ex-wives, who were now permitted a degree of financial independence. In the 1920s states gradually changed their laws so that custody was no longer automatically given to fathers. In many states the sex of the parent was not to be considered a factor in determining parental preference; only criteria related to parental capacity were to be utilized. During the next half century these statutes were generally interpreted in favor of mothers. A father had to prove a mother grossly unfit (e.g., an alcoholic, drug addict, or sexual "pervert") before he could even hope to gain custody. The notion that mothers were intrinsically preferable to fathers as child rearers came to be known as the "tender years presumption."

In the mid-1970s men began to complain that the notion that females are intrinsically superior to males as parents was sexist. Many courts and state legislatures agreed, and judges were instructed to be sex blind when hearing custody disputes and to focus on parenting qualities regardless of the sex of the parent. As a result the pendulum has shifted back slightly, and courts now do not automatically grant custody to mothers. In contested cases, they try to grant custody to the parent deemed more fit to take care of the children, and subtle criteria of parental capacity are given weight in the deliberations. One need no longer prove gross neglect or obvious incapacity for parenthood in order to win custody. Fathers are more frequently gaining custody of their children. And the stigmatization of mothers who choose to give up their children to their husbands also seems to be lessening; it has become more socially acceptable for a woman to admit that she has little maternal interest and that her children would be better off with their father.

In spite of these trends, however, the vast majority of children still remain with their mothers after separation and divorce.

The kinds of custody. Just as courts are no longer adhering strictly to the view that the mother's receiving custody is necessarily in the children's best interests, more flexible kinds of custody arrangements are also being recommended. Until the late 1970s, the most common type of custodial arrangement was *sole custody* (also referred to as *primary custody*). In this arrangement, the children live primarily with one parent but spend some time with the other during visits as specified in the divorce decree. The parent with whom the children live makes most of the important decisions regarding their welfare, especially the day-to-day ones that the other parent is not available to make. Both parents, however, generally participate in such major decisions as education, religious training, and vacations.

In *divided custody,* which is also called *alternating custody,* the children live about half the time with one parent and half the time with the other. Both parents participate in the important decisions of the children's lives. When the children are living with one parent the other has visitation privileges. Obviously, such an arrangement is most workable when the two homes are in the same school district. Otherwise, it may involve twice-yearly upheavals from both school and neighborhood—a situation that most would consider psychologically harmful. Another form of divided custody is an arrangement in which the children remain living in one home throughout the year; however, the parents alternate living in the home for six months at a time. In this way the problems of neighborhood and school changes are avoided and each parent has the opportunity of living half the year with the children.

In *split custody* the children are divided between the two parents. Some live permanently with one parent and some with the other. Working on the principle that half a loaf is better than none, some parents give serious consideration to this form of custody so that they will not be deprived completely of living with the children. Generally, I believe it is best to try to keep the children together. They can provide support for one another and a sense of continuity of the family. Children who have been isolated from one or both parents tend to form surrogate families in which the older children help serve as substitute parents for the younger ones. An older brother can serve as a father surrogate, and an older sister as a mother surrogate.

There are situations, however, in which split custody may be advisable. A parent, for example, may be so rejecting of or hostile toward a particular child that it is best to have that child live with the other parent. It may be difficult (even for skilled evaluators) to make decisions in such matters, but under these circumstances, the benefits to be derived from removing the child are likely to be greater than the losses from separating the child from the sibling support system. Some also claim it is important for an adolescent to live with the parent of the opposite sex—in order to have an opportunity to learn how to live with an opposite-sexed person before finding a mate—and that the children should be split up if necessary to accomplish this. Although I cannot deny the basic idea, the adolescent usually has anxieties about sexual feelings toward the opposite-sexed parent, and living alone with him or her is likely to intensify these. Accordingly, I am not inclined to make this recommendation. There are other theories that provide various psychological justifications for splitting up the children. My own opinion remains that the children do best if they remain together, and I do not subscribe to any basic formulas regarding their being split up. There are, however, situations (generally rare) when it may be in a child's or the children's best interests for them to be split up.

In recent years the term *joint custody* has become popular. While there is some disagreement about the definition of every custodial term, disagreement about the meaning of joint custody is probably most widespread.

I use the term joint custody to describe a custodial arrangement that approximates as closely as possible the flexibility of the original two-parent home. In such an arrangement both parents have equal rights and responsibilities for their children's upbringing. Neither parent is designated as the sole or primary custodial parent. Central to the concept is that there is no *structured visitation schedule*. The children *live* in *both* homes; they do not *live* in one home and *visit* the other. This distinction separates joint custody from traditional custodial arrangements. When successful, joint custody offers many advantages to both children and parents. Psychologically, joint custody is probably the healthiest and most desirable of the various custodial plans. As a result, it has become quite popular—perhaps, in many cases, too popular.

The term joint custody is sometimes used to refer to an arrangement in which there *is* a structured visitation schedule. Often, however, the arrangement turns out to be one of the traditional custodial arrangements going under the name joint custody to provide a sense of egalitarianism between the parents—when there is in fact none or very little. It is naive to call sole custody joint custody in order to protect the ego of one of the parents. Judges and lawyers do this especially frequently.

Since the middle to late 1970s we have witnessed a marked upsurge in the frequency with which joint custody is being recommended. One factor in the recent popularity of joint custody has been the changing concept of the role of fathers in the child-rearing process. As long as mothers were deemed the preferable parent, joint custody was not considered seriously. But in the 1970s the joint custody option became more viable. The popularity of joint custody has reached the point where many states require judges to order joint custodial arrangements for all divorcing parents unless there are compelling reasons not to. As I will discuss below, I think more harm than good will come from such laws.

Joint custody provides children with certain distinct benefits. First, of all the custodial arrangements it most closely approximates that of the original marital household. It does not impose artificial schedules; it allows children a freer flow of involvement with both parents; and it creates in children less of a sense of impotence, in that they have some input into what happens to them. (Of course, the older the child the greater the input.) There is the danger that a child will try to use the greater flexibility of joint custody to manipulate the parents, avoid responsibilities, or express hostility. A child will often say, "If you don't stop making me do such and such, I'm going to my mother's (father's) house." Healthy parents, of course, consider the child's wishes seriously but utilize their own adult judgment and retain veto power as well. Healthy parents do not allow the children to use their input as a way of fleeing from working through difficulties. They do, however, recognize that at times transfer to the other home can be a useful way of decompressing conflict-laden situations.

With joint custody, each of the parents is protected against the terrible sense of loss that comes with the sole custodial arrangement—in which the noncustodial parent often feels extraneous, expendable, or an outcast. The feeling often is that the primary parent has gotten the cake and that the visiting parent is merely groveling for the crumbs. Another advantage of joint custody is that it avoids the controversial element of the sole custody situation when one parent is placed in a position of authority over the other, inevitably producing resentment. The joint custodial arrangement may also reduce hostility by giving the noncustodial parent greater opportunity to be with the children, thereby reducing the frustration and hostility vented on the custodial parent. Still another fringe benefit relates to support; if a father has joint custody, for example, he may be more motivated to contribute to the support of his offspring than if he is a visiting noncustodial parent.

Joint custody also avoids the problem of discrimination between the sexes, in that the court does not have to award the child to either the father or the mother. Joint custody reduces the possibility of the father's being viewed as the good-time guy and the mother as disciplinarian. In addition, the arrangement allows the child to see the father getting involved in housekeeping and child rearing while the mother may also assume work functions outside the home. The children, then, have a chance to view both parents in a more balanced way. The situation increases the likelihood that the children will be comfortable in both domestic and nondomestic roles when they become older.

However, joint custody is not without its drawbacks. One of the most important is that joint custody may be a judicial cop-out. It is certainly easier for a judge to award joint custody than to consider the voluminous evidence often presented in a custody conflict. A judge may rationalize avoidance of the problem by following the joint custody trend. And as mentioned above, in some jurisdictions statutes actually require the judge to award joint custody unless there are compelling reasons for considering an alternative. But joint custody should not be imposed on a parent who does not really want it. The likelihood that the unmotivated parent is going to assume the degree of responsibility entailed in the joint custodial arrangement is small, and the plan may be doomed to failure.

The drawback here is that automatic or too-frequent granting of joint custody may do children much more harm than good. Because there are no restraints on the parents in the joint custody arrangement, the plan increases the chances that the children will be used as weapons or spies in parental conflict. Children may be placed in a no-man's-land in which they are up for grabs by either parent and may suffer formidable psychological damage. Although sole custody cannot protect children completely from such use, it certainly reduces the opportunities for the parents to involve their children in a tug-of-war. Sole custody lessens the likelihood of arguments over when the children shall go to whose home, when they shall come home, and so forth. Automatic award of joint custody often fails to take into consideration the logistics of school attendance, and thus it can cause problems in the educational realm.

A common criticism of the joint custodial arrangement is that it can produce confusion in the child who is shuttled back and forth between different homes and exposed to different life-styles, rules, disciplinary measures, parenting styles, and even socioeconomic milieus. In addition, critics claim that joint custody invariably means a detrimental lack of environmental continuity. I believe that these drawbacks are most relevant for young children, especially those under the age of three or four. Above that age, I believe that most children can accommodate well to the arrangement and need not suffer from confusion over lack of continuity. It is the parenting qualities of the mother and father that make the difference. If the parents are indeed providing optimum parenting, then the drawbacks of frequent transfer are reduced significantly. Even if a young child experiences some mild degree of psychological harm from environmental discontinuity, this disadvantage is generally more than outweighed by the advantage of the child's having access to both parents in a less structured and less artificial arrangement than is found in sole custody.

In recent years the terms *physical custody* and *legal custody* have been introduced in an attempt to clarify joint custodial rights and privileges and to reduce the opprobrium of the sole custodial label. Physical custody relates to the parent with whom the children primarily live. Legal custody refers to decision-making powers. For example, a mother may be granted physical custody and both parents given joint legal custody. Basically, what is being said here is that the children shall live primarily with the mother and have visitations with the father, and that both parents shall participate in important decisions such as education, medical care, and religious training. (Despite the new terminology, this still sounds like the old sole custodial arrangement to me. But many people feel strongly about these labels.)

Another approach is to use the term *parenting plan*. In some states, this term has been incorporated into statutes. Subsumed under this rubric is information about the time the children will spend in each of the households, whether scheduled or nonscheduled, and what each parent's decision-making powers will be.

By whatever name, I believe that joint custody is viable only when these provisions are satisfied:

1. Both parents are *reasonably and equally capable* of assuming the responsibilities of child rearing. When there is a significant disparity between the parents in this area, another custodial arrangement should be considered. Both availability and psychological stability are important here. For example, if the father is a traditional breadwinner and the mother a homemaker, a joint custodial arrangement may not be practical. And if one parent suffers a significant psychiatric disorder, the healthier parent cannot reasonably be expected to acquiesce to the impulses of the more unstable one.

2. The parents must have demonstrated their capacity to *cooperate* reasonably in matters pertaining to raising their children. They must show the ability to *communicate* well and must be willing to compromise when necessary to ensure the viability of the arrangement.

3. The children's moving from home to home should not disrupt their school situation.

Although the first and third provisions may be satisfied by many parents involved in custody disputes that go to litigation, the second is not likely to be. Litigating parents have proven themselves to be deficient in their ability to cooperate, otherwise they would not be going to court. Litigating parents are not likely to be communicating well either, otherwise they would not be resorting to attorneys to communicate for them. Accordingly, I consider people who are litigating for joint custody to be by definition poor candidates for the arrangement.

Because the animosity between parents may be greatest at

the time of their divorce, that often is not a good time to recommend a joint custodial arrangement. The adversary system may actually reduce parents' capacity to qualify for the joint custodial arrangement. It may worsen parental communication and polarize parents even further. Mediation (chapter 1) may increase the likelihood that a joint custodial arrangement will be viable. Sometimes a court will make a joint custodial arrangement temporary and finalize it only after the parents have had an opportunity to demonstrate that they truly can handle it. As mentioned, however, this arrangement results in a prolongation of the litigation and its attendant psychological stresses.

On occasion, one parent will be fighting for joint custody, the other for sole custody. It often turns out that the parent who ostensibly is litigating for joint custody really wants sole custody and is using the "joint custody" label as a cover-up. The details of the proposed "joint custodial arrangement" will often reveal a stringent visitation arrangement and significant restriction of decision-making powers for the other party. But again, even if this is not the case, the fact that the parents are litigating in itself suggests that the joint custodial arrangement is not likely to work.

People who desire joint custody (and even litigate for it) are generally viewed as highly parental. However, their motivations may be mixed. A mother, for example, may welcome joint custody because it makes the father bear more of the responsibility for the children's upbringing. Or vengeance may be a motive; a father, for example, may seek joint custody as a way to deprive the mother of some of the time with the children that she might ordinarily have under the sole custody arrangement. Some parents, too, will request joint custody in order to reduce guilt. In other words, a parent may request joint custody solely in order not to appear undesirous of having the children as much as possible. The increasing prevalence of the joint custodial arrangement makes some parents feel even more guilty if they do not request it. But child rearing that stems from guilt is not likely to be very effective. For two parents who constantly shift to each other the responsibility for raising their children, joint custody may merely afford latitude for avoiding parental duties.

Joint custody is commonly requested (and even granted) as a compromise when parents cannot agree. This may appear to be a reasonable course, but it represents confused thinking. In such situations, instead of the parents having a *joint custodial arrangement,* they have a *no custodial arrangement.* The children find themselves exposed to the crossfire of the parents and in danger of psychological trauma.

A court-ordered custodial arrangement invariably involves a certain element of prediction of the future. In the joint custodial arrangement, this factor is crucial. To order joint custody is to assume that hostilities will be reduced, passions will die down, and cooperation will increase. Obviously, this is not always the case. But even when it is, other factors may jeopardize a smoothly running joint custodial arrangement. A parent who takes a job with increased responsibility or travel may no longer have the flexibility of scheduling necessary for joint custody. If one parent moves far from the children's school, joint custody may become impractical. Even a smoothly running joint custodial arrangement may run into difficulty when one of the parents remarries; this parent then has many more obligations, and a stepparent may not be receptive to cooperation with the ex-spouse. And finally, parents who appear capable of cooperating and communicating well at the time of their divorce may later find their relationship deteriorates, precluding a successful joint custodial arrangement.

As mentioned, the term joint custody is variously defined, not only by state statutes but by attorneys, mental health professionals, and clients. Therefore, the parties involved in discussing a potential joint custodial arrangement may each have a different concept of the meaning of the term—a situation that causes confusion, expense, and waste of time. Or attorneys will haggle over the definition of the term and/or whether a particular client's custodial arrangement warrants the designation. In such conflicts the parties become sidetracked onto issues that may be basically irrelevant to the decision.

I believe that this semantic problem could be eliminated if all concerned avoided using *any* of the common terms for the various custodial arrangements. I suggest that all arrangements be subsumed under a rubric such as *residential and decision-making arrangement or parenting plan*. This is what we are concerning ourselves with anyway. We want to decide where the children should be at any particular time and what powers each parent should have—the substantive considerations that are relevant to the particular family.

Judges, lawyers, mental health professionals, and others involved in deciding what kind of custodial arrangement would best suit a particular family should focus on whether the parents are equally capable of parenting and equally available to assume parental obligations. Also, have the parents demonstrated the capacity to cooperate and to communicate? Can the children move freely back and forth between the two residences while attending the same school? When these issues have been explored, an evaluator should consider whether the parents need a court-imposed schedule or whether they can be relied upon to adhere to a nonscheduled arrangement. Generally, people who are equally capable as parents and who can communicate and cooperate can be trusted to a nonscheduled arrangement for visitation and place of residence. Those who cannot may need a court-ordered schedule.

Next, are both parents fairly equal as to decision-making capacity, or are there some areas where one parent should be given priority? Simply to designate one parent to make primary decisions may not reflect the reality of the situation. Of course, considerations of cooperation and communication also have a bearing on judgments about decision-making powers.

When all these issues have been explored, a suitable program should be formulated. The only name given should be *residential and decision-making arrangement* or some equally neutral name. This kind of name will circumvent the problems resulting from the use of any of the traditional terms and will direct attention to the substantive issues. And it has the fringe benefit of reducing the likelihood of litigation. One may choose to fight for sole custody, split custody, and so on; but one is far less apt to fight for a "residential and decision-making arrangement," because one has it already. Without the win or lose element, without the opportunity for wrestling something from the spouse, the impetus to fight is reduced—though of course not completely removed.

I recognize that this proposal comes at a time when mental health professionals, members of the legal profession, and state legislators have spent tens of thousands of hours defining the term *joint custody* and incorporating their definitions into statutes. The implications of my proposal are that most of this time has been wasted. That should not be a reason, however, to refrain from modifying these statutes.

The mother vs. the father as the more suitable parent. This is a very controversial subject. The opinions I express here are those that seem most reasonable to me at this time, and I recognize that they are not shared by some mental health professionals.

In recent years many have proclaimed that the notion of the mother's being superior to the father as a child rearer is not valid, that this is a social prejudice, and that both parents are equal in this regard. In many states this position has been incorporated into statutes that require judges to be sex blind and to focus only on parental capacity when deciding which parent to designate the primary custodial parent.

Although it may be an unpopular thing to say, I do not believe that sex-blind custody decisions necessarily serve the best interests of the children. In the mid to late 1970s, men proclaimed that the *tender years presumption* (the idea that women are intrinsically superior to men in child-rearing capacity) was basically sexist. State legislatures for the most part agreed, and laws were changed in accordance with what came to be known as the *best interests of the child presumption,* in which gender egalitarianism regarding child-rearing capacity was the central factor. But I do not accept this assumption of gender equality in child-rearing capacity. I would further state that the younger the child, the less the likelihood that this assumption is valid.

No one can deny that men and women are different biologically. No one can deny, either, that it is the mother who carries the baby in her body for nine months. It is she who is continually aware of its presence and its movements. It is she who is ever reminded of the pregnancy by formidable changes in her body, and it is she who gives birth. Even the most dedicated fathers cannot have these experiences. And it is the mother, too, who may very well have the breastfeeding experience, something the father cannot do. All these factors create a much higher likelihood that at the time of birth the mother will have a stronger psychological tie with the infant than will the father. I believe that most people would agree that, if parents decided to separate at the time of birth and both were reasonably equal with regard to parenting capacity, the mother would be the preferable parent.

Many people argue, however, that mothers' superiority stops at the time of birth and men are thereafter equal to women in parenting capacity. Even here I am dubious. It is reasonable to believe that during the course of human evolution there was a selective genetic survival of women who were highly motivated child rearers. Such women were more likely to seek men for the purposes of impregnation, more likely to be sought by men who desired children, and so more likely to have children to inherit their genes. Because of this evolutionary heritage, I believe, the average woman today is more likely to be genetically programmed for child-rearing functions than the average man. One could argue that environmental influences enable us to modify our genetic inheritance. I do not deny this, but there are limitations to environment's impact on heredity. Environment modifies heredity primarily—many would say exclusively—by the slow process of selective survival of the variants particularly well adapted to a specific environment. Accordingly, I believe that genetic factors are strong enough in today's parents to merit serious consideration in custody decisions.

What I recommend is that we give preference in custody disputes to the parent (regardless of sex) who has provided the greatest degree of healthy child-rearing input during the children's formative years. Under this principle, because mothers are still more often the primary child-rearing parents, more mothers would be given parental preference in custody disputes. If, however, in spite of the mother's superiority at the time of birth, it was the father who was the primary care-taker—especially during the early years of life—the father might very well be the preferable primary custodial parent. This principle is essentially sex blind because it allows for the possibility that a father's input may outweigh the mother's in the formative years, even though he starts at a disadvantage. It utilizes the *psychological bond* with the child as the primary consideration in custody evaluations. And I would add that the longer the time between infancy and the time of the custody decision, the greater the likelihood that environmental factors will modify (strengthen or weaken) the psychological bonds that the child had with each parent during the earliest years. A mother may be good with infants and toddlers but may do poorly with adolescents. A father may be uncomfortable with an infant but may excel as a parent when he can share sports and other activities with older children.

I refer to this as the *stronger, healthy psychological bond presumption.* This presumption, I believe, would best serve the interests of the child in a custody dispute. I am not referring here to any kind of psychological bond at all, but a *healthy* psychological bond. Clearly, the parent who had the greater involvement with the child during infancy is the one more likely to have the stronger psychological bond. However, if the early parenting was not "good," then the bond may be pathological. A paranoid mother who has so programmed her son that he too has developed paranoid feelings about his father may have a strong psychological bond with her son. But this is certainly not a healthy bond.

In summary, a custody decision based on the stronger, healthy psychological bond presumption should give weight to these factors:

1. Preference should be given to the parent (regardless of sex) with whom the child has developed the stronger, healthy psychological bond.

2. The parent (regardless of sex) who was the primary caretaker during the earliest years of the child's life is more likely to have developed the stronger, healthy psychological bond.

3. The longer the time gap between the earliest years and the time of the custody decision, the greater the likelihood other factors may tip the balance of parenting capacity in either direction.

The parental alienation syndrome. Starting in the late 1970s, in association with what can justifiably be called a custody litigation explosion, I began to see a disorder that developed almost exclusively in children exposed to and embroiled in custody disputes. *Parental alienation syndrome* refers to a disturbance in which a child is obsessed with unjustified and/or exaggerated deprecation and criticism of one parent and idolization of the other. It is as if the preferred parent can do no wrong and the nonpreferred parent can do no right. Such children have not merely been "brainwashed" or programmed by one parent to denigrate the other parent. The parental alienation syndrome does have a brainwashing component but is much more inclusive. It incorporates not only conscious but subconscious and unconscious drives in the preferred parent that contribute to the child's alienation. Furthermore, it includes factors that arise within the child— independent of parental contributions—to foster the development of the syndrome.

Typically, the child is obsessed with "hatred" of a parent. (I put the word *hatred* in quotes because there are still many tender and loving feelings toward the parent that are not permitted expression.) The child speaks of the hated parent with every vilification and profanity in their vocabulary— without embarrassment or guilt. The vilification of the parent often has the rehearsed quality of a litany. With only minimal prompting, the record will be turned on and a command performance provided. One often hears phraseology identical to that used by the "loved" parent. (Again, the word *loved* is in quotes because there may also be hostility toward and fear of that parent, similarly unexpressed.) My experience has been that in about 80 to 90 percent of cases the mother is the favored parent and the father the vilified one; in the remaining 10 to 20 percent of cases the opposite is true. It is important to note that when the child's anger is warranted by bona fide abuse (physical, emotional, or sexual), the parental alienation syndrome concept does not apply.

The child may justify the alienation with years-old memories of minor altercations with the hated parent. Usually these are trivial and relate to experiences that most children quickly forget: "She used to say 'Don't interrupt,'" and "He used to make a lot of noise when he chewed at the table." Asked to give more compelling reasons for their hatred, these children are unable to provide them. Frequently, the loved parent will agree with the child that these professed reasons justify the ongoing animosity.

The hatred of the parent often includes that parent's complete extended family. Cousins, aunts, uncles, and grandparents with whom the child previously may have had loving relationships are now detested. Greeting cards are not reciprocated. Presents are refused, remain unopened, or even are destroyed (generally in the presence of the loved parent). When the hated parent's relatives call on the telephone, the child will respond with angry name-calling or quickly hang up. The rage of these children is so great that they become completely oblivious to the privations they are causing themselves. Again, the loved parent is typically unconcerned with the untoward psychological effects on the child of the rejection of these relatives.

Another symptom of the parental alienation syndrome is complete lack of ambivalence that characterizes normal parent-child relationships. In this syndrome the hated parent is viewed as all bad and the loved parent as all good. The hated parent may have been deeply dedicated to the child, and a strong bond may have been created over many years. The hated parent may produce photos that show clearly a joyful and healthy relationship of affection, tenderness, and mutual pleasure. But all these experiences appear to have obliterated from the child's memory. When shown these photos, the child usually rationalizes the experiences as having been forgotten, nonexistent, or feigned: "I really hated being with him then. I just smiled in the picture because he made me. He said he'd hit me if I didn't smile."

The child may exhibit a guiltless disregard for the feelings of the hated parent. There will be a complete absence of gratitude for gifts, support payments, and other evidence of the hated parent's continued involvement and affection. Often these children will want to be certain the alienated parent continues to provide support payments, but at the same time will adamantly refuse to visit. Commonly they will say that they *never* want to see the hated parent again, or not until their late teens or early twenties. To such a child I might say: "So you want your father to continue paying for all your food, clothing, rent, and education—even private high school and college—and yet you still don't want to see him at all, ever again. Is that right?" The child might respond: "That's right. He doesn't deserve to see me. He's mean and paying all that money is a good punishment for him."

Those who have never seen such children may consider this description a caricature. Those who have seen them will recognize the syndrome immediately, although some children may not manifest all the symptoms. The parental alienation syndrome is becoming increasingly common—a direct result, I am convinced, of social and legal changes underlying judicial decisions in custody disputes.

Let me review these changes briefly. First, in the replacement of the "tender years presumption" with the "best interest of the child presumption," the best interests of the child became uniformly equated with the notion that custody determinations should be sex blind. Equating these two concepts, I believe, has caused considerable difficulty. I believe that in their desire to keep up with the seeming egalitarianism of the best interests of the child presumption, the courts have not been giving proper credit to the strength of the psychological bond in most families *today* (I am not predicting the future) between children and their mothers. And I believe that many women have responded to the threat of removal of their children by the utilization of maneuvers that have contributed to the development of the parental alienation syndrome in their children. Children, too, have been threatened by disruption of the mother-child bond. They have selected maneuvers that—although they may seem absurd—basically represent mechanisms of defense against the disruption of this bond. And the animosities engendered by these maneuvers have contributed to the increase in and intensification of custody litigation.

Second, the joint-custodial concept has contributed to an increase in the development of the parental alienation syndrome. In what becomes essentially a no-custodial arrangement, the children are used as ropes in a tug-of-war between the parents. These circumstances intensify the viciousness of the litigation, especially in cases where separated women—all too often at an economic disadvantage compared to men—program their children against their husbands in a desperate attempt to win the custody battle.

I believe that the utilization of the "stronger, healthy psychological bond presumption" that I have described would reduce the frequency of custody litigation and so help prevent the development of the parental alienation syndrome.

For example, let us envision a situation in which a couple has one child, a boy. During the first four years of the child's life, the mother remains at home as the primary child rearer and the father is out of the home during the day. When the child is four the mother takes a full-time job. During the day the child attends school and then stays with a woman in the neighborhood. At the end of the workday and over weekends both parents are involved equally in caring for the child. When the child is seven the parents decide to separate. Each parent wants primary custody. The father claims that during the three years prior to the separation, he was as involved as the mother in the child's upbringing; the mother does not deny this. The father contends that the court should make its decision solely on the basis of parenting capacity—especially as demonstrated in recent years—and claims that any custody decision taking his sex into consideration is sexist and is an abrogation of his civil rights. In the course of the litigation the child develops typical symptoms of the parental alienation syndrome. He becomes obsessed with hatred of his father and creates outlandish scenarios to justify his animosity. In contrast, he views his mother as faultless and all-loving.

I believe that in this situation the child's psychological bond is strongest with the mother, and the symptoms of alienation are created by him in an attempt to maintain that bond. If the father had been the primary caretaker during the first four years of the boy's life and had shared equally in subsequent child rearing, then the child might well have the stronger, healthy psychological bond with the father. And if he did, I would recommend the father be designated the primary custodial parent.

If the stronger, healthy psychological bond were the central criterion, when the mother had been the primary caretaker, the father would hesitate to seek custody. Accordingly, the likelihood of the mother's "brainwashing" the child and of the child's developing parental alienation syndrome would be obviated. Similarly, when the father had been the primary caretaker during the formative years, the mother would be discouraged from embarking on the custody litigation course. This would then obviate the brainwashing/parental alienation syndrome.

False abuse allegations in child custody disputes. Since the early 1980s we have witnessed a burgeoning of allegations of child sex abuse. Some observers claim that the vast majority of these allegations are false and that they are a manifestation of mass hysteria. Others claim that the majority are genuine and that the only new development has been the exposure of what was previously a widespread secret. The one thing that both sides agree upon is that the public media are giving much more attention to child sex abuse in recent years.

I believe that the conflict here is artificial and unnecessary. I believe that we are dealing not with an *either/or* but with a *both* phenomenon—namely that there are two epidemics going on simultaneously. We probably are witnessing an actual increase in bona fide sexual abuse of children, and in my view this is related to the general fragmentation of community values and upheaval in sexual mores that are generally agreed to have taken place in western society. We are also experiencing an increase in fabricated claims of child sex abuse, especially in the context of child custody disputes. In the 1980s many parents who were embroiled in these disputes found the sex-abuse allegation to be an extremely powerful weapon. Courts are notoriously slow in making decisions. Angry parents found that the sex-abuse accusation would speed up the litigation. And merely making the allegation could result in the court's immediately removing the alleged offender from the home. By the time a full investigation was conducted, six months or a year might elapse—during which time the accusing parent could entrench his or her position with the children. Understandably enough, the sex-abuse allegation thereby became incorporated into the parental alienation syndrome discussed above.

Programming a child into making such an allegation is not difficult, especially when the child is under the age of five. Children are ever trying to ingratiate themselves to their parents. Furthermore, young children normally have difficulty differentiating fact from fantasy; for example, most believe in the existence of Santa Claus and the Easter Bunny. It is also normal for children, even young children, to entertain a wide variety of sexual fantasies. It is relatively easy for a parent to use these fantasies as a nucleus for a false sex-abuse allegation. Another phenomenon that may be operative here is that of projection: the process by which a person deals with an unacceptable impulse by projecting it onto another party. Projection reaches its extreme form in paranoia, where individuals project malicious motivations onto other people and view themselves as innocent victims. A parent who may have incestuous designs on a child may disown them by projecting them onto the other parent. The accuser may actually believe the allegation, but it is basically a delusion.

Before the early 1980s, the general consensus among those who worked with sexually abused children was that children rarely, if ever, fabricated sex abuse. The main argument given was that children had no direct access to the details of the sexual encounter, so if a child did describe such details there must have been an actual experience. But this is no longer the case. Sex abuse has become a common topic in the public media. Television programs have become increasingly more explicit; even standard fare such as soap operas is sex laden. Sex-abuse prevention programs, in which children are given specific information about sexual activities, have been introduced into most schools, even down to the nursery school level. There are even sex-abuse coloring books and sex-abuse cassette tapes. Such exposure provides information and experiences that are readily incorporated into the children's contribution to the parental alienation syndrome.

Sex-abuse allegations are also being made in schools and day-care centers, especially with regard to younger children. In some of these cases genuine sex abuse has occurred. In others, no such abuse has taken place; the allegedly abused children and their parents have been swept up in an epidemic of hysteria. Often these allegations arise in situations in which the child is "evaluated" by overzealous sex-abuse workers who are committed to finding sex abuse in just about every child referred to them.

As a result of these developments we are being confronted with a grave problem: how to differentiate bona fide from fabricated sex-abuse allegations. A false accusation can have terrible consequences. The careers and reputations of innocent people have been ruined by such allegations, even after they are proven not guilty. Although we have accumulated a vast amount of information about the signs and symptoms of bona fide sexual abuse in child victims and about those who perpetuate sex abuses, we are just beginning to learn about the characteristics of the child fabricators and of adults who initiate and promulgate false allegations.

Parents can do certain things to increase the likelihood that a proper differentiation between genuine and false sex abuse allegations will be made. First, parents should insist upon an examiner who is truly objective. An examiner with an extremely high frequency of findings of abuse or—conversely—who always seems to find the alleged perpetrator innocent is probably biased. Examiners who utilize the so-called anatomically correct dolls are likely to conclude that many nonabused children were indeed sexually molested. These dolls clearly depict body orifices (the mouth, vagina, and anus), pubic hair, and full breasts (often with pointy nipples). In many the genitals are enlarged beyond proper proportion. The dolls are highly suggestive and provide children with food for thought. An increasing number of scientific studies demonstrate these dolls to be powerful contaminants to the sex-abuse evaluation. At this time, the findings derived from such dolls are not permitted as evidence in the state of California, and the American Psychological Association has not accepted them as bona fide testing instruments.

Furthermore, parents should insist upon an examiner who will evaluate all three parties—the accuser, the alleged perpetrator, and the alleged victim—both individually and in varying combinations as warranted. There are many examiners who feel no hesitation examining only the child and then deciding that the accused (who was never even interviewed) was the abuser. This is unconscionable and probably unconstitutional, yet it is a widespread phenomenon. Joint interviews are the best source of information, because they enable each of the individuals to talk directly with the other: the accused and the accuser, the accuser and the victim, and the accused and the victim. I am not saying that a joint interview between the accused and the alleged victim should automatically be conducted, as sometimes this can be psychologically detrimental. But an examiner should be given the freedom to conduct an interview if he or she considers it warranted.

Regardless of who initiates it, the deliberate false sex abuse accusation is a despicable act. It can cause lifelong psychological damage to both the falsely accused person and the child. In addition to the psychological trauma of numerous interrogations by lawyers, mental health professionals, prosecutors, detectives, and judges, the child is also subjected to the further trauma of being "treated" for sex abuse when there was no such molestation. There are thousands of children who are receiving such "treatment." Such "therapy" engenders the belief that a person betrayed them when that person did not do so, which produces further confusion about reality versus fantasy. The "treatment" then may produce long-standing (if not lifelong) alienation. And it can, I believe, predispose children to the development of psychotic thinking. Parents who contemplate the false sex-abuse allegation as a weapon in custody disputes must consider these effects on their children.

Although sex-abuse allegations are receiving the most attention (and probably causing the most difficulty), allegations of physical abuse and emotional abuse are also commonplace in child custody disputes. Each type of abuse may present difficulties for examiners trying to establish the facts. In many cases physical abuse is easy to establish because of obvious medical findings, photographs, X-rays of broken bones, and other physical manifestations. Proof that the child *was* physically abused, however, does not often provide information about *who* the perpetrator was. In custody disputes each parent will point the finger at the other. A parent will commonly make many trips to the emergency room or the pediatrician's office in the hope that the doctor will confirm physical abuse. Physicians become well aware of parents who are trying to make a case out of a normal, everyday injury, cut, or blemish. There are, of course, children who are genuinely getting hurt and require outside authorities to protect them from further abuse. But there are also false allegations of physical abuse. The differentiation, even by skilled examiners, may be difficult, especially when there are no physical signs.

Emotional abuse, unlike physical abuse, is extremely difficult to verify. Objective signs are not likely to be present. In addition, there is a continuum between normal, healthy disciplinary and punitive measures that all good parents utilize and those forms of parental negative feedback that would generally be considered emotional abuse. For example, a normal form of discipline is to send children to their rooms for a cooling-off period. Most would agree that fifteen to thirty minutes of such "solitary confinement" is humane and reasonable. Most would also agree that twenty-four hours is cruel and inhumane. How many hours, then, should we consider to be the upper range of normal? Two hours? Three hours? Four hours? But even this question is far easier to answer than more subtle forms of emotional abuse—such as criticism. Most would agree that some constructive criticism is necessary for a child's proper upbringing. But what about criticisms directed to the child in a state of frustration and anger? Every parent has a limit of tolerance for children's inevitable frustrating behavior. Criticisms made in moments of anger are often unconstructive: "You're driving me crazy" or "I can't stand you any longer and I hope your father comes home soon. Let him deal with you." We then move on to communications in which the child is humiliated, downgraded, and scorned—especially via the use of profanities. But here again the average parent may still occasionally degenerate to such a state. Where do we draw the line between the occasional use of profanities and use that would be considered pathological and a form of emotional abuse? Here, even more than for sexual or physical abuse, the examiner is going to have to rely heavily on the testimony of each parent, and the likelihood that parents litigating for custody will agree is almost zero.

Since the early 1980s, social agencies have been describing an ever-increasing rate of referrals about these three forms of abuse. In most states people who accuse others of such abuse are immune from retaliatory lawsuits. Therefore, many who are potential targets for such accusations are running scared. Divorced fathers are afraid to bathe their children during visitation; it is not hard to convince a three-year-old girl that her father, while washing her crotch, was utilizing "bad touches." Nursery schools have recruited extra personnel whose sole job is to be on-site observers at all times—just to ensure that no child is ever alone with an adult. Teachers and other school administrators leave their doors open at all times from the fear that if they are alone with a youngster behind a closed door an allegation of sex abuse may be impossible to disprove. I am convinced that there are countless people in prison for sexually abusing their children when in fact there was no such abuse—just as there are many others who have perpetrated such abuse but have escaped prosecution or been released for lack of evidence.

In short, society is having a hard time dealing with accusations of child abuse. And in my view the primary problems relate to the system that is used to find out the truth, namely, the adversary system. I consider this system to be hopelessly flawed as a means of learning "the truth" from children. Evaluators in the mental health professions are rarely given the opportunity to bring together in joint interview the accused, the accuser, and the alleged victim, but these joint interviews provide the best hope for verifying allegations or smoking out fabrications. Divorcing parents who are involved in such disputes should insist upon the utilization of evaluators who will conduct these joint interviews.

Asking the children whom they wish to live with.

Most often both parents agree that the children will do best living with the mother, and the children are not consulted about this decision. When there is a conflict over who shall have custody, the children's opinions may be enlisted. The responses children may provide to the direct question as to whom they would prefer to live with are very difficult to interpret and utilize properly. Most would agree that older children's wishes should be given consideration. However, children (and the younger they are, the more true this is) are generally ill equipped to make a judicious decision on their own. Furthermore, the question itself is a very anxiety-provoking one for most children. They may hesitate to express preference for one parent for fear the nonpreferred parent will react punitively or consider them disloyal. They appreciate that making a choice may jeopardize their relationship with the nonpreferred parent and may result in lifelong alienation. Many years later the child may regret a decision that may have been the result of childhood naïveté or distortion. All in all, if the child does not wish to express a preference, that wish should be respected.

When the conflict over custody is so great that the parents cannot resolve it themselves, they may resort to litigation in an attempt to resolve the dispute. This, however, is a misguided approach. It will inevitably cause both parents and the children psychological trauma, and it often produces parental alienation syndrome in children.

Inevitably, the children will be asked by mental health professionals, lawyers, and judges what their parental preferences are. Sometimes this is done subtly, sometimes directly. The legal and mental health evaluators generally take the children's wishes into consideration but do not automatically go along with them. There are times when children (especially older ones) will have a definite preference but will be afraid to reveal it directly. These children may subtly reveal the preference in the hope that the court will assign them to live with the preferred parent. They would rather have the decision made by the court in order to avoid the guilt they would feel if they were forced to state their preferences openly. Lawyers, judges, and mental health evaluators should recognize that they may be doing such children a disservice by trying to extract a definitive statement from them regarding their preferences.

A good example was Ralph, an only child, who was thirteen years old when his parents separated. He absolutely refused to express a preference for either parent; he even denied any knowledge of his parents' difficulties. His father was a well-known alcoholic but was able to keep his job in the insurance business and function adequately in it. He would often come home drunk, yet Ralph flatly denied that his father had a drinking problem. Ralph's mother was obsessed with cleanliness and hounded all members of the family about keeping the home clean and neat. Furniture was constantly being replaced in its exact position, particles of dust removed, and so on. Again, Ralph denied that his mother's pressures bothered or concerned him. Yes, he had overheard his parents fighting on occasion; but "I never listen to them; I just don't want to get involved."

When asked whom he preferred to live with, he emphatically stated that he had no preference and would leave that decision up to the court. "I'll live with whoever they force me to," he stated. In discussing his mother, however, he described how easy it was for him to talk to her, how they often shopped together because she knew exactly what to buy him, and how good it is to have mothers around during the day for carpools; whereas fathers have to work all day and don't have as much time for their children. I became convinced that Ralph basically preferred to live with his mother. However, I was also convinced that he wanted the court to be the one to "force" him to live with his mother so that he would not appear disloyal to his father. And this was the recommendation I made after taking all factors into consideration.

Many professionals recommend that children involved in custody litigation have their own lawyers. Obviously, a child so represented is more likely to get proper treatment from the court as well as from the parents and their advocates. But this recommendation (besides adding to the expense of litigation) has the disadvantage of further intensifying the problems of adversary proceedings. We have enough difficulties with *two* lawyers. Adding a *third* compounds the problems immeasurably. Consider the morass of conflicting data; we have enough trouble with two lawyers doing everything possible to suppress information detrimental to their clients' positions. Should we add a third to confound us further? I have serious reservations about this recommendation—in spite of its potential benefits to the child—and instead recommend the use of professionals as impartial mediators or arbitrators.

Parental sexual behavior as a determinant of custody.

In past years the sexual behavior of the mother, and to a lesser extent of the father, was an important consideration in the custody decision. Although adultery by *either* spouse was (and still is) generally considered grounds for divorce, adultery by the mother (but not generally by the father) was often considered grounds for depriving her (but not him) of custody. The courts would consider the mother's sexual life in great detail, and if she was having sexual experiences, even though she was not bringing her partners into the home, her maternal capacity would be questioned. Even one extramarital sexual experience before the divorce was legal could be in itself evidence to the court of her unfitness as a mother.

This punitive attitude has been moderated to a certain degree, and the courts have become less quick to use sexual behavior as a criterion for determining custody. I think, however, that it would be a mistake to go completely in the other direction. If a separated parent with temporary custody were, for example, to bring into the home a succession of lovers for overnight stays, I would consider this behavior potentially harmful to the children and an argument against such a parent's obtaining custody. (There might be counterbalancing considerations, of course. All pros and cons are to be weighed in relation to others, not to be taken in isolation.)

It is out of purely psychological considerations that I believe such behavior to compromise a parent's capacity. A *parade* of lovers through a parent's bedroom can be psychologically detrimental to a child. If, however, a mother who was not having sexual relationships with other men were to bring a man friend into the home to live, I would not necessarily consider this a reason for withholding custody. In fact, if the children had a good relationship with this man, it might even be an argument for her to have the children; she would after all be providing them with a male presence in compensation for their own father's absence. Children can maintain a good relationship *both* with their father and with their mother's cohabitant; one need not preclude the other. If such a mother, however, were to enlist the aid of the children in keeping her man friend's presence a secret from her friends, relatives, and neighbors, then this would be detrimental to them. She would be placing a burden on them in addition to the worries they are already suffering.

Custody and the homosexual parent. Now to the difficult and controversial subject of homosexuality. As explained in chapter 2, no one can claim to know with certainty the causes of homosexuality. I believe that there is a continuum with strong heterosexuality on one end and strong homosexuality on the other. No individual, no matter how strongly heterosexual, is completely without homosexual tendencies. And no individual, no matter how strongly homosexual, is completely without heterosexual inclinations. All individuals, therefore, are at some point between the two ends of the continuum. I believe, however, as stated in chapter 2, that an *obligatory* homosexual, who cannot or who has no desire to function heterosexually, is suffering with a psychiatric disorder that is primarily environmentally induced—although there still may be genetic (or constitutional) contributing factor(s). Such an individual has a problem that might readily be classified in many cases as a kind of phobia or inhibition. As with other kinds of phobias, such as agoraphobia or claustrophobia, there may very well be a genetic predisposition. But in my opinion, the fact that a genetic component may be operative does not warrant our declassifying homosexuality from the list of psychiatric disorders. Although I am less firm in my belief that bisexuals are suffering with psychopathology, I suspect that many (not necessarily all) are. And again, because of the homosexual potential in even the strongest heterosexuals, I would not consider pathological a rare homosexual act engaged in by a heterosexual person, especially when heterosexual opportunity is not available.

Let me emphasize that I am not claiming to know with certainty that my views are correct. They are the views I hold at this time on the basis of my present understanding of human sexual behavior. It is important for a therapist to take a position on this issue if he or she is to be making recommendations for people who present with homosexual urges and are considering treatment. For example, a mother brings a four-year-old boy for consultation because he is preoccupied with dressing in her clothing and has been showing effeminate behavior. One therapist may take the position that the child's behavior is normal and/or that the child is genetically programmed to be homosexual. Accordingly, that therapist will not recommend treatment. Another therapist may consider the child to be exhibiting pathological manifestations and will recommend therapy. (I am in the latter category.) A fourteen-year-old boy asks his parents to find him a therapist because of homosexual preoccupations. One therapist may consider the boy's thoughts to be part of a normal homosexual variation and may endeavor to help the youngster become more comfortable with his homosexuality. Another therapist (include me again in this group) may consider the boy to be showing signs of pathology and may recommend treatment for the alleviation of the homosexual tendencies.

I consider the average male obligatory homosexual to be suffering with more psychological difficulties than the average female obligatory homosexual. In our society, where the mother is still the primary caretaking parent in most families, the earliest primary sexual attachment for infants of both sexes is the mother. In the normal development of the boy, he transfers his affection from his mother to girlfriends and ultimately to other adult females. For the average boy the progression is a relatively smooth one and does not involve the kind of shift required of the female. The girl, in contrast, must transfer her sexual involvement from a female (her mother) to male figures: boyfriends and then adult males. It is reasonable to assume that remnants of the attraction to the mother will linger at subsequent levels of development. A woman who becomes a lesbian is fixated at an earlier level of development: the level at which she was attracted to her primary sexual object, the mother. But the male homosexual must abrogate mother and all her derivative surrogates. He must shift toward an intense sexual involvement with a father surrogate that has no continuity with his previous psychobiological track. The psychological processes involved in such a path are complex and extremely powerful. The distortions of thinking necessary to effect such a transfer are profound. It is for these reasons that I consider the obligatory male homosexual to have a deeper psychopathology than the obligatory female homosexual.

Although I believe that the obligatory homosexual is suffering with a psychiatric disorder, I do not believe that an obligatory homosexual (or any other kind of homosexual for that matter) should be deprived of his or her civil rights. One's private sexual life should not be a factor in employment, housing, and so on. If a homosexual's activities interfere with job functioning, then that must be taken into consideration—but this is equally true for heterosexuals. If a homosexual man is an elementary teacher and encourages homosexual activities among his students, then he should be fired. But if a heterosexual teacher does the same thing, he should be fired too.

By the same token, a parent's homosexuality should not in itself be a reason for depriving that parent of custody. It should merely be one factor considered in the decision. Removal of children from a homosexual parent can deprive them of valuable experiences, as homosexuality does not necessarily impair parental capacity. In custody evaluations involving homosexual parents, I try to determine whether the parent is trying to raise the child to become homosexual. This can be done overtly, with the parent stating directly that he or she wants the child to be homosexual, although this is rare, in my experience. More commonly, the homosexual parent who encourages homosexuality in the children does so more covertly, with comments such as "I'll tell my children that I have no particular preference regarding whether they become homo- or heterosexual." Healthy parents generally *do* have a preference—and strongly so. They want their children to be heterosexual. This has to do less with the social stigma that the homosexual suffers (which, fortunately, is lessening) than with the appreciation that such a way of life is more likely to be unrewarding and painful than a heterosexual existence.

Although a homosexual parent provides, in my opinion, an unhealthy model for sexual identification, this fact should not necessarily be a reason for depriving the parent of primary custody if the child is above the age of three or four and exhibits definite heterosexual orientation. By that time the child's sexual orientation is fairly well established and is not likely to be altered—unless there has been unusual and prolonged indoctrination into homosexual attitudes and behavior and/or ongoing exposure to environmental factors that can contribute to the development of homosexuality. When involved in custody evaluations of homosexual parents, I examine carefully each child's sexual orientation and look for signs of sexual identification problems—both present and potential.

For boys, the signs of a potential homosexual problem include effeminancy; fear of or withdrawal from rough-and-tumble play; the *frequent* desire to put on the mother's makeup and to wear her shoes, underwear, and other articles of clothing; a preference for the role of mother in playing house; and a marked preference for playing with girls rather than boys. These criteria are especially valid when they have taken on an obsessive or compulsive quality. Tomboyishness in a girl is not a very valuable criterion, however, especially nowadays, when girls' involvement in traditional male activities is becoming more common.

During the prepubertal and pubertal periods special problems may arise that can affect my recommendations regarding custody and visitation. If a homosexual father, for example, is frequently bringing his thirteen-year-old son together with his homosexual friends, he is providing the boy with a detrimental exposure. Even if the boy shows no sign of homosexual orientation, the atmosphere is bound to be a charged one for him. It may not result in his becoming homosexual, but it can add to the sexual anxieties and confusions that he will normally have during this period. I would consider such exposures an argument against granting this father primary custody. I would certainly encourage visitation, but I would recommend that such exposures not be permitted during the visiting times.

If a homosexual parent is reasonably private about his or her sex life and is not trying to induce homosexuality in the children or expose them to sexual activities, then I would not consider the homosexuality a reason for disqualifying the parent as the primary custodian. Nor would I recommend that there be any reduction or restriction of visitation rights.

More difficult is the question of what recommendations to make regarding custody for a parent who is living with a homosexual partner. Those who argue that homosexuality is not a psychiatric disturbance compare such a live-in relationship with a heterosexual one and argue that the same criteria should hold for both with regard to the granting of primary custody. If the court would grant primary custody to a mother with a live-in boyfriend or a father with a live-in girlfriend (and courts commonly do so in both of these situations), then, they contend, the court should not discriminate against the parent who lives with someone of the same sex.

I support the courts' more frequent granting of custody to a parent who is living with a heterosexual partner. Because I believe that homosexuality is most likely a psychiatric disorder, however, I believe that a child in a home in which both "parents" are of the same sex is being unduly exposed to an unhealthy psychological environment. I do not believe this environment is likely to reverse the sexual identity of children over four who have already established a heterosexual identity and orientation. Rather, I believe that such exposure can create confusions, anxieties, and compromises in sex role identification that might otherwise not have developed. Also, just as the heterosexual parent who exposes the children to a parade of lovers is, I believe, providing a detrimental exposure, a homosexual parent who brings a series of partners into the home compromises the parental role. Like all the other criteria I use, no one of these is overriding. I might still recommend custody for such a parent if other factors counterbalanced this one. Homosexuality in itself should not be a reason for reducing a parent's visitation or custody rights. But when there is an imposition of homosexuality, one should consider limiting the parent's privileges.

In Joan's case, for example, I recommended that a lesbian mother not be given custody of her child and that there be a curtailment of her visitation rights. Joan was thirteen-years-old when her parents separated because of her mother's homosexuality. Joan, who was an only child, initially went to live with her mother. At around the time of the separation Joan's mother became a gay activist. Many homosexuals visited the home, where meetings often took place. In fact the mother was so busy with meetings that she had little time for Joan. The apartment was flooded with literature and pamphlets supporting the gay cause. In addition, many homosexual magazines were strewn about the apartment, magazines with pictures depicting various kinds of homosexual activities. Joan's father instituted legal proceedings to gain custody of his daughter. As the result of my examination of Joan and both parents, I supported his request. Although Joan showed no evidence of a homosexual orientation at that time, I concluded that the intensive exposure to the homosexual environment was sexually titillating and confusing to her. The court agreed with my recommendations. Joan's father was granted primary custody. The mother was granted liberal visitation privileges but was not allowed to involve her daughter in gay liberation activities or to bring her to her apartment, because of the intensive homosexual environment there.

Before closing this discussion of homosexuality, I wish to emphasize again that I make no claims to be infallible. I claim only that my conclusions appear to me to be the most reasonable I can come to from my knowledge of and experiences with people who are homosexual. The recommendations I make regarding custody and visitation for the homosexual parent are based on this presumption.

Real vs. phony demands for custody. In recent years courts have been awarding custody to the more suitable parent, regardless of sex. A father now has a greater chance of gaining custody of his children; we are seeing more custody litigation in which fathers genuinely feel that they would be the better parent. We are also seeing legal contests in which the father is using his new opportunity for manipulative purposes, psychopathological gratification, or other inappropriate reasons.

A father, for example, may not really feel that he would be the preferable parent, but may selfishly try to gain custody of the children rather than suffer the pains of loss. Or a father may not actually want custody, but may claim that he does as a way of hurting the mother. Or he may know from the outset that he is not going to press this issue to the end; rather, he will use his custody demand as a bargaining maneuver in the negotiations over alimony and support payments. But custody litigation is invariably traumatic to children—pulled as they are between parents, lawyers, and other adults. The parent who places personal gain over the children's well-being reveals a serious defect in his or her parental capacity.

On occasion a parent will press vigorously for custody in an attempt to reduce guilt over the divorce. A father, for example, who never particularly distinguished himself as a devoted parent, may fight viciously for custody. But—consciously or unconsciously—he may not even wish to be granted custody. What he really wants is to put up a good fight so that he can convince himself and others that he really loves his children. Such a parent, while going through the motions of fighting for custody, may do things during the litigation to ensure that he loses the battle. For instance, whereas most parents spend maximum time with the children during custody litigation in order to impress all concerned with their devotion to their children, parents who basically wish to lose custody may not use this common maneuver. Or they may choose a lawyer who is obviously incompetent. Such parents are secretly relieved when they are not granted custody.

The lawyer may realize that the client does not deserve custody, but will nevertheless vigorously support the client's fight for the children. At times, this stems from the desire to use the custody claim as a weapon in the litigation to gain concessions in other areas. However, more benevolent considerations may also be operative. The lawyer may recognize that such clients may need the custody litigation in order to lessen guilt. Or the lawyer may hope that the exposure of the client's parental deficiencies in open court may help the client gain insight into the fact that he or she would be the less desirable custodial parent.

Choosing expert witnesses in custody litigation. In the typical courtroom custody conflict, each side brings in its own parade of professionals to testify on its behalf. As will be clear by now, I don't like parades. And when parades are held in a courtroom, and there are two of them (one for each side), and the parade consists of mental health professionals, I find them disgraceful to the profession and a disservice to the court.

Custody evaluations are really evaluations of two people. The mental health professional who is invited to testify in a custody trial is really being asked which of the two parents—

all things considered—would make the more desirable (or less undesirable) primary custodial parent for the children. It is somewhat ludicrous for an evaluator to get up in court after having examined the mother, for example, and simply to testify that she is a capable mother. The opposing lawyer should reasonably ask: "Have you seen the father?" In many cases the therapist will not have seen the father and will therefore not be able to comment on him. This is a gross omission, because one is really evaluating relative degrees of parental capacity. In most cases both parents *are* adequate, and the professional commenting on this issue should see *both* parents. Lawyers, with their deep faith in the adversary system, often hold that a custody decision is best accomplished in an adversarial proceeding—where each party's position is presented as strongly as possible. The better parent will then *win* custody. Although this system may have merit in determining the guilt or innocence of an alleged criminal (and even here I have reservations), it has little relevance to the determination of who is the better parent.

Parents should do everything possible to work out their custody conflicts themselves. This is not only the least expensive way but the least stressful for the children. Parents must recognize that once they go to court they are *putting the custody decision in the hands of others. They are giving up their right to make the final decision as to what will happen to their own children*. And from what I know of court decisions in such matters I cannot say that I have been impressed by their wisdom. The amount of data before judges is often mindboggling, and it is rare that time and money permit them adequately to assimilate all the evidence. Parents should be aware of the capriciousness of the legal solution before resorting to it. They should consider how difficult and expensive it may be to reverse a court's decision once it has been made. They should also consider the formidable amount of psychological trauma litigation will cause both to themselves and to their children. Custody litigation, especially when protracted, predictably makes preexisting psychiatric disturbances worse and often brings about such disorders when they have not previously existed. If the parents cannot resolve the custody problem themselves, they should first try mediation and should consider litigation only as a last resort.

If parents do decide to pursue the litigation course, they make a serious error if they each try to enlist their own team of experts, each of whom has been chosen to provide strong testimony on one parent's behalf. I believe that it is unethical for a mental health evaluator to agree to do a custody evaluation with the understanding that if the findings support the position of the inviting (and paying) party they will be used, but if they do not then the court will never hear the opinion. It is our legacy and our duty in medicine to provide our opinions impartially and not to cooperate with those who would use our medical opinions for their personal advantage or who would suppress our findings if they do not suit their purposes. Therapists who allow themselves to be used as weapons are not really helping lawyers or their clients. They are only prolonging and complicating the proceedings and adding to the expense and agony of the parents and children. Parents would save themselves expense and grief if they would insist on a mutually agreed-upon impartial examiner.

In recent years courts have become increasingly conscious of the depravity of the situation in which each parent brings in adversary mental health professionals. In many jurisdictions court-appointed impartial examiners are being used more frequently. Sometimes, in an attempt to avoid the problems attendant to the examiner's seeing only one parent, the court will order each parent to be interviewed by the other side's examiner. Unfortunately, this well-intentioned policy is injudicious, cruel, and exploitive. Most often, such hired guns support the position of the party who originally paid them. Accordingly, the parents forced into the interview by court order have everything to lose and nothing to gain. Everything negative they reveal about themselves will be used against them, but nothing positive is likely to convince the examiner to abandon the spouse who originally hired him or her. Parents who are placed in such a position have every reason to be incensed. It is a no-win situation. If they refuse to be interviewed, they will be in contempt of court and can even be fined and jailed. If they submit, they are providing ammunition to the other side. Parents should do everything possible to convince the court of the injudiciousness of such an order.

If a child is in therapy, one or both parents may wish to bring in the child's therapist to provide testimony in the custody conflict. This may appear to be a reasonable course, because the therapist generally knows the family well and may be in a good position to provide useful information to the court. However, it is inevitable that if the therapist does provide such testimony, the child's treatment will be jeopardized. Therapists' testifying in court in support of one parent cannot but cause the other parent to harbor deep resentments toward them, which predictably will compromise the child's therapy. Such betrayed parents will express these resentments openly in therapy, and even when attempts are made to hide the anger, the child will sense the hostile feelings that the parent harbors toward the therapist and will feel caught in the middle of a tug-of-war. This situation is bound to reduce the child's positive feelings toward the therapist. Therapeutic gratifications notwithstanding, a parent (even with problems) provides the child with more than the therapist—and the child has little choice but to side with the parent. Therefore, parents should separate these roles and, if the child is in treatment, get another professional to provide testimony.

At times parents will take a child to a therapist for treatment when actually a custody determination is desired. Parents may really believe that treatment is what they want; or they may say that treatment is what they want but have the custody consideration very much on their minds. They may withhold this from the therapist at the beginning because they fear the therapist will not want to become involved in the legal aspects of the case, or will not want to take the child into treatment at all if appearance in court is also being considered. Such parents may know of therapists' reluctance to go to court, though they may not understand the dangers that court appearances pose for therapy. (They may have been turned down by a series of therapists who refused to get involved once they suspected that their services were being requested for the purpose of litigation.) The parent may not appreciate that the therapist will be indignant when forced to testify in a case that was initially presented without any reference to the litigation plans. Accordingly, I warn parents once again that therapy and courtroom testimony cannot be combined. Parents who dupe therapists into providing testimony by presenting themselves and their children as "patients" are really deceiving themselves, because the resentment engendered by this deceit will compromise significantly the therapist's testimony.

After over twenty-five years of serving as an impartial court-ordered examiner, I have removed myself from direct involvement in custody litigation. Many factors led to this decision. The ones most pertinent to this book have to do with my belief that mediation is the far more sane and civilized way of resolving custody disputes; I am now devoting myself to this method of helping parents. Furthermore, I became increasingly aware of the psychologically damaging effects of adversarial proceedings, and I became conscious that even when I served as an impartial examiner I was implicitly conceding that this method of child custody dispute resolution had merit. I became increasingly convinced that even this level of participation was a disservice to parents, because their involvement in litigation inevitably contributed to the development and perpetuation of psychiatric disturbance. In the course of my involvement with custody litigation I personally observed three deaths by heart attack, one suicide, and one homicide—all of which would have been prevented had the parents not involved themselves in adversarial proceedings. Since 1988 I am not only devoting myself to mediation but promulgating other methods of child custody dispute resolution, methods that do not involve adversarial proceedings at any level whatsoever.

PARENTAL CRITICISM OF ONE ANOTHER

"Never criticize your ex-spouse to your child" is among the most common advice given to separated and divorced parents, and even mental health experts often profess it enthusiastically. The rationale is that it is important that children have respect for and admiration of each of their parents. The theory holds that if too many of a parent's deficiencies are revealed to the child, that parent will not become an object of identification, and so the child's healthy psychological development will be compromised.

Although well meaning, this advice is misguided. All of us, whether or not our parents are divorced, should have as accurate a picture as possible of our parents—both their assets and their liabilities. Children tend to identify with and unquestioningly accept their parents' characteristics. They operate on the principle: "If it's good enough for them, it's good enough for me." When young they swallow the whole bag, so to speak, indiscriminately identifying with many qualities that are not in their best interests. As they grow older, healthy children learn to accept parental qualities that are desirable and reject those that are not.

In a healthy home each parent can be a source of information for the children about undesirable qualities. Ideally, such information should be imparted in a benevolent fashion; for example, "Your father thinks that just because a person is black he is less worthy than others. I don't agree with his thinking." Or "Your mother thinks that something terrible will happen to you if you don't eat everything she gives you. I don't agree with her." In addition, parents should admit their own defects to the child—for instance, "I'm afraid to swim. I know there's nothing to be afraid of. I just can't help it. However, I hope that you'll learn to swim, because I can see that it can be a lot of fun."

Divorced parents as well owe their children this kind of information. To deprive children of it not only contributes to their developing difficulties in their interpersonal relationships but also produces confusion as well as distrust of the parent who withholds this vital information. Hearing nothing but good things from Mom about a divorced father, the child can only wonder: "If he's so great, why have you divorced him?" Moreover, the children's picture of the praised person is likely to be distorted, because they do not believe their primary source of information; so their fantasies can be validated or refuted only by their own, often primitive, observations.

The healthiest approach in such situations is to try to give the children as accurate a picture of their parents as possible. The children should grow to respect in each parent those areas that warrant respect and to hold in low esteem those qualities that are not worthy of admiration. If parents' defects far outweigh their strengths, so be it. This is not a reflection on the children. They may suffer from having a less admirable figure with whom to identify, but is this worse than emulating a contrived person whose assets exist only in words—words the children cannot fully believe? Respect is earned; it cannot be obtained by order or deceit. Children will ultimately see through facade.

Admittedly, separated parents are not famous for their objectivity when providing such information. The rage that often exists may be blinding, and distortions and exaggerations may be extreme. Nevertheless, I still advise separated parents to impart to their children what kinds of people they consider their spouses to be. Often this is best done when the parent is actually acting in a way that confirms the opinion. When a father misses his visits, his lack of interest should be labeled as such. When he exhibits genuine interest in the child's welfare, his involvement should be given credit. When a mother leaves her child in the care of a seven-year-old, this is neglect and should be defined as such. When she deprives herself of a new dress to buy her children clothing, she is showing true concern, and her children should know it. Parents do best to communicate information about one another during quiet discussion. (In my therapeutic work with children, I advise them to be somewhat skeptical of criticisms made while a parent is enraged.) I also advise parents to preface criticisms of ex-spouses with terms like "In my opinion" and "As I see it." In this way they convey their awareness that what they are saying may not be completely accurate.

I am not suggesting that every single defect and private failing of the parent be disclosed to the children. But the details of a parent's behavior toward them, no matter how contempt-ible, are the *children's business* and should be discussed at a level comprehensible to the children and at a depth appropriate to their ages. The children will then be far better prepared to relate effectively with their parents as well as others whom they will encounter.

There are parents who appear not to criticize the ex-spouse but who communicate in other ways their profound condemnation. For example, if a boy asks his mother about the reasons for the divorce and she tells him to ask his father, the child is likely to conclude that the truth is so bad that it cannot be told by a nice woman like his mother. When asking children if they want to see their father, a mother may say, "Do you *really* want to see your father?", communicating by the tone of her voice her hatred for her ex-husband. The father who says, "I would not want to say anything *against* your mother" gets across the message that there are terrible things that could be divulged, but that he is just too much of a good guy to tell about them. Because the details are not provided, the children are likely to imagine the defects to be far worse than they really are. Parents who continually speak with pride about how carefully they refrain from criticizing their ex-spouses provide the children with much food for terrible imaginings about the other parent's despicable crimes and heinous behavior.

Parents often ask what they can do when the ex-spouse continually disparages them and bombards the children with lies about them. I usually advise such parents that their best defense is to give the children living experiences that prove they are not what the ex-spouse describes them to be. I try to impress upon such parents that if they are loving and con-cerned, the children will ultimately come to appreciate this (even though at times they may be confused by the contradic-tory messages). I discourage such parents from questioning the children about the particular criticisms and attempting to correct them one by one. Such an endeavor is usually futile (the children cannot remember them all and they may be endless), and the parent's defensiveness may tend to make the children disbelieve the refutations. Parents who involve themselves in such continual disparagement of the ex-spouse are harming their children, and I try to get them to understand this. I also try to get them to appreciate that their children will (if they do not already) respect them less for involving themselves in such a campaign.

When working with parents who continually disparage one another, I try to help them reach the kind of relationship that often exists between countries that are basically antagonistic but find it in their mutual interests to maintain civilized relations. In the divorce situation the children can benefit when the hostile parties so conduct themselves.

The same professionals who suggest that one never criticize the absent spouse often advise divorced parents to reassure the children that the absent parent still loves them. This advice is certainly valid in most situations, because the absent parent generally does love the children. However, in some situations the advice is obviously misguided. The father who has not been heard from in many years is said still to love his children "but just can't show it." The mother who has disappeared is described as "keeping her love inside." As chapter 4 explained, children who are provided with such excuses cannot but become confused, sense the absurdity of the reassurance, and become distrustful of their only remaining parent. Telling the children that the abandoning parent still loves them is not going to provide any feeling that they are really loved. These children have to be given the truth and be helped to find ways to become comfortable with the angry feelings they will probably have. And they have to have *living experiences* that there are others with whom they can have affectionate and loving relationships. Only then will they really be convinced that the deficiency does not lie within themselves.

USING CHILDREN IN THE PARENTAL CONFLICT

A common error that separated parents often make (especially in the period immediately following the separation) is to use the child as a source of information about the ex-spouse. It is natural for a parent to be curious about what the former partner is doing (especially with regard to dating and spending money), and children can be an excellent source of information about such activities. Occasionally, the data so obtained is used in legal proceedings. Often parents are so eager to extract information from their children that they blind themselves to the harmful effects of using children as informers. Children are usually ashamed of themselves for disloyalty, yet they provide the information so as not to alienate the inquirer. The parents may also suffer a loss of self-respect for turning their children into spies. And the children lose respect for the parents.

Some parents, although not actively trying to extract data from the children, may find it impossible to avoid hearing the news. Johnny returns from a weekend visit with his father and speaks glowingly to his mother: "Dad's new girlfriend, Fran, is terrific. She makes the best pizzas I ever ate. And you should see the beautiful gold watch Dad bought her. It has jewels and everything!" During a weekend visit, Jimmy excitedly tells his father about his mother's new friend, who has moved into the home: "Dan's a great guy. He's a lot of fun to be with. He doesn't work, so he has lots of time to play ball with me when I come home from school." There are few parents who could restrain themselves from indulging their curiosity further in such circumstances.

In my psychotherapeutic work with children I try to discourage them from spying and try to get them to be self-assertive enough to refuse to answer each parent's questions about the other. For example, I might say to a boy, "No one respects a spy. The people he spies for know that he can't be trusted with a secret. And the spy can't even like himself, because he knows that what he's doing is wrong because it hurts other people." I also point out to such children that their spying is contributing to the continuation of the parents' fighting. If one or both parents are motivated to discontinue this shameful game, I suggest that they try this approach with their children.

The converse of using the children as sources of information is using them as couriers of messages. Although this may appear to be a harmless and expedient practice, it can easily deteriorate into another way of using the children in parental conflict. For example, a father, speaking to his six-year-old child on the telephone, says: "When we finish talking don't forget to tell your mother that I won't be picking you up this Saturday." The child can be relied upon to forget the message, causing the mother no end of frustration and inconvenience. The father knew, either consciously or unconsciously, that this would happen, but can play Mr. Innocent when his wife has a fit over his not showing up. Or Mom may say to her daughter, "When you see your father, tell him yourself that you need a new dress." By having the child make the request, the mother hopes to play on his guilt, or perhaps she knows that the father is unable to say no to his cute little daughter. In more extreme cases the warring parents may actually carry on prolonged conversations through the children: "You tell your mother that who I have in this house when you come here is none of her damn business." "You tell your father that I'll spend my money any way I please." "You tell your mother that if she doesn't have you ready on time next week I'll call my lawyer." "You tell your father that if he doesn't get here on time this Sunday I won't let him take you at all." Obviously, the bearers of these messages suffer strain and trauma and parents who so use their children are doing them a terrible hurt.

On occasion, each parent will try to get children to serve as allies. Many children, in an effort to please, will take the side of the parent with whom they are with at the time. Because of the dishonesty involved in such shifting loyalties, the children lose respect for themselves. They also live with the fear that their deceit will be revealed (which it most often is) and that they will suffer the alienation of those who have learned off it. Other children consistently side with a particular parent against the other and thereby compromise what could have been a rewarding relationship. This is especially the case for children who exhibit the symptoms of parental alienation syndrome.

I urge such children to try to assert themselves and refuse to take sides. The older the children, the more likely they will have the strength to say to each of the parents: "Please don't involve me." This does not mean, however, that I discourage children from gaining information about each of the parents and fighting their own battles. If, for example, a father gambles, then both children and mother suffer. The children of such a father should be encouraged to tell him how much the gambling bothers them. If the children's reform efforts prove futile (most often the case when the gambling is compulsive), then they have to be helped to resign themselves to this defect in their father and gain their gratifications elsewhere. A different situation would be one in which their mother intensely dislikes their father, but he loves them. The deficiencies that the mother sees in the father in no way affect his ability to love and care for his children. The children would do themselves and their father a disservice if they joined forces with their mother against their father. I try to help children appreciate that their parents' criticisms about one another (especially when made in anger) may not be completely trustworthy. Children should form their own opinions about each parent *on the basis of their own observations*.

Children are often used as scapegoats in the parental battle. Because Dad is no longer available, Mom may vent the hostility she feels toward him on her son who lives with her. Such scapegoating may be fostered by qualities—real or imagined—of the son that remind her of her former husband. A related phenomenon is that of the child's generalizing from the mother's hatred of the father and assuming that she therefore hates all males. It is an easy next step for him to imagine that she hates her son as well.

Some children take advantage of parental hostilities for their own ends. When with the mother they will try saying critical things about the father in order to gain special favors, privileges, or presents from her. And they may act similarly when with the father. Divorced parents are particularly susceptible to this maneuver because they so relish hearing critical things about one another; when it comes to critical information about the ex-spouse, they may exhibit amazing gullibility. Children should be shown that they cannot respect themselves when they engage in such deceitful maneuvers. And parents should interrupt the game once they are alerted to its occurrence. Some parents quickly catch on. Others are so angry that they cannot avoid getting sucked in and so are continually manipulated by their children—an unfortunate situation for all concerned.

DATING, SLEEPING TOGETHER, LIVING TOGETHER, AND REMARRIAGE

Children living in an intact home have to resign themselves to the fact that the same-sexed parent, and *only* the same-sexed parent, shares intimacies and has prerogatives with the opposite-sexed parent that they do not enjoy. They can do little but resign themselves to the jealous rivalries engendered in the typical family situation. But such resignation does not come easily. Children of divorce, whose parents are dating, have a much more difficult time alleviating their jealous possessive and sexual rivalries. A boy living with a dating mother—especially one who meets a large number of dates in her home—is likely to conclude that just about every man in the world shares intimacies with his mother that he does not. He need not know that sexual encounters are occurring to feel rejected. The fact that his mother spends time alone with his rivals and goes out with them, while he has to remain at home, is enough to produce feelings that he is a second-class citizen and feelings of resentment toward both his mother and her dates. A girl living with a dating father, or whose father exposes her to numerous women friends during visitation, is likely to react similarly. In addition, if the child looks forward to the parent's remarrying in order to compensate for the loss of a parent, each new date may raise hopes. Conversely, children who dread the thought of parental remarriage are being provided with exposure to the objects of their concerns.

It is common in such situations for a child to become very antagonistic to both the parent and the date and to employ various maneuvers to prevent the dating or alienate the date.

Last-minute temper tantrums; crying spells; "sickness" (often involving vomiting, soiling, diarrhea, and other dramatic and date-alienating manifestations); fierce sibling fighting; and sudden homework crises may be utilized. Or the child may be overtly hostile to the date in an effort to derail the relationship with the child's parent. Recognizing that embarrassing questions may have alienating value, the child may inquire, "Are you going to be my new daddy?" or, even more provocatively, "Are you going to sleep over here like some of the other men do?" A child may say, "Daddy's going to be angry at you when he finds out what you're doing," or "Does Mommy know that a lady is going to sleep over here tonight?" Sometimes the hostility the child feels toward the absent parent may be displaced onto a date—a safer target, whose total alienation would be no loss to the child whatsoever.

An adolescent girl whose mother has a whole series of affairs is likely to identify with her mother. She may come to adhere to the view that the greater the number of men she can attract, the more attractive she is. In addition, her awareness of her mother's activities can be very titillating, as she is stimulated to fantasize exactly what her mother is doing, and this can contribute to her desire to gain similar gratifications herself. Her jealous rivalry with her mother may cause her to compete with her. Such competition may be confined to boys of the daughter's own age, but at times she may seek older men and even her mother's lovers. She may be more seductive with her mother's men friends than with her father—viewing the latter (generally correctly) as less sexually available. Resolution of this problem in such girls is very difficult; they are so stimulated by older men that there is little desire to have a peer as the source of satisfaction. Similarly, a father who flaunts his popularity and sexual prowess with women in front of his adolescent boy is likely to produce strong jealous rivalries in his son. The youngster may then become obsessed with sexual conquests of large numbers of girls, even beyond the usual adolescent boy's obsessions in this department.

Youngsters exposed to parental promiscuity may occasionally react in the opposite way; that is, they may find sex repulsive and become sexually inhibited. In my experience, however, promiscuity is more likely than inhibition. This relates to the formidable power of the modeling effect and the desire to join the fun. But youngsters who do become promiscuous themselves under such circumstances are generally less concerned with the intimacies and pleasures of the sexual relationship than with the number of partners they can attract. Accordingly, they lose out on the deeper pleasures that may be derived from such relationships.

For all these reasons, I strongly urge parents not to expose their children to each new date but to meet their dates outside the home. When a parent has formed an ongoing relationship with someone, then the children should meet that person. Although such contacts are still likely to generate jealous rivalries, they can also provide children with many benefits. Ideally, the new person can help compensate the children in part for the absence of one of the parents—and this benefit cannot be underestimated. In addition, children should appreciate that this new relationship makes the parent with whom they live a happier person, and this promotes their own well-being. For example, when Mom is lonely, she may be grouchy; when she is happy, she will be more fun.

Some parents may go in the opposite direction and hide all dates, short-term or long-term. They often do this in order to avoid their children's hostile reactions. But such hiding is not in the children's best interests. It only entrenches the children's manipulations and deprives the children of the growth experience of dealing with something they find unpleasant. Such parents are probably afraid of anyone's anger and do well to look into this problem for their own sakes as well as that of their children.

Parents are sometimes concerned about the effects on the children of an opposite-sexed friend staying overnight in bed with the parent (without, of course, the child's observing or overhearing sexual activity). If such experiences occur with many different lovers, then the effects can be quite detrimental. If such intimacy is reserved for deep, ongoing relationships, I see no reason why the child should develop untoward reactions. It is the parade that is the dangerous thing, not sexual intercourse performed out of the child's presence or awareness.

Just as younger people are more frequently living together before marrying, many divorced people are doing so as well. And others may choose to live together without marriage necessarily being considered. The question is often raised about the psychological effects on children of such an arrangement. I believe that if a parent has the full conviction that the decision is a wise one, then the children are likely to accept it as well. If the parent has the strength to tolerate any social stigma that may result from such an arrangement (a stigma that has lessened in recent years), then the children are likely to tolerate it as well. If, however, the parent is ashamed of the arrangement, tries to keep it a secret, and also tries to enlist the children's aid in hiding it, then the children are likely to become confused and suffer unnecessary shame themselves. Maintaining a conspiracy of silence in which the children are sworn to secrecy places a terrible burden on them. They may have to forgo inviting their friends to the home, create excuses for not doing so, live with the fear that in spite of their efforts the secret may be revealed, and suffer guilt if they contribute to the secret's being divulged (which, of course, usually occurs). That parent's feelings about living together with another person become the children's.

Occasionally parents will seriously consider marrying people they are not sure about because they feel it would be good for the children to have a father or mother figure living in the home. Just as I generally discourage parents who are considering divorce from staying together "for the sake of the children" (at least as the primary reason), I similarly discourage single parents from remarrying for the children's sake. I am not suggesting that the children's needs be totally ignored in such deliberations, only that they not be given highest priority. Although I believe strongly that children do best in a situation in which mother and father figures are present, this does not mean that *any* mother or *any* father figure will do. The mother who has mixed feelings about remarriage but who is considering it for the children's sake must take into consideration the fact that a poor relationship between her and her new husband is likely to have harmful effects on the children. And she must consider her prospective husband's relationship with the children as well.

Occasionally a single parent will wonder about remarriage to someone who seems suitable and desirable in every way except that the person does not seem to have a good relationship with the children. Such a parent should try to determine whether the problems are the result of deficiencies in the potential spouse or are caused by distortions or difficulties in the children. If the potential spouse is the problem, the parent should try to determine the extent of the deficiency. If it is only a defect with regard to children, then the parent should be clear about this beforehand and recognize that it will be a drawback of the marriage. If there is a broader problem in human relationships, then the parent might do well to get a clearer picture of the potential spouse before making a definite decision. (Some joint counseling might be useful here.) On the other hand, if it is the children's problems that are compromising the relationship with the intended spouse, then it is inappropriate not to remarry for this reason. It is not in the children's best interests psychologically to comply with their inappropriate or unreasonable demands; to do so would only encourage their maladaptive behavior.

Remarriage to someone who enjoys financial security is often very tempting. If alleviation from financial pressures is the primary or even exclusive reason for remarrying, then the children (and both partners in the new marriage as well) are bound to suffer. Financial privation produces psychological difficulties; but a second unhappy marriage is likely to produce even greater ones. I cannot discourage parents strongly enough from entering into such an ill-conceived arrangement.

One of the single parent's greatest dangers is remarrying for the same unhealthy reasons that brought about the first marriage. In all marriages there is a dovetailing of healthy and unhealthy behavior patterns that exist in each of the partners. In the relatively stable marital relationship there is a preponderance of the healthy factors; in the unstable marriage (whether or not it ends in divorce) there is a predominance of the unhealthy. Since the unhealthy, psychopathological factors are often unconscious, a divorced parent may gravitate, without realizing it, toward involvement with a new partner who will provide the same sick gratifications as the old. Parents may resolve never again to get involved with a person who has the same personality patterns that contributed to the deterioration of the marriage, yet they may unconsciously do so. They may believe that the new marriage is different, being unaware that the new spouse has the same psychological illness(es) as the old and that the same sick patterns of interaction are bound to ensue. This fact may be obvious, however, to others. Friends and relatives often remark: "You know, it's amazing. Alice vowed never again to get involved with someone who's going to exploit her like Harry did. Her new husband is Harry in another body. I don't know how she doesn't see it. He's a loser from way back. In six months she'll be supporting him. How can she be so blind?"

Single parents should be ever alert to this danger. If the prospective spouse has been married before, they should find out exactly what caused the breakdown of the previous marriage(s). (I am truly amazed by the number of people who do not make such inquiries; even after they have remarried they may know very little about the reasons for the failure of the new spouse's former marriage.) The failure to gain such information may serve the forces that compel the person to find someone to complement the sick patterns of interaction. The refusal to make such inquiries is often justified with such rationalizations as "It's none of my business," or "It's water under the bridge; nothing can be accomplished by bringing it up," or "I never discussed it because I knew it would upset him (her)." If, when contemplating remarriage, a couple begins encountering difficulties in the new relationship, they should seek counseling in order to determine whether they are involving themselves in the same old sick type of relationship. I have seen many remarriages that were uncannily similar to the previous ones—with the same tragic consequences to both the spouses and their children.

An example of such a parent was John, who first came to me because of difficulties in his relationship with Brenda, his second wife. John was a commercial artist who, although not ambitious or a large earner, had gained a solid reputation and had a secure position with a large advertising firm. He married his first wife, Joan, a very wealthy young woman, while he was still a student, and they were supported by her parents. Following graduation John suffered little anxiety over his lack of advancement because he was secure in the knowledge that his wife's money would always be available. However, Joan became less and less respectful of him, started to have affairs with other men, and after eight years of marriage asked John for a divorce.

John came for marital counseling during the fifteenth year of his second marriage because he and his wife, Brenda, were always squabbling over how to deal with the children. John believed that Brenda was overindulgent of them, whereas Brenda considered John to be jealous of any attentions she gave to the children. As it turned out, Brenda's view of the situation coincided with mine. John actually viewed himself as a rival of the children for his wife's affection and would basically have been happier if he had had no children, even though he professed great love for them. Brenda had many real estate holdings, which she had acquired from her father, with whom she was still in business. Although her money was kept separate for such things as vacations and the children's education, it was clear that her income gave John much greater flexibility regarding what he could do with his earnings. Brenda, like John's first wife, Joan, had little basic respect for him. I saw John in therapy over a period of about a year, during which time Brenda joined us about ten or fifteen times for marital counseling. But John never really understood his dependency on his wife; and Brenda had little interest in changing qualities within herself (such as controlling attitudes and sexual inhibitions) that were compounding the marital problems. The marriage ended in divorce, at Brenda's initiation.

Following the separation and divorce John continued in

individual treatment with me. Although a passive and shy man, he did date—but mainly women who were assertive enough to initiate contact and to communicate fairly openly that they would be receptive to dating him. Although John gained some insight into his passivity, the pattern was too ego-enhancing for him to give it up and start risking rejection by being the initiator.

About a year after his separation John told me about a new woman he had met, a widow named Yvonne, whose husband had left her fairly well off and who also had a very good income from a business of her own. From what John said about her, and from what I observed during two interviews with John and Yvonne, it was clear to me that Yvonne was materialistic and domineering and had little basic respect for John. It was clear, however, that she was desperately intent on getting married again and that John was going to be the man. Although it was not my role to tell John whether or not he should marry, it was my job to help him see how he was reproducing his old patterns. John married. Six months later he left Yvonne because he felt that she was leading him around by the nose. Perhaps it was a sign of health on John's part that he initiated the separation. Soon afterward John got a job in another city, and I never saw him again. I considered it likely that if he did not get more therapy he would probably involve himself once again with the very same woman, though once again in a different body.

6

The Children's Involvements with Others

The effects of separation and divorce extend beyond the nuclear family to grandparents, stepfamilies, and the larger community. Chapter 3 discussed problems with children's peers and how best to deal with them. This chapter focuses on children of divorce in their various other relationships.

GRANDPARENTS

Just as in-laws may play a significant role in a couple's decision to marry, they can also contribute to a couple's marital difficulties. A wife may complain, for example, that her husband is still a child in his relationship with his parents. A husband may displace onto his in-laws his hostilities toward his own parents—thereby causing a loyalty conflict in his wife. Often in-laws feel that their son- or daughter-in-law does not live up to the image they had of what their son- or daughter-in-law would be like. Parents generally tend to idealize their children. (Such overvaluation, within reason, is probably useful to the growing child, because it can serve to enhance self-esteem.) And when the child becomes of marriage age, parents tend to assume that the only suitable mate for their wonderful son or daughter is another perfect person. When the son or daughter marries a mere human being, disappointment is often communicated to the couple. And the son or daughter's involvement with the new spouse may thereby be compromised. When marital problems arise, each set of in-laws may side with their own son or daughter. In-laws may play a significant role, too, in helping a son or daughter decide either to dissolve or to maintain an unhappy marriage. They may, for example, encourage the couple to stick it out to spare the older generation embarrassment over the divorce. Or a woman's parents may discourage her from divorcing because they fear that she will once again become dependent on them or even move back home—this time with the children.

In an intact family the two sets of grandparents sometimes compete with one another (sometimes openly, sometimes covertly) for the affection of the grandchildren. When this competition is kept within reasonable bounds, the children may benefit, because it can provide them with much attention, affection, and a deep sense of family belonging. However, when the children are subjected to interrogations about which grandparents they like better or are asked to take sides in conflicts between the two sets of grandparents, the benefits of such affection are significantly diluted. When marital problems arise, the grandparents may become embroiled in the couple's conflict—contributing to the problems that beset children at such times. But if the grandparents can rise above the feuding, both they and their grandchildren may enjoy the benefits of their continued good relationships with one another.

Returning to the home of the children's grandparents. Following the separation, a mother with children may return to live with her parents. (Although fathers with custody of the children may also do this, it is far less common for them to do so.) Often financial considerations make this a reasonable and possibly the best decision. If the mother has to work, it is often good for the children to be taken care of by their

grandparents, who may make excellent parental substitutes—especially the grandfather as a replacement for the absent father. Grandparents usually love the children more deeply than any housekeeper the working parent could provide. However, there are a number of drawbacks to such an arrangement. Although the grandparents can enjoy a joyful relationship with their grandchildren when they visit on Sundays, living with the children is an entirely different story. When one has to change diapers, get up in the middle of the night with a sick child, break up sibling bickering, and so on, the joys of grandparenthood may diminish rapidly. In addition, the grandparents are likely to become resentful of the new obligations that they now have to assume. They've been through the child-rearing bit; and they've looked forward to a little more relaxation in their old age. Now they suddenly find themselves having to go through the whole scene again. And such resentment can contribute to conflict between the grandparents and their daughter. Having just moved out of one home that was filled with strife, the children now find themselves in another. Or the resentments that the grandparents may feel toward their daughter for providing them with this new and unanticipated burden may be displaced onto the children. Or the unhappiness the mother feels in such a situation may make her less loving as a mother to the children. In all these cases the children suffer psychologically.

Another problem that may arise when mother and children move into the grandparents' home relates to the mother's dependency on her parents. A more mature and independent mother will generally be willing to suffer many deprivations and inconveniences rather than move back with her parents. But a more dependent and immature mother may more readily choose the alternative of living once again with her parents. Unlike the more independent woman, she may see nothing inappropriate about the situation, may suffer no embarrassment over it, and may even welcome it. The children of such a dependent woman ultimately appreciate that their mother is really still a child in her relationship with her parents. Their respect for her is diminished, as is their confidence in her as a protector and source of guidance. They may look then to their grandparents as their true sources of strength—a situation that is quite detrimental to their relationship with their mother. Children in such a situation may consider themselves to have suffered two losses: (1) their father from the household and (2) their mother to their grandparents.

Martha married Bill when she was seventeen and he twenty. During the first three years of their marriage they lived in the home of Martha's parents while Bill studied accounting at a nearby college. Martha worked as a secretary during the first year of marriage, then became pregnant and stayed at home with her new baby. Even during this early period, Martha sensed that things were not going well between Bill and herself. He often liked to stay out late with his single boyfriends, whom he described as still "free." Martha felt that Bill still had some growing up to do and had to get youthful escapades out of his system. From the outset, as well, there were frequent fights over what Bill felt was intrusiveness by his in-laws into his and Martha's marriage. Particularly, he felt that his mother-in-law was forever telling his wife what to do and that she was always complying. He felt his wife didn't "have a mind of her own."

Soon after graduation Bill got a job and the couple decided to find their own apartment. Martha was pregnant again and decided it would be a good idea to find a place near the home of her parents, so that her mother would be available to help with the children. Although Bill would have preferred a place farther away, he reluctantly agreed to Martha's request. Martha's mother spent hours at the house, and there were three or four telephone calls each day to Martha's parents' home.

During the next few years Bill spent less and less time at the apartment. Ostensibly this was related to long working hours. Actually, he felt excluded from the continuing close relationship between Martha and her parents and came to feel more and more uncomfortable at home. Not surprisingly, he met another woman, began to have an affair, and finally told Martha that he wanted a divorce. Not surprisingly, Martha and her two children then moved back into the home of her parents, and there they stayed.

I met Martha when Tom, her oldest child, was nine years old. Tom was doing poorly in school in spite of high intelligence, concentrated on his schoolwork only when his teacher gave him one-to-one instruction, and had few friends. He was easily taken advantage of and would go home crying to his mother when teased. He was frequently called "Momma's baby" and "Sissy." Tom was a very immature child who had been overprotected by his mother and grandmother. He had become quite dependent on others, and this interfered with his applying himself independently to his schoolwork. In addition, he had never had the toughening up that enables most youngsters to get along with their peers. Beside the overprotection of his mother and grandmother, Tom got little if any guidance or protection from his father, who rarely visited. Although Martha dated, she had not remarried because Mr. Right had not yet come along. On further inquiry, it emerged that Mr. Right would have been someone who appreciated the value and beauty of the close relationship Martha had with her mother.

In his first session Tom drew a picture and told me a story about it. The picture showed a tree, on the branches of which a bird had landed. Each time the bird alighted the branch broke, and so it tried a lower branch. And each subsequent branch broke as well, even though the bird was very light. The bird then went on to a second tree and suffered the same experience. Finally, the bird found a big tall tree, on the top of a high mountain, with branches that held it. It seemed to me that the first tree represented Tom's father, who had proved unwilling to provide Tom with emotional support. The second tree, I believed, symbolized Tom's mother, who, because of her dependency on her own mother, was not seen by Tom as someone who could support him either. And the tree on the top of the mountain stood for his grandmother, the one who really had the power in the family. This interpretation of Tom's picture and story was confirmed in a dream that Tom related during his second session. In the dream Tom walks past his mother and goes up to his grandmother and asks her for some money to buy ice cream. His grandmother gives him the money and he happily skips off to the store. I considered the dream to reflect Tom's feelings that his grandmother was the source of power. In addition, the ice cream well symbolized all the material things and affection that a loving person could provide. And it was the grandmother, not the mother, who was seen as the provider of such goodies.

In Tom's case I felt that work with Martha as well was important if I was to help Tom. It would have been extremely difficult to help Tom with his overdependency problem if the only parent he had to identify with was an overdependent person herself and if, in addition, she was continuing to overprotect him. In this case, things went well in treatment. Martha began to see how much a child she still was in her relationships with her parents, and as she matured in treatment, Tom became more respectful of her and identified more with her maturity. In addition, Tom himself was helped to become more independent. After about fifteen months of treatment, Martha got a job and moved out of her parents' house. Although it was rough going at times, Martha managed to function on her own. About a year after leaving her parents she met a man whom she ultimately married—this time forming a relationship that was much more mature and egalitarian than that which she had with Bill.

Another possible source of difficulty when a mother moves back to her parents' home is that the mother and grandmother may become quite competitive with one another over who "knows best" how to take care of the children. The children may be subjected to very different schools of thought regarding their upbringing and can become confused and divided in their loyalties. Mother may consider herself to be using child-rearing techniques reflective of the latest advances in psychological thinking. Grandmother, however, may have the deepest respect for the good old-fashioned methods that she was raised on and that served her so well in the upbringing of her daughter. Or the grandmother may be ambivalent about disciplining the children. She may consider this to be the role of their mother. Or she may want to avoid giving the children any reason to be angry at her. In this way she enjoys the reputation of the all-loving, all-giving, good Grandma, and her daughter is looked upon as the family witch—again, not a situation conducive to the children's having a healthy relationship with their mother, or their grandmother.

The joy of grandparents. At times these potential drawbacks to the mother's returning to the home of her parents may not exist (or they may be negligible), and the children may profit greatly from the arrangement.

After all, much of what I have said about mothers who return to the homes of their parents is applicable only to Western culture in the last hundred years or so. Previously, and in many parts of the world even today, a newly married couple could not enjoy the luxury of a separate home, or even room(s). Not only did three generations often occupy the same home, but an assortment of the children's uncles, aunts, cousins, or other relatives as well. Divorce or abandonment by a parent in such an arrangement was probably far less traumatic than it is for children in twentieth-century Western culture. In the extended family arrangement the children have many familiar surrogates—people with whom they have lived all their lives—who can take over the parental role when a parent leaves the household. And grandparents today have the potential to provide children of divorce with similar security and gratifications. More people today are reaching old age than ever before, and the elderly sometimes find themselves feeling useless in a society that is not optimally designed to utilize their talents, skills, and experience. For many grandparents the presence of grandchildren in their home can provide them with a new lease on life, and a new sense of purpose.

Separated parents do their children a terrible disservice by drawing grandparents into their conflict or by allowing themselves to be polarized further by grandparents' involvement. Ideally, parents should be able to see the grandparents as important sources of emotional gratification for their children and as people who, possibly more than anyone else, have the interest and capacity to provide their children with love and affection—the most effective preventives of and antidotes to the harmful psychological effects of divorce.

STEPPARENTS

When stepchildren are involved in remarriage, the couple commonly fantasizes that the new marriage will provide a normal and natural family life. But such expectations are rarely realized, because of the multiple problems that predictably beset such new families. If the children have been given promises of a rosy new life after the remarriage, they too are likely to be disillusioned, even though the new arrangement may be far superior to any they may have previously had.

The wicked stepmother. In legend and fairy tale, stepmothers have traditionally been cruel and wicked. In real life as well, stepmothers are not commonly portrayed as benevolent. So deeply ingrained is the stepmother's bad reputation that the name itself is almost intrinsically disparaging. The word has become so associated with unpleasant connotations that many stepmothers insist that the term not be used, especially when they themselves are being referred to.

I believe that one of the reasons for this tradition is the fact that a stepmother is a convenient person upon whom children can displace unexpressed hostility against their natural mothers. When a mother dies, her children may harbor feelings of resentment toward her for having "abandoned" them— in spite of their awareness that she did not wish to die. Obviously, such hostility cannot usually be expressed in any way. A stepmother, as a maternal figure who is very much alive and available, may serve as an ideal target. And when a natural mother is alive but divorced, guilt over and fear of her loss and rejection may prevent a child from directly expressing anger to her. Again, a stepmother may serve well as a substitute.

Another factor is that the stepmother may not love the

stepchildren as much as their natural mother. This is not surprising; it would be unreasonable to expect the bonding between stepmothers and stepchildren to be as strong as that between biological mothers and their children. The children inevitably sense this difference and are apt to view it as a manifestation of the stepmother's "meanness." The problem is often further enhanced, of course, when the father and the stepmother have their own children.

The mother vs. the stepmother. Natural mothers and stepmothers, almost predictably, are rivalrous. A stepmother, in order to ingratiate herself with her husband, may endeavor to form a good relationship with his children. It is rare for a natural mother to respond with enthusiasm to these overtures. Mothers are usually somewhat possessive of their children. They do not take well to others who try to mother them, attempt to give them significant maternal affection, or otherwise take them under their wings. The children are thereby placed in a conflictive situation. With their loyalties divided between their mother and stepmother, they usually side with their mother—the one with whom they usually have the deeper and more important relationship. One could argue that a really mature mother would appreciate that a stepmother can offer her children many satisfactions and that three loving adults are better than two. But I myself have met very few such women. And it is probably unrealistic for a husband to hope that his former wife will have anything more than a formal and somewhat stiff relationship with his new wife. Although it would probably be better for the children if there were friendliness between the two women, and on occasion I have seen it happen, it is an unrealistic goal to hope for or pursue.

The competition between a stepmother and her husband's former wife is intensified by the fact that the presence of the children requires their father's continual contact with his ex-spouse. When stepchildren are not present, a new wife has far fewer fears about her husband's maintaining a relationship with the woman with whom he was previously involved. The stepchildren situation requires it. Even though the husband may have achieved a state of true psychological divorce, the other woman is still there as a rival for his time, interest, money, and involvement. And if the husband has not achieved a satisfactory resolution of his conflicts with his former wife, the maintenance of the malevolent involvement not only deprives the new spouse of a relatively content husband but threatens the new relationship, because such maintenance of hostilities represents a closer tie than a neutral involvement. In such situations the rivalry between the two women is likely to become quite intense.

Stepmothers should face up to the fact that the cards may be stacked against them with regard to their forming a loving relationship with their stepchildren. Even when the natural mother has totally rejected or abandoned the children, the stepmother may find herself the butt of displaced hostility. She must try not to take all such anger personally. If she is genuinely affectionate, the children will come to appreciate her and develop a warm and even loving relationship with her.

A stepmother should also be aware that she probably harbors some misconceptions about her husband's former wife. She may have spent countless hours listening to her husband describe the various indignities he has suffered at the hands of his former wife. Naturally, she will tend to side with her husband. If he is still trying to wreak vengeance on his former wife or maintaining other forms of hostile interaction, she is bound to become his ally in the battle. In such an atmosphere it is not likely that she will be able to form a good relationship with the stepchildren, because of their ties with their natural mother. This is just another example of the harmful effects of postmarital warfare and another reason why it behooves divorced parents to do everything possible to bring about a truce.

Fathers and stepfathers. Stepfathers, in my experience, do not seem to develop the same kinds of hostile relationships with their wives' former husband as stepmothers do with their husbands' former wives. Men, it appears, do not seem to be as jealous and possessive as women with regard to the children's developing affectionate relationships with others. This is probably related in part to the closer relationship that the mother, as the bearer of the children, has with her offspring. But social factors are very important here as well. A society that does not provide the female with opportunities for self-fulfillment in areas other than childbearing and child rearing is likely to produce women who jealously covet their children—their primary source of feelings of self-importance. In such a society men, having sources of ego-gratification in their careers, are likely to be less dependent on their children to give their lives meaning and less jealous of those who share their children's affection.

Stepfathers often believe it is important that they strictly refrain from criticizing their stepchildren's natural father in front of them. (And many professional authorities warn about the detrimental effects on stepchildren of such criticisms of their father.) But I think this is a mistake. Children do best when they have as accurate a picture as possible of their parents—their assets as well as their liabilities. The stepfather can be a source of valuable information about the children's father. He should be reasonably balanced and objective when providing such information. The fact that he may not always be completely objective is not reason for suggesting that he shut up entirely. The children have to be helped to determine when such information is likely to be inaccurate (when it is provided in a state of rage, for example) and to rely, as well, on their own observations.

Children's affection (or lack of it) for their stepparents. It is common for stepchildren, viewing the new marriage as a source of pain, to fantasize breaking it up. They particularly enjoy the idea of harm befalling the stepmother, whom they may view as the source of all their woes. Fairy tales certainly derive their power from such fantasies. In the typical tale the stepchild suffers a series of pains and humiliations but ultimately ends up in a far happier state than the stepmother and her allied persecutors. Snow White ends up marrying a handsome prince, whereas her wicked stepmother, the queen, is forced to dance to her death wearing red-hot iron shoes (or, in the Walt Disney version, to leap into a bottomless chasm). Hansel and Gretel first kill the witch (who symbolizes their cruel stepmother), then return home to find out that their stepmother has conveniently died. Cinderella escapes from her stepmother and stepsisters by marrying a handsome prince. She ostensibly forgives her stepmother and stepsisters and invites them to her wedding. Then, as fate would have it, doves pluck out the stepsisters' eyes—right at the wedding. Subsequently they too conveniently die.

Besides the use of the stepparent as a target for displaced hostility toward the natural parent, other factors may contribute to difficulties between children and their stepparents. We all experience some fears in new relationships, and children, being less competent to handle them, even more so. Children of divorce will usually be even more hesitant than children from an intact home to involve themselves with a strange adult. Having lost one important adult already, they anticipate a recurrence of the abandonment and are likely to need time to warm up. Adults do well to take these factors into consideration. Coming on too strongly and overwhelming the potential stepchildren may make it even more difficult for them to get involved.

Another factor is children's projection of their own hostility onto the stepparent. A child may reduce guilt over anger by disowning it and attributing it to a stepparent. It is as if the child were saying: "It is not I who have hateful feelings toward her (him); she (he) is the one who hates me." A stepparent is preferable to a biological parent as a target for such projections because of children's need to view their parents as good and kind and wise. Furthermore, because stepparents have already been considered an expendable commodity, their rejection and removal for hating the child would not be viewed particularly as a loss. The child, however, will not so readily wish to remove a natural parent upon whom hostility has been projected.

Hostile behavior toward a stepparent can serve to test a natural parent's loyalty. When a stepmother, for example, is provoked by a child and an argument ensues, Dad is often called upon to intervene or mediate. In such situations the child can learn with whom Dad's true feelings lie: his own flesh and blood or his chosen wife.

When a parent leaves the home, children are generally deeply resentful. The appearance of a stepparent on the scene may cause additional anger. When stepsiblings are brought in as part of the bargain, children may become even more embittered. And the stepparent, as the one who has intruded in the relationship between child and natural parent, and as the one who has brought along a horde of other intruders, can readily become a target of formidable anger.

Sexual rivalries may contribute to problems in children's (especially adolescents') relationships with their stepparents. A factor that operates in such conflicts is the incest taboo. In the distant past, it was probably recognized that the survival of civilized society depended upon a stable family life, and that free sexual access of family members to one another could be a disruptive influence on such family stability. Accordingly, incest taboos were created—not out of moral or ethical principles, I believe, but from the very practical observation that the very survival of the society depended upon them.

Our sexual hormones, however, know nothing of incest taboos. They produce sexual cravings with little concern for whether the object happens to be a relative. We have to learn that certain people are "off limits." Even in the relatively stable, intact home, however, children may be quite obvious about their physical desires toward the opposite-sexed parent. Such desires may not be specifically for heterosexual intercourse, but they do include various other kinds of heterosexual activities; erotic play, for example, or the observation of undressing and toilet functions. And if there is parental seduction, then the child's sexual cravings are likely to be intensified.

In the adolescent period, when sexual desires become markedly intensified, these urges may become particularly strong—even toward a biological parent. And whereas in childhood the likelihood of reciprocal sexual interest by the opposite-sexed parent was small, in adolescence the child's sexual development may be a source of sexual stimulation to the parent. It is quite common for such mutual attractions to be repressed by both parents and children. However, like most repressed impulses, they often find release though disguised expression. For example, an adolescent girl may complain how "disgusting" her father is when engaging in everyday physical functions. She may become "nauseated" by his chewing at the dinner table or the sounds of his brushing his teeth. Such disgust generally serves to repress from conscious awareness the sexual titillation that results from physical activities—which may suggest sexual activity to the teenage daughter, as she generally has no closer access to her father's more directly sexual forms of animal functioning. Or father and adolescent daughter may cover up their sexual attractions to one another by frequent bickering. Angry interchanges can hide underlying loving feelings and serve to distract the individuals from the feelings that press for release.

With stepparents the incest taboo is usually less strong on the part of both the children and the adults. Neither has had years of living together to internalize the incest taboo. Also, years of familiarization lessen novelty. Stepparents and stepchildren are very new to one another and therefore more likely to be sexually stimulated by one another. Accordingly, the situation becomes much more highly charged, and the maneuvers to decompress it more formidable. Violent arguments between stepfather and stepdaughter or between stepmother and stepson are one of the more common ways in which both may protect themselves from their sexual feelings. Furthermore, before separation, the children may have resigned themselves to the fact that the parental bond is unbreakable and that sexual-possessive cravings for the opposite-sexed parent are futile. But when the parents break up and a newcomer replaces one of the parents, the child is less likely to view the marital relationship as inviolable. A boy living alone with his mother may consider the arrangement a fulfillment of sexual-possessive fantasies. The appearance of a stepfather on the scene robs him of his total possession of his mother. Accordingly, the rivalry with and hostility toward the stepfather may become very intense. A girl living with her divorced father may have similar reactions to her new stepmother.

Prior to the separation the child had to come to terms with *one* rival for the affection of the opposite-sexed parent. Now that that one has been displaced, a second has suddenly appeared on the scene. Sometimes the sexual titillation, rivalries, guilt, frustration, and hostility produced by the sexual feelings between teenaged stepchild and the opposite-sexed stepparent can become so intense that the youngster's leaving the home (to live with the other parent or go to boarding school, for example) may be the only viable solution to the problem.

Myra's situation provides an example. Myra was sixteen when her parents separated because her father was having an affair with Gail, a twenty-five-year-old woman. Following the separation Myra and her two brothers lived with her father, because her mother did not feel that she could cope with raising the three children herself. One year later the father married Gail, who had never been married before.

Since Myra's father was about fifty at the time, Gail was much closer in age to Myra than she was to Myra's father. In addition, Gail claimed that she hoped to be a "friend" to Myra rather than a mother. In fact, it was quite apparent that Gail was so immature herself that she could not have assumed a mother role to an infant, let alone to a seventeen-year-old girl. Gail was demanding of her husband, kittenish, and self-indulgent. She thought about little other than clothing, jewelry, cosmetics, and decorating her new home. Myra ostensibly welcomed Gail's decision to be a friend rather than a mother, but in my work with Myra it became apparent that she was disappointed; she still basically wanted guidance and protection, even though she could not openly admit this.

Soon after Gail moved in, she and Myra began lending one another clothing, confiding in one another (even personal matters between Gail and Myra's father), and often passing as sisters. The honeymoon, however, was short-lived. Myra began to complain that her father always took his wife's side over hers. Myra resented her father and Gail going out without her. On a few occasions Myra knocked on her father and stepmother's bedroom door and was told to go away with reasons such as "we're resting." Myra was convinced that they were making love and bitterly complained: "They're just like animals. They have no sensitivity to the feelings of others." Within two months, bitter fighting between Gail, Myra, and the father became almost incessant. It was clear that Myra was furious at her father for choosing a "peer" over her for a wife. And she was jealous of Gail's intimacy with her father, a jealousy made worse by Gail's flaunting her relationship with her father under the guise of divulging intimacies to a close friend.

It quickly became apparent to me that all three would probably require years of intensive therapy to have any hope of dealing successfully with this problem. Myra was in her third year of high school at the time of the marriage, and I concluded that her being out of the home would probably be the most expedient (if not the only) way of decompressing the situation. I decided that the pains of yet another separation would be less than those she was suffering in this intolerable situation. Accordingly, I raised the question of boarding school. Each member of what had psychologically become a mènage á trois had mixed feelings about the recommendation, but all finally agreed that it would probably be best for all concerned—which it proved to be. Although Myra's example is an extreme one, the basic rivalries exhibited in her situation are common.

Other factors may contribute, in varying degree, to children's impairments in their relationships with stepparents. Stepchildren may feel guilty over their resentments toward their stepparents and believe that there are other good, upstanding children who harbor no such hostilities. Parents should reassure such children that their hostile reactions are normal and inevitable. If the parents themselves believe that children should be capable of unadulterated benevolence toward stepparents, then they are placing an unnecessary burden upon the children and contributing to their feelings of guilt. Parents should encourage their children to form good relationships with their stepparents in the hope that the painful angry feelings will be replaced by more enjoyable loving feelings.

Children often blame stepparents for the breakup of their parents' marriage. Obviously, in certain cases, from the children's point of view, it does appear as if the new partner brought about a breakup of the marriage. Children often do not appreciate that the new partner did not come upon the scene of a loving, secure marriage and then by force, seductivity, or other disruptive maneuvers lure away one of the partners. Rather, there has usually been fertile ground for marital destabilization. It may be very difficult to convince children that this was the case, especially if the rejected partner professes strongly that the marriage was a good one until the appearance of the third party. There are situations in which the new partner did not appear on the scene until after the separation—and even then children are likely to blame the new person for breaking up the marriage. They may entertain fantasies that if the new partner hadn't appeared on the scene the parents might have reconciled. Remarriage represents a final statement of the demise of the original marriage and is likely to shake children's reconciliation fantasies at their very foundations. Even after remarriage, however, children may persist with such fantasies, making comments like: "You divorced Daddy and married Marc. Why don't you just divorce Marc and marry Daddy again?" Children sometimes view marriage and divorce as a flip-flop situation where parents can slide easily out of one marriage and into another, then vice versa. Blaming the stepparent for the breakup may also be a manifestation of displaced hostility; and again, the stepparent serves well as a target for such anger because he or she is expendable anyway. Parents should try to understand the factors behind the children's blaming the stepparent and should try to correct distortions in the hope that the animosity that derives from such blame might be reduced.

The better the children's relationships with their natural parents, the greater the likelihood of their developing good relationships with their stepparents. If children, for example, have a relatively healthy relationship with their mother, they will tend to generalize and view other adult females (including potential stepmothers) as benevolent and will anticipate good treatment from them. In contrast, children whose relationships with their mothers have been bad, who have been significantly rejected or neglected by their mothers, will expect similar treatment from a stepmother, and this is likely to interfere with their forming a good relationship with her. Obviously, the stepparent's own personality and attitudes toward the children will play some role in whether a good relationship develops.

Stepparents' affection (or lack of it) for their stepchildren. Because of the many factors that may interfere with children's feeling affectionate toward stepparents, stepparents are likely to be slowed down in developing loving feelings toward the children. Genuine love must involve reciprocity. If the object of our affection shows little inclination to respond, our ardor tends to diminish. There are however, additional factors present in the stepparents—factors independent of the children—that contribute to difficulties in their relationships with their stepchildren.

First, it is unreasonable to expect stepparents to have the same strong bonds of affection for stepchildren as they have for their biological children. We are more likely to develop a strong psychological bond with a child of our "own flesh and blood" than with a child born of other parents. I am not claiming that it is not *possible* for stepparents to love a stepchild as much as their own; I am only saying that it is entirely reasonable that they may not, and that this is no cause for self-reproach. There are stepparents who, although they feel a preference for their natural children, feel that it would be harmful to reveal this to the stepchildren. "They're all the same to me," they profess. "Sometimes I forget which ones are mine, which ones theirs, and which ones ours." I find such "forgetfulness" incredible and so, I believe, do the children involved. Such a stepparent would do better to convey to the stepchildren, in the appropriate context, thoughts along these lines: "Yes, I do love my own children in a special way. I have known them much longer and there has been more time for our love to grow. I do feel great affection for you children, and the more loving things we do for one another, the more our love should grow. And that's the same with my children as well." The last statement should let children know that love must be worked at—whether one is a natural child or a step-child. Along these lines, the stepparent is well advised to take it slowly and let the relationship grow. Overwhelmingly step-children with kisses, fulsome praise, gifts, and so on is bound to turn them off and retard, if not squelch, the development of healthy, affectionate relationships.

A factor that also predictably contributes to stepparent hostility toward stepchildren is that they are an ever-present reminder of the previous marriage—the marriage that once was, the marriage that both partners might like to forget. The stepchildren also require continual involvement with former spouses, a situation likely to engender in the stepparents resentment that may be directed toward the stepchildren.

Another common problem relates to the marked differences between premarital fantasy and postmarital fact. A woman with no children of her own, when in love with a man who has children, may entertain fantasies about how wonderful life will be with him and his children. In her enthusiasm to get married she may underestimate the problems she will face after she has achieved her goal. Or she may feign affection for the children, recognizing that such displays will make her more attractive to her would-be husband. After marriage, and after the lessening of romantic euphoria that inevitably occurs, the bride may become oppressed with the new burden she has taken on. A mother eases into the role of motherhood and gradually becomes accustomed to its frustrations. A step-mother has parenthood thrust upon her and may feel trapped and overwhelmed. Such a stepmother often becomes resentful and is likely to focus her resentment on the children, whom she will consider the basic cause of her difficulties. Even when the children live with their mother and visit on weekends, the stepmother may discover that instead of spending weekends alone with her, her husband is either off with his children or entertaining them in the house. Her anger toward the children, inevitably sensed by them, results in a further deterioration of the relationship.

One of the most common complaints made by stepmothers is that they are not appreciated by the stepchildren. The stepchildren come on weekends and "eat, slop, demand, and take, take, take—there's never a 'thank you' or one word of appreciation." The children, of course, are just treating the stepmother like their own mother. Who ever heard of children saying "thank you" to their mother for feeding them? From the stepmother's vantage point, the children "are guests, should behave as such, should be polite, and should at least show token appreciation for what is being given them—even though they may not mean it." Pleas to the father that he try to engender in the children a little more appreciation often prove futile. The children's motivation to consider the stepmother's feelings is likely to be further reduced if they see the stepmother as someone whose presence they have to tolerate if they are to spend time with their father. The situation then may deteriorate to one in which the stepmother feigns desire that the children visit, but in which her false smiles and stiff manner betray her lack of commitment. The children sense her underlying rejection, hesitate to come, and when they do, are even less prone to be appreciative of the stepmother's efforts on their behalf.

Loyalty conflicts are inevitable when stepchildren are on the scene. In conflicts between the stepparent and stepchildren, the father's or mother's loyalty to both sides is continually being tested. When more kids are in the home ("his, hers, and ours") a stepmother needs to devote significant time to the children's upbringing. The father, although he may recognize the necessity of his new wife's time-consuming involvements with the children, feels rejected. And when the stepmother directs her attentions to her husband, the children become resentful. The woman may feel continually guilty, unworthy, and resentful of the children. Loyalty resentments are further compounded by each parent's natural tendency to view the children as an extension of him- or herself. When a stepparent criticizes a spouse's children, the spouse may consider himself or herself to be the one who is being criticized. Last, when a father spends time with his new wife's children, who live with him, he cannot but feel some disloyalty to his own children, who are living with their mother. Resentment of the children who by their very existence produce such guilt is common if not inevitable.

There is no perfect solution to these loyalty problems. Every party appears to feel that he or she is being shortchanged or neglected. The best one can hope for is that each party be sympathetic to the other's loyalty conflict and all resign themselves to the fact that with more people around, all have to spread themselves a little thinner. All have to give more and take less.

Because stepparents are not natural parents there is a danger that they will be less committed to the children's upbringing. For example, the children may not get the parental support and encouragement of educational pursuits that play such an important role in the children's motivation in school. On the positive side, the stepparent is less likely to have the kind of exaggerated commitment to the children's growth and development that can place inordinate pressures on them and may result in their pursuing their goals with less, rather than more, enthusiasm.

What should stepchildren call their stepparents? It is the basic relationship between the stepparent and stepchild that is important, not the names they use to address one another.

Parents should not try to force stepchildren to use a name that they are not comfortable with. Often this is done in an effort to provide an appearance of intimacy and closeness for an uneasy relationship—but such coercion only makes the relationship worse. For example, insisting that the children call a new stepparent *Mom* or *Dad*, when the children hardly know the person, is likely to produce resentments. The child's using terms like *Mom* or *Dad* can also be confusing, in that people may not know whether the child is referring to the natural parent or to the stepparent. In addition, natural parents generally object to the child's using these terms with the stepparent. And the child will generally feel some disloyalty when doing so. Because the special relationship that most often exists between a child and a natural parent cannot so easily be formed with a stepparent, referring to stepparents as *Mom* and *Dad* is often contrived and probably should be avoided. When, however, the child's relationship with the natural parent is either significantly deficient or impaired and there exists a genuine desire to use these terms with the stepparent, then I can see no objection to them.

In the more common situation, in which the children still have a healthy relationship with the natural parent, many children will use some combination of *Mom, Ma, Momma, Daddy, Dad* or *Pa* and the stepparent's first name. Some may call the natural mother *Mommy* and the stepmother *Mom;* the natural father *Daddy* and the stepfather *Dad*. Others will just use the stepparent's first name. Some stepparents are comfortable with this, others not. Some may ask the child to use a special pet name or made-up name. Just as the stepparents should respect the child's wishes, the child should respect the stepparent's as well. A situation to be avoided is the one in which the children do not use any name to address the stepparent and go to all sorts of trouble to structure their conversations in such a way that they will not have to speak directly to the stepparent by name. Such a situation suggests not only that the individuals are not communicating with one another about this problem but that there are probably other sources of estrangement as well.

Stepchildren may resent another woman's taking on their mother's surname. There is only one Mrs. Smith, and that's their mother; this second Mrs. Smith is an intruder, she can't use that name. In their resentment the children may purposely continue to refer to their stepmother by her previous surname, in spite of both her and their father's requests that they stop.

It's important to remember that no name is intrinsically good or bad; it is one's attitude toward a name that determines whether it is acceptable. And it is the relationship between the two individuals that counts, not the names they use when addressing one another. If the relationship is good, most reasonable names will be mutually acceptable. If not, names are not going to improve it, no matter how affectionate.

The problem of the stepparent's disciplining the children. Disciplining the stepchildren often presents special problems for a stepparent. A stepmother may hesitate to be as firm with the stepchildren as she otherwise might be, lest she alienate her husband. If she has children of her own in the home, they will immediately recognize the preferential status being granted their stepsiblings and will become resentful of both their mother and the privileged characters. Such a woman is doing her husband no favors. If she leaves the heavy disciplining to him, he becomes the bad guy and she the good guy—reputations that are bound to interfere with the children's relationships with both of them. A stepfather, also, may get sucked into a child's ploy: "You can't punish me; you're not my real father." The best thing stepparents can do for the children and themselves is to utilize the same disciplinary measures that they ordinarily would use with their own children. Children want and need proper and humane discipline—their protestations to the contrary notwithstanding. Accordingly, a good answer for such a stepfather to give is: "Yes, you're right, I'm not your real father. However, you're wrong when you say that therefore I can't discipline you. You wouldn't say to me that I can't give you ice cream because I'm not your real father. You wouldn't say that I can't clap at your school play. Like your father, I try to do all the things that are best for you. And that will include things that you like, and things you don't like."

Adoption by a stepparent. When a biological parent has totally abandoned a child, then it can be psychologically beneficial for the stepparent to adopt the child. This tends to lessen the child's feelings of rejection. However, once again, parents should realize that the human relationship that exists between child and stepparent is more important than the child's legal name. If the relationship is a good one, the adoption can be a small fringe benefit; if it is a bad one, it will be of little value.

Questions occasionally arise about this issue. A biological father, for example, may ask if he should give his daughter up for adoption by her stepfather. He may claim that he still loves his child and wants to maintain a good relationship with her, but that she feels awkward in school and with peers because she has a last name different from that of her half-siblings, mother, and stepfather. If this father is really just using the child's request as an excuse to give the responsibilities of his daughter's upbringing over to her stepfather, then I would generally suggest that the adoption process proceed. However, if the father's claim of deep involvement is valid, and he wishes to remain the legal father but is considering giving up his daughter because he believes that it may be in her best interests to do so, I generally try to dissuade him from allowing her to be adopted by the stepfather. In such a case it is likely that the adoption will be psychologically traumatic to the child and the benefits of having the same last name as others in her household will be outweighed by the rejection implicit in the adoption.

There is, however, a compromise that is most often workable, namely, that the child use the last name of the stepfather but legally retain the last name of the natural father. Most schools, in my experience, will go along with a parent's request for this. When older the youngster can decide which last name to use. Switching back to the legal name is easier then, because the youngster is no longer so deeply identified with the family. Or he or she can then legally change the last name to that of the stepfather—without having to be legally adopted by him.

Financial considerations may sometimes play a role in a stepparent's decision to adopt, because once one adopts, one usually assumes financial responsibility for the children's upbringing—even if the marriage dissolves. For example, a stepfather, sensing that the new marriage is a shaky one, may hesitate to adopt because he knows that if the marriage breaks up the children's natural father will still have to contribute to their upbringing. His wife, however, may be very eager to have her new husband adopt the children because of the greater financial security she believes they will enjoy if their stepfather is obliged to support hem. Such deliberations may be complicated by lawyers, who tend to advise stepfathers, on the one hand, not to adopt, and mothers, on the other hand, to do everything possible to get a new husband to adopt the children.

Another question concerning adoption is whether a child who is adopted in early infancy, and who has never had a relationship with the biological parent, should be told of the adoption. For example, a boy is totally abandoned by his mother in infancy. The father soon remarries, the stepmother adopts the infant, and the boy is brought up with no distinction made between himself and his half-siblings. Having no memory of his natural mother, the only mother he knows is his stepmother. The question is whether this boy should be told the truth about his natural mother. My answer is yes for a number of reasons. Should the child ever learn from others of his true origins he would be angry that his father and stepmother had withheld such important information. The shock of such a disclosure could result in lifelong distrust of them. And the argument that the boy will probably never find out is not convincing. In such a situation there are usually dozens of people who know the story, and the likelihood is great that either they or their children, by design or error, will sooner or later mention what happened. Also, our knowledge of human genetics is expanding enormously; and with this new knowledge has come increasing use of genetic counseling—for both its preventive and its curative potential. Obviously, individuals who have been misinformed regarding their true genetic heritage will have difficulty taking advantage of genetic counseling. In fact, if the counseling is sought after the parent and stepparent have died, the secret may never be known to the child, now adult.

Furthermore, no matter how hard the stepmother may try to treat her adopted child the same as her natural children, she may not be able to do so completely. Even though she may have adopted the child in early infancy, the absence of psychological bonds forged in pregnancy and childbirth may make her feel that the adopted child is somewhat different from her biological children. We are living at a time, too, when people who were adopted as children are seeking their natural parents with increasing frequency. Similarly, though to a lesser degree, individuals who have given up children for adoption are also seeking them. And organizations have been set up to help such parents and children find one another, even using illegal tactics at times to accomplish their goals. (We are moving in the direction, I believe, of making such information more accessible, so that illegal tactics may not have to be resorted to.) Accordingly, the couple's belief that there will never be any contact with the natural parent is less likely to be realized today than it was in the past.

As is obvious, the stepparent-stepchild relationship has many antagonisms working against its success that are intrinsic to the new family situation. Because of the parents' desire to make this new marriage work, there will often be a tendency to suppress such resentments, and this is likely to result in many kinds of personal and interpersonal problems. All concerned must try to express their feelings about the situation, in the most civilized way. And all must have great tolerance for ambivalent feelings, because ambivalence is characteristic of all human relationships.

If these difficulties can be avoided or overcome (and they can in many cases), the stepchildren are likely to derive many benefits from the new relationship. Most important, the presence of a stepparent provides them with a second chance either to live in or to experience an intact home.

The stepparent can serve as a surrogate for the absent parent. When the relationships between the children, their parents, and their stepparents are good ones, the children can feel that they have "two parents" of each kind, the original parent and the stepparent. Often new grandparents, uncles, aunts, cousins, and other members of the new extended family can enrich the stepchildren's lives. Furthermore, stepsiblings, the new rivalries notwithstanding, can help fill the partial vacuum caused by the divorce. For some children, especially those who have never had siblings, stepsiblings can be a dream come true. Now, almost miraculously, the child has siblings who may be of the same age and thus serve as excellent playmates—even better than the younger siblings the child had hoped would come along. And the stepparent home, when it is a stable one, may prevent or reduce any psychiatric disorders that develop in connection with the separation. It is the absence of such a home that is at the root of many of the problems that children of divorce may develop.

SIBLINGS, STEPSIBLINGS, AND HALF-SIBLINGS

Normally, sibling rivalry is fierce. All children wish to be the favorite of the parents. All find one another convenient scapegoats on which to vent hostilities too dangerous to release elsewhere—for example against teachers, parents, and peers. Siblings are excellent targets because they are a captive audience; they cannot run away, and younger ones are often helpless to retaliate effectively. Children are egocentric and greedy (they don't differ very much from most adults in this regard). With siblings children are forced to share. And the more siblings there are the more sharing there must be.

In the home where children of different marriages live together, such rivalries may become even more intensified. In the intact home a child has a chance to accommodate gradually to each new sibling. But the brood of stepsiblings arrives all at once. They suddenly descend like a horde and camp permanently. Rarely do children have more living space for themselves when stepsiblings are on the scene than when the first marriage was intact. And then there's the problem of different ways of doing things: "They like foods that would make us vomit, and half the time that's what they put on the table. They want to watch the stupidest TV programs, so often we can't watch our favorites (and Daddy says we can't afford another TV set now)." With such frustrations it is no surprise that rivalries are more intense among stepsiblings than among full siblings. And when half-siblings appear (fortunately at a slower rate), a third category of intruder arrives on the scene. As products of an entirely new family, they have their own strange habits, infantile demands, and inordinate need for the parent's time, and they encroach further on the family's already compromised living space.

What I have described so far are the inevitable and predictable rivalries that would exist even if the parents handled the situation in the most ideal manner and even if there were no other intensifying factors. With regard to handling such rivalries, I have no simple solutions. In fact, I have no simple solutions to any of the problems of child rearing. Parents have to adjust to the reality that a significant amount of sibling bickering is normal, that even more will take place when there are more kids, and that when stepsiblings live together there will be even more fighting. Parents must try to tune out and ignore a fair amount of the noise. One errs in trying to find out "who started it." It is better to place both combatants in separate rooms for some "solitary confinement" for a fifteen-minute "cooling-off period." Although at times an innocent party will suffer by the implementation of such indiscriminate punishment, things tend to even out. Recognizing that even innocent parties can get punished when battles get too much out of hand helps children remember to keep them under control. Traditional disciplinary techniques such as deprivation of a favorite television program or removal of a pleasurable activity may also help. However, these methods are not likely to result in a cessation of the fighting; they are designed more to preserve parental sanity.

Such rivalries can be intensified, however, by certain things that the parents may be doing. The normal preference that parents will have for their own offspring is bound to be appreciated by the stepchildren. They will therefore see evidence of favoritism that cannot but intensify jealousies. Parents should not deny such preferences; that only makes the situation worse. Admit they are there and do everything possible to reduce them.

As I've said, a stepparent may hesitate to discipline the stepchildren properly, and intensified sibling rivalry can result.

Sometimes a stepparent's hostility toward the stepchildren can be transmitted to his or her natural children and this can increase sibling rivalry problems. At times, a stepparent may use the natural children to act out the hostility felt toward the stepchildren—for example, by not appropriately disciplining the natural children when they bully the stepchildren. The natural children appreciate the parental encouragement for their scapegoating, even though it is not verbalized.

Sibling problems are so complex as to be mind-boggling. The remarried partners may never have imagined before their marriage how much of a drain on their relationship problems with the children would be. Some remarrieds actually divorce again, not so much from dissatisfactions in the marital relationship as from the desire to remove themselves from all the new problems that have arisen because of the children. Parents who are considering remarriage should consider in great detail the kinds of lives they will be leading, not just between themselves, but with their children as well.

THERAPISTS

How to tell whether a child needs to consult a therapist. Divorce does not necessarily result in children's needing therapy. The situation does, however, increase the risk that psychological problems will develop and that therapy will be warranted. How does one decide, then, whether a child needs treatment? Although this is a question that a trained therapist can best answer, there are certain behaviors parents can look for to help them decide whether to bring a child for consultation. And on the basis of a consultation the therapist can determine whether treatment is warranted. It is important to emphasize at the outset that there is hardly a person who could not benefit from therapy. How does one differentiate, then, those who *need* treatment from those who do not, since most could profit from it anyway?

Generally, most parents recognize that children will develop acute reactions (i.e., those of sudden onset) to the separation. Symptoms such as temper tantrums, crying spells, and disruptive behavior are predictable, and most parents do not consider such behavior to warrant psychiatric treatment. They understand that such reactions will lessen and even disappear as the children get used to the fact that they will be living with only one parent. It is hard to specify the normal duration of such acute reactions, but generally, four to six weeks is a reasonable period for them to exist. When they persist (especially unabated), then therapy, or at least parental counseling, may be warranted. Sometimes, the initial reactions may be so severe that therapy and/or parental counseling is warranted during the acute reaction.

The child who needs therapy is generally one who has exhibited difficulties for a significant period prior to the separation and whose symptoms have intensified as a result of it. There are children, however, whose symptoms date from the time of parental separation but have persisted for many months and even longer. In such situations, the parents are usually involving the children in various psychologically detrimental maneuvers (using them as spies and weapons, for example) or exposing them to constant traumas of a new kind (endless conflicts, for instance). The key factor, then, is the duration of the difficulties. Acute symptoms, especially those that arise in a response to the trauma of the separation, are not likely to require treatment. Such children are likely to work out their reactions themselves by natural psychological processes. Children often accomplish this through repeated questioning, preoccupations that serve to help them become used to the new situation, and release of feelings through play fantasy. When these natural adjustment processes become blocked, either through parental inhibition ("See how brave you can be" or "Stop asking me so many questions") or through internal inhibitive processes already present in the child, then therapy may be necessary.

With regard to the long-standing problems, there are a number of behavioral manifestations that parents can look for to help them decide whether consultation is warranted. One of the important areas to investigate is school. The school is the first testing ground to prove whether the parents have been successful in turning the primitive newborn infant into a civilized human being capable of functioning in a complex and demanding group situation. Accordingly, it is a sensitive— if not the most sensitive—area of inquiry for determining whether a child is psychologically healthy. One would want to know if there has been a deterioration of academic performance and/or classroom behavior. Discussion with teachers is crucial here, because they have been the direct observers of the child's classroom behavior. In addition, they know better than parents (and often better than many therapists) what is normal behavior for a particular age and what is atypical or excessive. Whereas in the home children's behavior is normally disruptive, healthy children are capable of inhibiting themselves to a reasonable degree in the classroom. They will differentiate between school and home authorities and are able to refrain from expressing many things in school that they would guiltlessly reveal at home. Children without such controls are in psychological difficulty and may need treatment.

Children's peer relationships can provide important information regarding whether they are suffering with a psychological disturbance. Normally, a child will fight fiercely with siblings. One cannot exhibit such behavior with peers; they have the power not only to retaliate but to reject and alienate. Accordingly, intense sibling fighting is a poor criterion by which to decide whether a child needs therapy, but poor peer relationships is a very good one. When evaluating children for therapy I particularly inquire into whether they seek peers and whether they are sought by them. If there is some impairment in either of these areas, I look into the reasons. I am also interested in knowing about the kinds of friendships my patients have; for example, whether the friends are age appropriate and whether they are relatively normal, mainstream children or are on the fringe because of atypical behavioral manifestations. A child with significant difficulties in peer relationships usually needs therapy.

Uncooperative behavior in the home is generally an unhelpful yardstick. Children normally balk at doing chores, keeping their rooms neat, getting up on time, going to sleep when they are asked, coming home when they are supposed to, and so forth. They generally take the path of least resistance, procrastinate as much as possible, and are happiest when their parents are off their backs. Accordingly, difficulties in these areas have to be quite severe before I will consider them valid reasons for therapy. When such refusal to cooperate is so marked that the child does practically nothing around the house and when frequent power struggles appear to be the rule, then the child may need treatment. And if such lack of cooperation exhibits itself in school and interferes with peer relationships, then it is even more probable that the child will need treatment.

Of course, there are additional kinds of problems that may warrant therapy if they are to be alleviated in the optimum way. I am referring to psychological symptoms such as phobias, obsessive ruminations, excessive tension, depression, and the variety of other manifestations of psychiatric disturbances with which children may suffer. However, it is beyond the scope of this book to discuss these. If parents observe a child to exhibit behavior that they suspect is caused by psychological diffi-culty, then a consultation is usually advisable. However, such symptoms, if severe enough to require treatment, will gener-ally interfere with the child's functioning in school, with peers, and at home. In short, if a child is doing well in school (both in the academic and behavioral areas), is getting along well with age-appropriate friends (both seeks them and is sought by them), and is generally (though not invariably) cooperative at home, the likelihood that psychiatric treatment will be war-ranted is small.

Resistances to treatment. Parents may be very resistive to the idea that their child needs treatment. They may consider it a sign of failure, and by denying that the child needs therapy they protect themselves from esteem-lowering feelings. And separated parents may be particularly prone to deny their children's psychological disturbance because of the guilt they may feel over their divorce. If such parents can convince themselves that their children don't need treatment, they will

335

feel less guilty over the potentially harmful effects of the divorce on them.

Most parents try very hard to do what is best for their children; yet in spite of their most dedicated efforts things may go wrong. Parents should understand that a child's needing treatment does not necessarily mean that they have been defective as parents. Child psychology is a very young field and there is still much that we have to learn. No therapist, no matter how skilled and experienced, is yet able to formulate a set of guidelines for bringing up a perfectly healthy child. In fact, we don't even know exactly what a fully healthy child would be like. Therefore, parents who resist getting therapy for their children in order to protect themselves from experiencing a sense of failure are being too demanding of themselves and at the same time are depriving their children of what might be an extremely useful experience—one that could benefit them for the rest of their lives.

Children also may resist the idea of having treatment. Generally, one of the most important determinants of whether a child will resist treatment is the attitudes of the parents with regard to therapy. If *both* parents have a deep commitment to the child's having treatment, then the child is more likely to respond positively to the idea than if one or both are basically resistive to the idea (even though they may go along with it). Even with full parental support, many (if not most) children resist therapy. Some may believe that their seeing a therapist means that they are crazy. Parents should talk with such children and make it clear that being in treatment does not mean that they are crazy and that most children in therapy do not look any different from others in their class or neighborhood. Rather, they have some problems in their lives (such as parental divorce) for which they need some help. (If, of course, the child's problems are so severe that he or she is called "crazy," then the child has to be helped to appreciate how cruel the taunters are.) Some children fear the stigmatization they anticipate they will suffer if others find out that they are in treatment. They have to be helped to recognize that being in treatment may be unfortunate, but that it is nothing to be ashamed about and that those who would tease them have something wrong with *their* own thinking. Children of divorce may have additional reasons for refusing therapy. They may already feel shame over having a divorced family and may not wish to suffer voluntarily the additional stigma of having to see a "shrink." Last, most children would much prefer to play with their friends, watch television, or just hang around rather than spending their time at the office of a psychotherapist talking about unpleasant things and touchy subjects.

However, there are children who may be receptive to treatment. They may understand that therapy can be of help to them. Probably the most important influence on a child's receptivity to treatment is the parents' genuine conviction for the process. Parents who are in therapy themselves serve as models for their children and are the most likely to engender conviction for treatment in their children. (Once again, we see here the importance of parental models in determining children's behavior.) Children of divorce may have an additional reason for being receptive to therapy. They may wish the therapist to assume the role of a surrogate parent in order to compensate them for the loss of the real parent. If this is one of the fringe benefits of therapy (to the degree that it can reasonably be accomplished in the therapeutic situation), fine; it should not, however, be the primary reason for a child's being in treatment. If therapy is necessary, it is generally preferable that the child work with someone of the same sex as the departed parent, unless other considerations dictate otherwise. But treatment should be suggested for therapeutic, not primarily social, reasons. There are far less expensive ways for the child to get a parent surrogate.

Divorced parents' involvement in a child's therapy. Children of divorce are most likely to be effectively helped with their psychological difficulties if the therapist works closely with one and even both parents, even though the parents are separated or divorced. Parental contributions to the psychological problems of children of divorce are so formidable that it is often difficult, if not impossible, to help a child if some additional work is not done with the parents. Such work may include a variety of therapeutic experiences: counseling with regard to dealing with the child (the most common type of involvement in a child's therapy); counseling with the parents for their own difficulties (either singly or together); therapy for each of the parents (either with the same therapist as the child's or with a different therapist); and active parental participation in the child's sessions.

In some cases one parent may absolutely refuse to be involved in any way in the child's treatment. In such situations I generally advise the parent who is receptive to involvement to inform the nonreceptive parent that his or her failure to contribute makes it less likely that I will be able to help the child. However, I will not refuse to treat the child, and my hope is that uninvolved parents will ultimately appreciate that their contributions can be useful and will increase the likelihood that the child's therapy will be successful.

Sometimes parents are willing to cooperate in the therapeutic process but absolutely refuse to see me together. This is especially true around the time of the separation, when the bitterness between the parents is most intense. I generally respect parents' wish in this regard and see them separately. My experience has been, however, that even around the time of separation most parents are willing to see me together. Sometimes the parents are so enraged during the joint session that it may not be very productive—other than letting the therapist observe firsthand the nature of the hostilities that exist between the parents. More often the parental hostilities are not so bitter that useful work is precluded.

Of course separated and divorced parents generally want to have as little as possible to do with one another. Generally, if it weren't for the children, they would have no contact with one another whatsoever. Yet when such parents bring a child to me for therapy, it presents a conflict for me. On the one hand, I know that they do not relish the idea of working with one another for the purposes of their child's therapy or of being seen jointly. On the other hand, the chances of my helping their child are increased to the degree that they can see their way clear to such cooperation. My experience has been that the more they can work jointly with me, the more successfully the therapy has gone. Accordingly, I strongly urge parents to make every attempt to work jointly with therapists who believe as I do (and there are many who do not share my views here) that such joint work is the best way to contribute to the alleviation of their child's psychological difficulties.

Situations that may appear to warrant treatment, but do not.

Not all unusual behavior patterns that may appear after the separation require treatment. What appear to be psychological symptoms may be manifestations of natural mechanisms to adapt to the trauma, as described in chapter 4. For example, a boy may become preoccupied with a television story depicting a parental loss. He may become "hooked" on the story because it provides him with the opportunity to get used to and accommodate bit by bit to the trauma of his parents' separation. Such a child may not need therapy. All he may need is his parents' permission to indulge himself in his fantasies. In all likelihood the time he is so preoccupied will diminish daily and therapy will not be necessary. Of course, if the preoccupation continues unabated and occupies a significant part of his life, then other factors are probably contributing and therapy may well be necessary.

There are parents who are quite insecure and fear that following the separation they will not be able to rise to the challenge of bringing up a child alone. Such parents may seek therapy to ensure that by putting the child in "good hands" they will avoid the harmful effects of their assuming sole responsibility. Sometimes such a parent will quite early comment to the therapist: "I want to put him in your hands, Doctor." The competent therapist will recognize in this situation that it may be the parent, rather than the child, who requires guidance and possibly treatment. Such a statement also hints that the parent thinks that the therapy is for the child alone and that little if any parental involvement is required. To dispel that unfortunate (yet common) view, I tell the parents at the outset that this is not the way therapy works.

I impress upon them that the more involvement I have on both of their parts—separated or divorced status notwithstanding—the greater the likelihood I will be able to help their child. I also emphasize that I am making absolutely no promises regarding the outcome; all I will promise is that I will devote myself to the treatment process. This statement helps further to dispel any parental fantasies about my role.

Some parents are very fearful about their children and may be quick to seek psychiatric consultation and even treatment for the most minor problems. Often such parents have had extensive treatment themselves and may be quite "sophisticated" about psychoanalytic matters. When a separation has occurred, they may be certain that the child is going to develop problems that will require psychiatric treatment. Even though the child has not exhibited any unusual reactions to the separation they may request preventive treatment. But treatment is not warranted if there are no significant problems to treat. The therapist needs some symptom, some handle on which to grab, some problem to be put out on the table for both the patient and therapist to view, if the therapy is going to have any effect. Furthermore, competent therapists generally appreciate the importance of listing at the outset the therapeutic goals. These are important to review at times in order to ascertain how the therapy is progressing and whether there has been enough symptomatic alleviation to warrant discontinuation of the treatment. Without a list of presenting symptoms, both the therapist and patient are deprived of this important aspect of treatment. Accordingly, such children should not be treated. However, the therapist might make an inquiry into the parents' anxieties and investigate whether these are exaggerated and/or inappropriate. In such cases the parents themselves might need some counseling.

Sometimes parents project their own problems onto their children; they see themselves as healthy and their children (or one particular child, singled out for this role) as sick. A therapist may have a difficult time convincing such a parent that the child is not the one with the described problems. Typically, such a parent will seek another therapist to treat the child. If the second therapist concurs with the first, the parent will go on to a third and fourth, until one is found who will provide the desired treatment. If one searches long enough, one will eventually find a doctor who will say what one wants to hear or will do what one requests. It is important for parents to appreciate that there is a sea of therapists out there: psychiatrists, psychologists, psychiatric social workers, pastoral counselors, nurse practitioners, family therapists, and a wide variety of self-schooled "psychotherapists." The supply of people willing to provide therapy is much greater than the demand of people needing treatment. Furthermore, differentiating common and even healthy reactions from pathological responses to the inevitable stresses of life can be difficult even for the most experienced therapists. Parents who want to cure themselves vicariously through their children are easy prey to overeager therapists. The competent and ethical therapist will recognize the situation and investigate what can be done to bring the parent—the bona fide patient—into treatment.

There are children who are not really in need of therapy but who are brought because of the parents' need to reduce the guilt they may feel over the separation. The parents wish to leave no stone unturned in ensuring that only good things will happen to the child, and they see therapy as a way of bringing this about. Such children, of course, should not be treated. The indications for therapy are psychiatric disturbance, not parental guilt feelings. Of course, such parents should deal with their guilt more appropriately and realistically. One of the more reliable ways to reduce such guilt is to avoid the kinds of postseparation problems that increase the children's burden and may cause difficulties beyond those that inevitably result from the separation.

Sometimes parents will attempt to use a child as an admission ticket for their own treatment. Such parents appreciate that in the course of the child's evaluation the therapist will ask questions about themselves as well. The parents thereby gain the opportunity of becoming familiar with the therapist and talking about themselves in the context of discussing their children. In this way they ease themselves into the therapeutic situation without having to admit directly that they are there for themselves. In the course of such conversations they also have the chance to look the therapist over and decide whether he or she would be acceptable as a therapist. Such parents may not be consciously aware that they are really coming for themselves, but they unconsciously appreciate that discussions about themselves may result in the therapist's recommending treatment for them. In these cases, of course, competent therapists do not treat the child but inquire instead into what problems these parents have that cause them to use such a devious route to obtain treatment.

Divorce in itself does not warrant a child's being in therapy. This is especially true if the child has a good relationship with both the custodial parent and the one who does not live in the home. If the absent parent is uninvolved with the child or unavailable, there is a greater chance that the child will develop psychological difficulties. However, if the remaining parent makes efforts to provide such a child with surrogate relationships, then harmful psychological reactions may still be avoided. If the separated parents can achieve a civilized relationship with one another, they will significantly lessen the likelihood of the child's developing psychological difficulties.

CLUBS AND ORGANIZATIONS

In recent years many clubs and organizations have been formed specifically for divorced parents and their children. Probably the best known of these is Parents Without Partners,* which has hundreds of chapters in the United States, Canada, and various other countries. Although many parents join in order to meet possible candidates for remarriage, the organization provides a variety of activities that are of value to divorced parents and their children. Most chapters have family activities, outings, picnics, and so on that provide children with opportunities for involvement with opposite-sexed parent substitutes. Discussion groups and lectures offer the members information that can be valuable to themselves and their children. Recreational groups for children and adolescent discussion groups help these youngsters feel less different and give them opportunities to work out some of the special problems that children of divorce often have.

There are numerous other organizations that provide similar opportunities for divorced parents and their children. Many are designed to attract specific groups, like college-educated people or members of a particular religious faith. The sense of belonging to a special club and the feeling of communality serve well as antidotes to the feelings of loneliness that many single parents and their children suffer.

An organization that can be useful for children who live alone with single parents is Big Brothers—Big Sisters of America.** Men and women volunteer to spend time with youngsters from single-parent homes. The most common arrangement is one in which a man will take under his wing a boy from a single-parent home who lacks a father figure, or a woman will involve herself similarly with a girl from a home without a mother figure. Attempts are made to form deep, ongoing relationships with these youngsters in the hope that involvement with a parental surrogate will help prevent and alleviate the kinds of difficulties that may arise when children grow up in such situations. It may also be helpful for children to join clubs that are likely to provide them with parental surrogates. Scouts, Brownies, Little League, Ys, summer camps, and various organized recreational activities can provide such parental substitutes for these children.

BOARDING SCHOOLS AND FOSTER HOMES

Loving parents derive deep gratifications from living with and rearing their children—at least until the teenage period—and

*National headquarters: 8802 Colesville Road, Silver Springs, MD 01612. **Headquarters: 230 North 13th Street, Philadelphia, PA 19107.

will suffer significant pain upon being separated from them. Such parents are willing to tolerate the frustrations, sacrifices, and privations of raising a child because of the joys and satisfactions that child rearing can also provide. I believe that parents who voluntarily send their children below the age of puberty to live elsewhere, when there is a reasonable possibility of their living at home, exhibit some deficiency in parental capacity and involvement.

Sending a young child (unless stated otherwise, I am referring to children below the pubertal period) to boarding school is, until proved otherwise, a sign of such parental deficiency. Some parents justify sending off their children with rationalizations such as: "It's better for him (her) to be away from all the conflict," "Private schools are the only places where one can get a really good education," and "Our home is split up; there they have good mother and father substitutes, all in the same place." When "family tradition" is used as the reason for sending young children off to boarding school, then the family tradition, I believe, is one of neglect and disinterest in children. The fact that sending children as young as four years of age off to boarding school is common practice in England does not make the practice any less harmful to children. When typhoid fever becomes epidemic it's still a disease.

When separated and divorced parents send their children off to boarding school they usually take pains to reassure the youngsters that they are not being sent away because they aren't loved. Professional authorities often strongly urge such parents to emphasize this fact. But the children know the truth—that (with rare exception) they are being sent off because neither parent wishes to assume responsibility for their care. The children know that their parents want them out of the way. Therefore, such reassurances in most cases only cause further distrust. It would be much better for parents and their children if the parents would openly admit that they are deficient as parents and that they are sending the children away in the hope that others may be able to do a better job. I recognize that this is not an easy thing for most parents to do.

In fact, many such deficient parents cannot even admit their parental impairments to themselves. But parents who have enough courage to admit the problem to themselves and the children do both a service. By such admission they avoid the lowered sense of self-worth that inevitably occurs when one tries to deceive one's children in such an important area. And the admission to the children helps them avoid the distrust of the parents that comes from being lied to about the reasons for their being sent away.

Some parents might argue that the pain of such distrust is less than the pain a child may suffer from being told that there is a deficiency in the parent's capacity to love. Parents who follow such an argument are fooling themselves into believing that they can dupe their children. How can an eight-year-old child, for example, not feel unloved when sent to live elsewhere at an age when the vast majority of children (even those whose parents are divorced) are still living at home? The parental affection impairment cannot be covered up, and therefore the parents should not add the additional distrust problem. Such parents should help their children know exactly in which areas the parents still show interest and affection and in which they do not. In such situations there is generally still some parental involvement, and the child should be helped to clarify its extent. Furthermore, the children should be helped to realize that such partial rejection does not mean that they themselves are unlovable. Rather, the defect lies within the parent. If the children are nice to others, others both in the present and future can love them.

Some children may consider being sent off to boarding school a punishment. It is not difficult to understand why this may occur. It is a painful experience just like punishment. In addition, the ultimate punishment for all children is loss of parental affection, and being sent away to boarding school most often symbolizes just that. Furthermore, such an idea may serve these children's need to gain control over an uncontrollable situation. When children can believe that they were sent away for "being bad," then they gain a sense of having control over a situation in which, in reality, they are usually impotent. Attempting to reassure such children that they are not being sent away as punishment is not likely to work (although the statement might very well be made)— because the reassurance does not address itself to the primary causes of the delusion. Rather, these children have to come to appreciate that they are being sent away because of deficiencies in their parents. In most cases they have not been particularly "bad." What has been bad is their luck. The best way to cope with the delusion of control is to help the children differentiate between those things they have control over and those they do not. They must learn to give up on foolhardy quests (such as trying to extract more affection than a parent can provide) and direct their attention to pursuits with a greater likelihood of success.

Some children prefer a boarding school because there they are removed from the strife and misery of their home life. But to believe that these children are better off than those in intact homes (even intact homes with a moderate amount of dissension) is misguided. These children are just expressing preference for the less painful of two detrimental alternatives. Even children who request to go are not generally asking to leave a relatively warm and loving home; rather, they see the boarding school environment as exposing them to less trauma than their homes.

The adolescent is in an entirely different situation. The adolescent's being sent off to boarding school is not necessarily a psychologically harmful experience and does not necessarily indicate rejection by the parents. If such a youngster has gained the benefits of good parenting from one or both parents (in either a divorced or an intact home), the boarding school experience can be enriching and maturing. But even in this period, the parents should keep up frequent contact with the youngster via mail, telephone, and visits. And I still believe that for the early adolescent (up to about age fifteen or sixteen) a stable home environment is better than the best boarding school. Such youngsters can still profit from parental model and guidance, and the boarding school is not likely to provide substitutes for these roles who are as dedicated and involved as loving parents.

Much of what I have said about boarding schools holds for foster homes. In the foster home situation, however, the children are more likely to be told that the reason for their placement relates to the fact that their parents cannot afford to keep them at home. Although financial considerations may very well play a role in such a decision, most loving parents manage to stay together with their children regardless of how difficult things may get. Parents and others involved in the care of children living in foster homes should help such children see through the rationalization of parental poverty, help them recognize the parental limitations, discourage them from the futile quest for affection from those who cannot provide it, and help them gain compensatory gratifications from others.

7

Concluding Comments

Divorce is painful and problematic for parents and their children; that is the reason for this book. Why is there so much divorce? What can be done to reduce the divorce rate and to minimize the sufferings of families that do separate?

SOME CAUSES OF THE HIGH DIVORCE RATE

A good way of understanding the reasons for divorce is to look into the reasons for marriage. If people involve themselves in a marital relationship for poor, and even sick, reasons, then the marriage is bound to be unstable and the likelihood of marital discontent and divorce great.

In the United States (and throughout most of the Western industrialized world) the reason for getting married nowadays is *love*, and more specifically *romantic love*. These days, individuals who marry for other reasons, or who fail to include love in their list of reasons for marrying, are likely to be considered strange, misguided, or possibly suffering with a psychopathological disturbance. People in love find that they experience certain ecstatic feelings when thinking about or being in the presence of a specific person. Lovers soon develop the conviction that these blissful feelings will last forever. They have probably never observed anyone—except on the movie or television screen—who has sustained this state of elation beyond a few years. Yet this does not deter people in love from making vows about how they will feel and behave toward one another many years hence, even for the rest of their lives. Predictably, the result is often divorce.

A type of romantic love that is particularly attractive to adolescents is the kind that I refer to as the *Some-Enchanted-Evening-Across-a-Crowded-Room* type. In this variety, two complete strangers, merely on viewing one another (from across a crowded room is desirable but not crucial to the phenomenon), are suddenly struck, as if by a lightning bolt, with intense feelings of affection and sexual attraction for one another. (I also refer to this type of romantic love as the *bifurcated lightning bolt* kind of love.) So magnetized, the two strangers make a beeline for one another, trampling people in between, and "read life's meaning in one another's eyes."

Closely related is the "acute infectious disease" type of romantic love. Here the individuals are suddenly afflicted with cravings for one another, as if stricken with an illness. In fact, in popular song individuals with this kind of love may refer to themselves as having been "bitten by the love bug." In medicine we have a term, *pathognomonic sign*, which refers to the sign that clinches the diagnosis of a disease. And the love-bug disease has a pathognomonic sign. A patient suffering with any other disease would be quite upset if a doctor announced that the patient would have to share a bed with another victim of the same disorder. But people with the love-bug disease have no such objections; they welcome being in the same bed together. This is the pathognomonic sign that differentiates this from all other diseases known to medicine.

In these cases of romantic love, the individuals view their attraction as coming from mysterious, almost magical forces that instantaneously and irresistibly draw them together. Although some see the cause of the overwhelming attraction as external (planned by God, for example), others attribute it to internal factors (such as "chemistry"). I, personally, suspect that internal psychological and biological factors are the most important elements in producing this phenomenon. The individuals enter the room predisposed to the experience, even hoping for it, because of a lack of meaningful involvement with anyone else at the time. Loneliness may intensify the craving for such an involvement. The need for an esteem-enhancing experience as an antidote to one's pains and frustrations may also be present. Perhaps the object of the intense attraction bears some physical resemblance to an earlier love object, such as an opposite-sexed parent or a former lover. Sexual frustration is in all probability present as well. All of these factors may be particularly potent at the time—a possible explanation for the suddenness with which individuals may be drawn to one another. All the factors together result in a copious outpouring of hormones into the bloodstream that enhances formidably the desire of the two individuals to spend as much time as possible with one another, both physically and psychologically. In fact, they may give such high priority to being with one another that they may ignore obligations vital to their well-being. And when the two people become more involved with one another, the attraction becomes solidified by a dovetailing of both healthy and (as I'll detail below) neurotic needs.

The risks that one takes when falling in love with a stranger are little different from those one takes when, for example, buying a used car from a stranger or lending money to a stranger. Yet it is both amazing and pathetic how many individuals who would never be injudicious enough to buy cars from or lend money to strangers are willing—under the influence of romantic love—to vow to live together for the rest of their lives with strangers from "across a crowded room."

Let's look at the important psychological factors operative in bringing about this state of romantic euphoria. First, I wish to emphasize that I do not necessarily equate psychological factors with psychological disturbance. Most, if not all, forms of behavior have psychological elements, but not all psychologically determined behavior should necessarily be considered psychopathological. Each of the psychological mechanisms I shall describe runs the gamut from the normal to the pathological. Each person who is "in love" utilizes one or more of these mechanisms. And each person may use them in either normal or pathological degrees and at any level between these extremes.

One factor operative in the romantic love phenomenon is compliance with social convention. In our society we consider "love" to be the most important reason for marrying another person. Of course, in other societies other criteria have been used. For instance, money and power have often been the criteria for matchmaking. Some of the ancient pharaohs married their brothers and sisters in order to keep power and wealth within the family. Unfortunately for the pharaohs, genes for intellectual retardation were quite common in their families—resulting in an unusually high percentage of retarded rulers. Among European royalty, marrying cousins and near relatives was a routine practice up to this century. Unfortunately for certain European dynasties, genes for hemophilia ran in the family; marriages between close relatives persisted, however, because of the great desire to hold onto wealth and power. In many cultures, marriages planned by parents are an ancient tradition, the parents considering themselves to be better qualified than their children to make such an important decision. Although I would not recommend that we adopt this tradition, I cannot say that the custom is not without its merits. Here again, considerations other than romantic love are generally operative in the parents' decision-making process.

Our social convention, however, deems it normal for people, especially when young, to have the experience of falling in love. In fact, people who claim that they have never had this experience are often viewed as being somewhat deficient and even unfortunate. We are much more like sheep than we would like to admit, and for many of us the social-compliance factor is an important one. When one's friends start falling in love, then one starts falling in love as well. The pattern is similar to the phenomena of anorexia/

bulemia and even adolescent suicide. When something becomes "the thing to do," many adolescents are likely to go along with the crowd, even if it means acquiring some dreaded disease and even if it means killing oneself. And such slavish adherence to social convention extends into adult years for many people—as the advertising industry well appreciates.

I believe that another important factor is the narcotic effect of romantic love. Like a narcotic, romantic love quickly produces intense pleasurable sensations. One need not apply oneself diligently over time to gain this intense pleasure; one can spontaneously induce the state within oneself and revel. (One need not even have encouragement or reciprocity from the object of one's affection; unrequited love can produce the same euphoric state.) In addition, like a narcotic, romantic love makes one insensitive to pain. There are many painful feelings associated with the idea of marriage—if one allows oneself to think about them. The prospect of living with the same person for the rest of one's life cannot but provoke extreme anxiety in an intelligent and sensitive human being. And the awesome responsibility of rearing children is calculated to produce further anxiety. But romantic love, an extremely potent tranquilizer, dulls all these anxieties. Like a narcotic, too, romantic love assists the lover in denying deficiencies in the partner, even deficiencies that may be obvious to almost everyone else. And with a narcotic, the ecstatic feelings of romantic love are experienced only early in its use. As time passes a drug becomes progressively less capable of producing the desired blissful state. Alas, such is also the case with romantic love.

Another important attraction of romantic love is that it is an esteem enhancer. We generally admire most those who have the good sense to like us. We cannot but find attractive a person who has selected us—from all the billions of other people on earth—to respect, to confide in, and to communicate sexual attraction to as well. Typically, lovers bestow praise on one another to a degree not generally seen in any other situation. All stops are pulled out. Even one's own mother does not hold one in as high regard as one's lover. The process may start, for example, with A bestowing on B some complimentary comment. B, flattered, returns the favor. A then thinks even more highly of B for having such high regard for him or her. A mutual admiration society thereby develops, founded on the agreement that "if you'll admire, praise, respect, and find me sexually attractive, I'll do the same for you."

Individuals with profound feelings of low self-worth often gravitate toward this aspect of the romantic love phenomenon because the praises provide compensation for low self-esteem. But unfortunately, there are only about 400,000 words in most unabridged dictionaries of the English language; only a small fraction of these words are useful in the service of complimenting one's beloved; and of that fraction, only a few words are in the repertoire of most individuals. As a result, lovers' praises tend to become repetitious and thus to lose some of their efficacy. In addition, maintaining a high frequency of compliments can be taxing and draining. Healthy people can allow the romantic love experience to simmer down somewhat and have ongoing experiences that enable them to supply fresh compliments. But others may become frustrated with this aspect of the romantic love experience.

Yet another element in romantic love enhances even further the feelings of self-worth of the individuals involved: If the object of one's affections is perfect, and if one is in turn loved by that perfect person, then one must be a most admirable person indeed. It is as if the young man in love were saying: "She is perfect. Among her perfections is wisdom. She loves me. If she is wise enough to love me, I must be unique, adorable, lovable, wise, and maybe even perfect like her. Why, she even tells me that 'we're a perfect match.'"

Sometimes, paradoxically, romantic love actually serves to conceal underlying anger. All human relationships include ambivalence, and love is no exception. But there are individuals who believe that they should have a relationship in which there is no anger expressed, lest the relationship be viewed—by themselves and others—as not "the real thing." In most (if not all) human relationships, angry feelings are going to arise at some point. We cannot satisfy one another's desires all the time; the frustrations that ultimately develop in all close human encounters must produce resentments at times. In healthy relationships, the individuals express resentment promptly and in a civilized manner, in the hope that the problem may be resolved. If a problem cannot be resolved, and if there are many such problems, then the individuals usually part ways. If, however, they succeed in resolving the conflicts that arise, they may then be in a position to maintain a relationship that may ultimately mature. But individuals who are too guilty to express their resentments, or who need to feel that there are none, are likely to use romantic feelings in the service of reaction formation. Obsessive love may then suppress deep-seated hatred. Accordingly, romantic love not only may provide a cover-up of angry feelings but may lessen the likelihood that the individuals will work out the problems that are producing the anger in the first place.

Romantic love can also be used to satisfy pathological dependency needs. It is much more socially acceptable to gratify pathological dependency with a spouse than with a parent. This is an extension of the shift in which the adolescent transfers dependency from parents to peers; but in romantic love, the dependency cravings may be even greater. A marriage based on such cravings is not likely to be stable, because in any parasitic relationship the host resents the parasite because his or her blood is being sucked, and the parasite resents the host because of his or her vulnerability. Such resentments may, over time, develop into hatred when the two individuals become "locked in" with one another.

Another element that may be operative in romantic love is the desire to outdo one's friends, even to arouse their envy. One can boast to friends that one is loved, adored, and admired. When one's friends are not at that time having that fortunate experience, one gains a superior position in the competition for success in the dating/mate acquisition arena. One can then flaunt the "good catch" to one's friends. Again, individuals with low feelings of self-worth are more likely to utilize this maneuver.

Let me reemphasize that these psychological factors in

romantic love should not necessarily be equated with psycho-pathology. Each factor, when present in mild degree, may very well be considered normal. But if romantic love becomes obsessive, prolonged, and delusional and interferes with important functions (school, work, etc.), it may be considered psychopathological. The healthiest situation for young people is to have a few such experiences but not to make any commitments under the influence of the romantic-love feeling. My advice to the adolescent or the adult who is in love is this: Romantic love is a wonderful experience. Enjoy it while it lasts, but don't make important decisions under its influence—like marriage, for example!

In moderation, romantic love can be an enriching, uplifting experience. It has served to inspire some of the world's greatest artistic and scientific creations. The person who has not tasted its sweetness has missed out on one of life's great pleasures. But when it is indulged in to excess, when people are so blinded by it that they enter into self-destructive involvements, I consider it a type of psychological disturbance. One can compare romantic love to the occasional alcoholic beverage. Used in moderation, love can ennoble our spirits; when we are addicted to it, it can destroy us. I think that it is possible that in recent years there may have been some decrease in the tendency of people to become addicted. The "tell it like it is" philosophy that became popular in the 1980s may signal the beginning of a social change. Perhaps in the future there will be less tendency for people to enter into this self-induced delusional state to such an extreme degree.

Apart from the effects of romantic love, many people marry because marriage is supposed to enhance one's personal happiness. Whatever miseries one may have (and each person has his or her own collection) marriage is often looked upon as the universal antidote. The fairy-tale ending "and they got married and lived happily ever after" is only one example of this traditional association between marriage and the state of happiness. Those who look upon marriage as a potential source of happiness generally believe that it is within the capability of human beings to "be happy," that is, attain a state of continual happiness. This belief seems to persist in spite of the fact that the believers themselves never seem to have been able to reach this state. Things always seem to be happening to interrupt the acquisition of the goal, and even when one seems to have attained happiness, it never seems to last very long. Those who view marriage as a source of continual happiness are bound to become disillusioned when it inevitably fails to provide them with such a state. And then they divorce, stating: "We are no longer happy."

Many marry because it is the "thing to do." Although they will profess "love" as their reason for marrying (the official, acceptable reason for marrying), their real motive may have less to do with affection than with the desire to do the socially accepted thing. As young people grow older, and more and more of their friends take the step, they feel increasingly pressured to go along. Married and single people often do not mix well socially (married people often play it safe by not placing themselves in situations with sexually available people), so people who remain single may find themselves becoming increasingly isolated. Most people dread being significantly different from the majority (professions of independent thinking and acting notwithstanding) and will marry in order to fit in with the crowd. Of course, in our society marriages based on factors external to the relationship are not likely to have the inner cohesion necessary to survive. In recent years the single state has become more socially acceptable. Accordingly, fewer people have probably married just to follow the herd (although I consider this still to be a very popular, though unadvertised, motive for marrying). And some who have married for this reason are coming to appreciate the absurdity of their decision and are divorcing.

Many believe that the ideal marriage is one in which the spouses enjoy doing together most of the important activities of their lives. Togetherness appears to be the ideal to be achieved. The individuals live together, sleep together, raise children together, and socialize as a couple. Invitations are invariably addressed to both together as a unit, and invitations are responded to with "We can't make it this week. How about next week?" I often refer to this as the Siamese Twin Theory of Marriage. No other human relationship makes such demands. And to the degree that the couple (that word again) adhere to this theory, to that degree will they suffer mounting resentments and a desire for freedom. Another name I give to this concept of marriage is the Three-Legged Race Theory of Marriage. As in a three-legged race, in which each pair of contestants have their adjacent legs bound together, the couple hobbles along. A marriage in which the two individuals are so tied together is bound to fall flat on its face.

In recent years, with increasing appreciation that too much togetherness can be a significant source of frustration and difficulty in a marriage, many couples have become more liberated and each has done his or her own thing. Certainly this is a good trend. However, certain problems have yet to be solved. Most will agree that greater opportunity for a variety of separate experiences is healthy for a marriage. The crucial question has been how much involvement in extradomestic activities is good for a relationship? When is the point reached where independent involvements may threaten the marriage or reveal a deficiency in it? People vary considerably in their interest in and tolerance for a spouse's activities with other persons.

When outside experiences include extramarital sex, many would say that things have gone too far. Many people believe that jealousy over a partner's involvement in extramarital sex is inevitable in a close human relationship. They believe that the closer the relationship, the more pained one will be over a partner's extramarital sexual activities. Others hold that such jealousy is socially conditioned and that the mature individual feels no such jealousy and places no such restrictions on a partner. I am inclined to agree with the first view and believe that anyone who experiences no pained or jealous reactions to a partner's extramarital sexual involvement has a somewhat superficial relationship. Obviously, the conflicts surrounding this issue contribute to marital dissatisfaction and divorce. And these conflicts arise from the feelings of restriction when there is too much togetherness, and the feelings of jealousy and other resentful reactions when there is too little. It is rare for a couple to reach the ideal point somewhere in the middle.

Economic fluctuations notwithstanding, we in Western society enjoy abundant material comforts and free time. Before the twentieth century people's primary interest was in survival; this is still true today in most parts of the world. Life is a practically endless struggle to stay alive. Few can indulge themselves in the luxury of seriously considering adopting a different way of life, especially one involving the support of a second household. And those who do consider it soon conclude that it is impossible. Most are locked in from birth to a particular path. But in the affluent developed nations we have the privilege of being free to seek self-fulfillment. We are encouraged to do everything to "maximize our potential." Although there are healthy aspects to such trends, many have used "self-realization" as a justification for self-indulgence. Expressing one's individuality has often been done with little concern for the harmful effects on others of such "self-fulfillment." And the mass media have added to the problem. We are bombarded with images of countless objects and experiences, only a fraction of which we can possibly acquire, which produce cravings and frustrations that might not have otherwise arisen. We are led to believe that we are not getting our share of the joys of life and are given exciting views of those who are allegedly getting theirs. It is not surprising, then, that many leave their marriages in the hope that they will thereby be free to fulfill themselves materially and/or experientially by joining in the fun and getting their share of the action.

Although in its early history, America was certainly a country of great mobility, there was much less mobility in the past than there is today. In our early years, when one went west, for example, one went to *settle* somewhere—to settle and remain there for the rest of one's life. Today we experience a much greater kind of mobility. People from rural areas move to the cities. People from the cities migrate to the suburbs. People from the cities and suburbs gravitate toward small towns. Companies relocate and take with them their employees.

Executives and their families are shifted around the country like chessmen on a board. Children grow up and spread themselves all over the country. In such a world there is little sense of having roots, little feeling for permanence, and little commitment to long-standing human relationships. And our comfort with loose bonds with friends and relatives may weaken the marriage bond as well and play a role in our divorce rate.

We are very much a youth-worshiping culture. There was a time when the elderly were revered for their experience; today we farm many old people out to nursing homes to spend their last years watching television. The youth culture reigns and beauty reigns supreme. The mass media contribute significantly to this mystique, as do advertisers and manufacturers. Many people consider themselves the object of envy because of the beautiful partner they have acquired. And the partner is flaunted like the expensive new car, jewelry, or fur coat. The self-esteem of such individuals, then, is dependent upon the maintenance of the physical attractiveness of the partner. A marriage based on the hope that such beauty will persist is inevitably doomed.

The Women's Liberation movement has contributed to the lessening of many prejudices that were deeply entrenched in our social structure. One of the outgrowths of this movement has been that many women have become freer to express their basic dissatisfaction with the childbearing and child-rearing role and have abandoned it entirely. And it has been easier for women to do this in recent years than in the past, because women have more of the education and skills they need to exist independently of a husband. In short, more women today can afford to divorce than in the past—and more are doing so.

No-fault divorce laws have also contributed significantly to the rising divorce rate. As I have mentioned, the idea that divorce should be granted only if one party has committed a "crime" such as adultery, addiction, or desertion is a legacy of the past. Although the passage of no-fault divorce laws has certainly eased the suffering of many, I am not convinced that these laws are an unmixed blessing. Because they make it so easy for people to dissolve a marriage, there are many who are too impatient with what I would consider the usual frustrations and resentments intrinsic to the institution. There is no question that many marriages that would have survived fairly successfully in former days, when there were more stringent divorce laws, have been dissolved too easily under the new laws, to the detriment of all concerned. If children are involved, even more damage is done. I am not suggesting repeal of these new laws, however; on balance, I believe they have done more good than harm.

Another factor that has contributed to our high divorce rate is our increased life span. In earlier eras and other cultures, most people married in the early to mid-teens; children came along quite quickly; one could not reasonably look forward to years of living after one's children grew up. But most people in the United States today can anticipate twenty-five or more years of productive living after their children are self-sufficient. Both in the past and today many stayed together for the sake of the children and/or found the children a bond that provided them with a mutual purpose. But in the past, one didn't have too many years after the children grew up to build up marital intolerance to the point where one got divorced; one died first. Today, there is so much life to live that many people choose to get out of a relationship that no longer seems to have purpose or meaning. In essence, if people live longer, marriages last longer, and the percentage of marriages that will end in divorce is bound to increase.

There is no question that in the 1970s and 1980s there was a significant shift in values in American society. The sense of commitment that people have toward one another has definitely diminished. There seems to be less guilt around, as evidenced by increasing crime rates, more exploitive lifestyles, more academic cheating, more professional plagiarism, and a general atmosphere of self-serving attitudes. In the 1960s and 1970s many best-sellers professed a "think of number one" philosophy. Such narcissistic attitudes cannot but contribute to divorce. One should be thinking not only about number one, but about number two, number three, and others upon whom one is dependent and with whom one is involved. When a person contemplates divorce, he or she should take all these individuals into consideration. The failure to do so has contributed to the divorce rate.

A variety of other factors have played a role in the prevalence of divorce. The weakening of organized religion has certainly contributed. Fewer people remain in unhappy marriages because of religious restrictions, and fewer feel guilty over violating religious strictures when dissolving their marriages. With the breakdown of many religious and racial prejudices we have witnessed a greater incidence of marriage between persons of different cultures, classes, races, religions, and creeds. It may be that such marriages are less stable than those between individuals of the same ethnic background. We live in a world where there is less veneration of marriage as an institution and greater social acceptability of divorce. In the past many stayed together in their unhappy marriages because they could not face the social stigmatization that befell the divorced person. Today there is little such stigma and this has made it easier for many to divorce who might not have in the past.

It may also be that my own field, psychoanalysis and the various forms of therapy that stem from it, may have played a role in the divorce rate. There is no question that psychotherapy has helped many marriages. However, there is no question as well that psychotherapy has also caused many divorces. How the balance tips, whether therapy has prevented more divorces than it has brought about, I have absolutely no way of knowing. As mentioned in chapter 1, when one partner is in therapy and becomes healthier, the other (whether or not he or she is in therapy) may rise to the occasion and become healthier as well. In such cases the therapy will have served to place the marriage on a securer footing. If, however, the other partner cannot or will not relate in a healthier way, the resulting conflicts may result in a divorce. The two individuals are no longer dancing to the same tune, so to speak; they are out of step with one another, and an ongoing relationship may become difficult if not impossible. Also, when one partner is in treatment for a marital problem and the therapist strictly refuses to see the patient's marital partner, then the likelihood of the marital problem being worked out is, in my opinion, extremely small. This type of treatment has brought about many divorces in marriages that could have been salvaged had the therapist been more receptive to some involvement by the patient's partner.

CHANGES THAT MAY REDUCE THE DIVORCE RATE

Many changes taking place today may ultimately slow the divorce rate. Some of these changes should lessen the likelihood of unsound marriages ever occurring in the first place.

The greater freedom for premarital sexual experience, the greater availability of contraceptive devices, and the relaxing of restrictions (social, legal, and religious) on use of contraception make it more likely that people will engage in premarital sex—and therefore that fewer people will marry primarily for sexual gratification. In addition, the more widespread use of contraceptives and legalization of abortion make it less likely that people will get married because the woman is pregnant. And the reduction of the stigma associated with obtaining an abortion makes it easier for women to undergo the procedure. The lessened stigma of unwed motherhood, also, is probably bringing about fewer injudicious marriages.

In the past a young woman who lived with a man before marriage was considered to be immoral—a disgrace to her family. In recent years the practice has become quite widespread, and such women do not suffer anywhere near the stigma they once did. Their parents may have to go through a period of adjustment, but they often come to accept their offspring's decision. I suspect (though one cannot be certain) that the practice has forestalled some misguided marriages.

I have discussed how the Women's Liberation movement may have contributed to the increased divorce rate by enabling women to gain the education, skills, and financial resources to remove themselves from unhappy marriages. However, the same opportunities for women may serve to keep other marriages intact. Having extradomestic opportunities may make many women less frustrated with their lives and more willing to tolerate many of the burdens of marriage and child rearing. Furthermore, with more skills and independence, women should be less hasty to enter into injudicious marriages. This factor, as well, may help lessen the divorce rate. (It is important to note, however, that many women do not seek independent and/or egalitarian relationships with their husbands. Polls in many states have indicated that many women voted against the passage of the Equal Rights Amendment to the United States Constitution. Further inquiry revealed that many of these women feared that the amendment might jeopardize the dependent-protective relationships they enjoyed with their husbands.)

There are other changes that I think could be instituted that might contribute to a reduction in the frequency of unfortunate marriages. In most education systems, courses in family living, family psychology, and child rearing are usually minor courses, sometimes still taught by the gym teacher, and they are not given the distinction of such major courses as history, mathematics, science, and English. Accordingly, students tend to take them less seriously. I believe that family living courses are the most important a youngster can take. I believe that they should be major courses from the sixth grade on and that youngsters who fail such courses should be required to repeat them. Many seem to take it for granted that child rearing and family living need not be taught. The assumption appears to be that with the physical capability of being able to have children comes the knowledge of how to adjust in a marriage and rear children. Although in recent years schools have certainly given more attention to such teaching, the courses are still not ranked as among the more important and, worse, are not taught by people specially trained to teach them.

The educational system can serve in other ways to bring about a reduction of the divorce rate. It can help children appreciate the fallacies advanced and perpetuated by the media and the advertising industry: of lifelong ecstasy provided by romantic love, of the "beautiful people" and the joyful lives they lead, of wives who (even when scrubbing the floors) are continually seductive to their husbands, and of husbands who never stop adoring and doting on their wives. Schools must also help engender in children the values of responsibility and commitment, not only by word but by deed. These qualities are essential to the survival of the family as well as society. People today, I believe, feel less commitment to and responsibility for their spouses and children then they have in the past. Many teachers have reflected this decline; they have failed to communicate these values to their students because they have not served as models themselves for them or been able to teach them with conviction. If we are to slow the divorce rate, society must once again bring about a general appreciation of and respect for these values. And both the family and school are crucial in serving to reach this goal.

Another change that I believe would also reduce the high divorce rate would be the establishment of a mandatory waiting period—three to six months—between the time a couple was granted a marriage license and the time they were permitted to marry. A couple can usually get married within a few days of making the decision; divorces, by contrast, even with no-fault divorce laws, can take many months, even years, to get. The mandatory cooling-off period would be waived only if the people could prove that they had been living together during the prescribed period or if the woman were pregnant.

Whereas before the twentieth century people in their teens may have been prepared psychologically to marry by the social customs and expectations of the time, this is not the case for many people in an industrialized society. Adolescents today are still very much children. The long training required before they can assume a responsible position in our complex indus-trial society requires a more prolonged dependency on parents. Teenagers are not considered adults by society, and they do not really consider themselves to be fully grown either—in spite of their strong professions that they are fully capable of assuming adult responsibilities. Accordingly, most adolescents today are not ready for marriage, and it is no surprise that the divorce rate is highest in this age bracket.

Anything that can reasonably be done to discourage adolescent marriages, then, will contribute to a lowering of the divorce rate. Parents should teach their children during their formative years about the inadvisability of marrying during the teens. Educational programs on family living would do well to drive home this message. All states require people to have reached a certain age before they can marry. The minimum age varies with the state. On the average, for the United States as a whole, males have to reach twenty and females nineteen in order to marry *without* parental consent. The minimum ages to marry *with* parental consent, which also vary from state to state, are lower. The average is about seventeen for males and sixteen for females. Although I believe that all these ages are too low, I do not think it reasonable to raise the ages at which one can marry without parental consent; but I would like to see a raising of the minimum ages at which one can marry with parental consent. I would allow for a waiving of the requirement if the woman were pregnant or if there were other special circumstances. (In most states today the court has the authority to marry couples below the age of consent, and a woman's being pregnant is one of the considerations that may result in the court's utilizing this authority.) In making such proposals I am fully aware that externally imposed legal restrictions are far less desirable than internal convictions as determinants of when one marries. Accordingly, I would rely more on parental and school educational exposures than on legal restrictions to discourage early marriages. However, the legal position can affect the psychological state of such youngsters and contribute to their deferring marriage until they are older.

CHANGES THAT MAY REDUCE THE SUFFERING OF DIVORCING PEOPLE

In earlier chapters of this book I have been very critical of lawyers and of certain aspects of the legal system. (I blame the system more than the lawyers. They are often the victims of a system that is not of their making.) I have been especially critical of the adversary system when applied to divorce and custody litigation. I believe that if one is going to find fault, one should provide constructive proposals to rectify the deficiencies that one is criticizing. Toward that end, I would like to make some recommendations that I believe can be useful in divorce and custody litigation.

In chapter 1 I spoke about mediation and the ways in which it can protect people from the psychological damage caused by custody litigation. Mediation is now available to those who wish to avail themselves of the procedure. However, if mediation breaks down (as it often does), the parties generally resort to adversary litigation. But it is my belief that we should remove divorce and custody disputes entirely from adversarial proceedings.

A three-phase plan for divorce.

In the service of this goal I offer a three-phase plan. This plan would deal with divorce and custody disputes in such a way that both lawyers and mental health professionals would be utilized, but under no circumstances would the parties have the opportunity to resort to adversarial proceedings.

In the first stage, *mediation* would be required as the first step toward resolution of a child custody dispute. This is already the situation in the state of California, where the Conciliation Courts routinely attempt to mediate all custody disputes at the outset. In recent years many other states, as well, have introduced mediation that is mandatory before parents are permitted to embark upon adversarial litigation.

In the system I propose, parents could choose to mediate their dispute within or outside the court system. They could avail themselves of the services of psychiatrists, psychologists, social workers, lawyers, mediators, arbitrators, pastoral counselors, clergymen, and others qualified to conduct such evaluations—either privately or in clinics. Crucial to the success of such mediation would be the reassurance that under no circumstances, at any stage, would the content of the deliberations be made available to outside individuals. No written reports would be formulated and no verbal conversations between the mediator and lawyers would be permitted. My hope is that such mediation would serve to resolve the vast majority of custody disputes.

The mediated parenting plan would be verbally communicated to the attorney preparing the separation agreement. Because divorce is still a legal matter (and probably will be for the foreseeable future), the services of an attorney would still be necessary. However, my hope is that other possible disputes related to the divorce would also be resolved by mediation. In any case, the custody dispute could not be dealt with—at any of the three stages of my plan—by proceedings within the adversary system.

But mediation, like everything else in the world, is not without its drawbacks. All of us are fallible, and the most skilled mediator is no exception. Mediation may break down for a variety of reasons. One of the most common reasons is the refusal of one or both parties to make full disclosure of finances. Or each spouse may be so convinced of the other's ineptitude as a parent that the necessary compromises are impossible. Or psychiatric problems may interfere. For whatever reason, when mediation breaks down, most people today have no choice but to go to custody litigation. But in the system I propose, the parents would now be required to submit their dispute to an *arbitration panel,* working within the court structure. I believe that the best panel would consist of two mental health professionals and one attorney. The panel members would be selected by the parents from a roster of properly qualified individuals provided by the court. Like a judge, the panel (especially the lawyer) would have the power to subpoena medical records, request financial documents, and so on. Most important, the parents would meet directly with the panel members. Although the discussion would be free and open, the panel would have the authority to prevent the proceedings from degenerating into a free-for-all. The panel would be free to bring in any parties who might be helpful, and such parties could include attorneys to provide independent representation within the structure of free and open discussion. By having three panelists there would be no chance of a tie vote. The majority decision would prevail.

The crucial question remains as to whether the findings and recommendations of the arbitration panel should be binding. On the one hand, one could argue that the process has to end somewhere and that such a panel is a good enough authority to make final decisions in matters such as custody disputes. On the other hand, one could argue that even three people could make a mistake. So I recommend an *appeals panel:* another panel of three individuals (again an attorney and two mental health professionals) with significant experience in child custody mediation and arbitration. This panel would have the power to make a final decision. These panel members, as well, would be selected by the clients from a roster provided by the court. This appeals panel would carry out a two-step process of review. The first step would be to review the case. At this stage the panel would have the power to refuse to consider the case further; or the panel might consider another hearing warranted. It could then hear the parties directly and conduct whatever further data collection and/or evaluations were necessary. Once again, traditional courtroom procedures of examination would be replaced by open and free discussion. Whereas traditional courts of appeal allow lawyers only to provide testimony, the appeals panel would have the power to interview directly any and all parties it considered useful to hear. And the conclusion of this appeals panel would be final.

The three-step procedure I have outlined (mediation, arbitration panel, and appeals panel) does not involve adversarial proceedings at any level. The plan would protect clients from the polarization and spiraling of animosity that frequently accompany adversarial procedures and contribute to the development and perpetuation of psychopathology. It bypasses the system that makes many people feel compelled to commit perjury, slander, and libel. The plan also replaces the cumbersome and inefficient method of evidence gathering used by the courts with the more flexible and efficient data-collection process used by mental health professionals. The parents would be given the opportunity to choose their own panel, thus escaping the sense of impotence suffered when parents are stuck with a judge known to be ill equipped to deal with custody conflicts. In short, parents would choose their own judges. The three-member panel would reduce the likelihood of bias. Last, and most important, this system precludes any possibility of involvement in adversarial proceedings by people involved in a custody dispute. There would be no such forum for such individuals. The law would thus protect parents from involvement in a system that was never designed to deal with the question of who would serve as a better parent for children of divorce.

Due process and constitutional rights. The system does not deprive the parents of any of the rights of due process guaranteed by the Constitution of the United States. First, parents have the right to representation by counsel at both the arbitration and appeals levels. (Nowhere in the Constitution is anyone, including lawyers, given the right to subject another individual to the frustrations and indignities of yes-no questions. In fact, I have sometimes wondered whether yes-no questions deprive witnesses of their right to freedom of speech, guaranteed under the Bill of Rights.) Also, the constitutional right of the accused to confront his or her accuser is protected. Even better, this system gives the accuser the opportunity for direct confrontation with the accused without the use of intermediaries (adversary lawyers) or the restriction of courtroom procedures. Although individuals now have the opportunity for such direct confrontations in the courtroom if they represent themselves (appear "pro se"), this is not commonly done. In the system I propose the parents are essentially operating pro se. And even when they choose to bring in attorneys to represent them, the discussion will still be far freer than that found in the courtroom.

The constitutional right of a hearing before an impartial judge is also protected. Here, the parents have not just one judge but three (serving in a sense as a tribunal). And protection against bias is enhanced by the requirement that the majority vote will prevail. Not only is the requirement that two of the "judges" be mental health professionals desirable for the purposes of the custody evaluation; it is in no way unconstitutional. Nowhere in the Constitution is anything said about the educational or professional requirements a person must satisfy to serve as a judge. Last, even for criminals the Constitution calls for a speedy trial. But only a bizarre interpretation of the word "speedy" would suggest that a speedy trial is conducted for the vast majority of litigants in custody disputes today. My proposal is more likely to provide speed, primarily because of the advantages of its method of data collection over that of traditional adversarial courtroom proceedings.

It is important for the reader to appreciate that this proposal is just that, a proposal. It outlines what I consider a reasonable approach to the resolution of custody disputes. I am not claiming that it is perfect; I suspect that in practice it would warrant modification. Still, there is no question that it would be far more efficient and less expensive than adversarial proceedings.

There are other changes that would increase the likelihood of such a system's working. One relates to the training of lawyers. Lawyers' traditional training has been deeply committed to the adversary tradition as a way of resolving conflicts. Wouldn't it be helpful for lawyers to receive more training in the roles of mediator and arbitrator? Their knowledge of the law relating to such matters as divorce makes them ideally suited to serve in this position. However, their training in adversary proceedings is so deep that it makes it very difficult for them to do this at this time.

Another change that would be helpful would be the establishment of formal specialties—such as exist in medicine—in law. A specialty such as matrimonial law, in which there would be rigorous requirements for training and certification, would provide more of the kinds of lawyers that one would want for the effective utilization of proposals such as the one I have presented here.

ALTERNATE LIFE-STYLES AND THE FUTURE OF MARRIAGE AS AN INSTITUTION

The recent trend toward greater social acceptability for divorced parents is healthy both for them and for their children. Such parents and their children have enough trouble already; they do not need the additional, unnecessary burden of being looked upon as freaks and made social outcasts. In an attempt to counteract some of these old biases, some have gone to the opposite extreme and extolled single parenthood as being superior to the married type. This idea substitutes one form of unhealthy thinking for another. Monogamous marriage—all its restrictions, frustrations, and difficulties notwithstanding—is still the best arrangement for a child's healthy psychological development. A child, regardless of sex, needs intimate involvement with a mother *and* a father. The parent who claims that he or she can be both mother and father is dealing in self-delusion. I am deeply sympathetic with women who, advancing in years and seeing little prospect of getting married, decide to have children out of wedlock. However, such women should actively involve their children with father surrogates as much as possible.

Many other types of intermediate situations are now becoming prevalent. Regardless of whether or not they have a divorce decree, many parents still maintain various kinds of contacts and involvements with one another. Some will spend two or three days a week with the family and live elsewhere the rest of the week. Some children live in the father's house half the time and in the mother's the other half. Future experience and research will give us insights into the effects of these and other alternative arrangements on the psychological lives of the children involved.

Such intermediate states are not new to the law. Yet many of the problems that arise as a result of them have yet to be settled. What of the unmarried woman, for example, who lives with a man, bears his children, and is then abandoned by him?

What are his obligations to her? Most courts consider him to be obliged to support the children, but he may have no obligation at all to pay a penny to their mother. What of the woman who lives many years with a man, bears no children, and is then left at an age when her chances of attracting another man are very low? Generally, this man has no obligation to her at all. Is this fair? Trial marriages may have advantages, but the risks (for women, much more than for men) of maintaining single status for long periods, especially when children appear, are formidable.

The rights of children born of parents who are unwed also have to be redefined in my opinion. The term "bastard" is still occasionally used in the law to refer to such children. The term "illegitimate" is still very much with us. Are these children indeed illegitimate? What of their rights of inheritance? Sometimes, they have absolutely none. Should they be so penalized because their parents were not married? What about their fathers' rights to visitation and their mothers' rights to prevent such if they wish? Should the fact that their parents were not married affect such decisions and increase the chances that the children will be used as weapons in the parental conflict?

We are told that marriage is just one of the many possible arrangements that men and women can involve themselves in and that it is no more or less preferable than a number of other possible arrangements. We are told that marriage has been upheld as the superior life-style and that those who are unmarried or who have involved themselves in other arrangements have been discriminated against. We are also told that there is no evidence that monogamy is necessarily the only, or the best, arrangement for children and that other family patterns may be equally good or superior.

There is nothing really new in the alternative life-styles that are being given so much publicity these days. There is no pattern that has not been tried many times over, somewhere, someplace, in the long history of the human race. There are just so many possible arrangements that one can devise between two sexes. The number of possible combinations between males and females is not that great, and we have had ample opportunity to try them all. Group marriages, communal living, polygyny, polyandry, homosexual marriage, and single parenthood have all been tried many times over. But I am still convinced that children do best when they grow up in a home where there is one recognized father and one identifiable mother—each of whom has established a close relationship with their children from the time of their birth. Such children are most likely to perpetuate their heritage and build upon it. I am not presenting monogamy as a perfect arrangement. But of the various possible *parental* arrangements for the upbringing of children, it is the one that will most predictably produce psychologically healthy children.

WHAT IS A "HAPPY MARRIAGE"?

There are some who would say that the expression "happy marriage" is a contradiction in terms. In this view happiness inevitably must be compromised by marriage, and marriage cannot coexist with the state of happiness. I do not take such a dim view. I do believe that there are reasonably good marriages in which individuals derive many gratifications in a number of areas. I present here what I consider to be the ingredients of such a good relationship.

I believe that love between adults is a composite of many factors, each of which is on its own continuum—from a very low to a very high level. One factor, of course, would be romantic love. Romantic loving feelings tend to decrease in ongoing close contact, such as when two people live together. The feelings do not survive well under the competition of hair in the sink, bathroom smells, snoring, and so on. But ideally, vestiges of the initial feelings survive over time to reexpress themselves in periods of relaxation, tenderness, and sexual intimacy.

Another factor is sexual attraction. Generally, these feelings are strongest in the earliest phases of the relationship, when there is much novelty and even a "forbidden fruit" element. In the healthiest relationship, sexual feelings may still remain strong over many years. But fluctuations from high to low may be present and still be considered within the normal range.

Another important factor is that of respect. Here, too, the continuum ranges from very low to very high. In a good relationship there is a high regard for the other person's opinions, rights, space, aspirations, and a wide variety of other needs. Related to respect is admiration. When there is admiration the loving relationship is likely to be even stronger. However, admiration must be based on qualities that are genuinely worthy of respect, not superficial attributes.

Another element in a good loving relationship is the desire to share with one another. Probably the most common area for sharing is child rearing. However, some couples may not enjoy this kind of sharing but other kinds of mutual endeavors. But I would not consider the ideal to be one of complete togetherness in practically every area of functioning. There must be opportunities for each to have his or her own areas of interest and opportunities to enjoy other relationships as well.

Loving adults ought to be willing to make *reasonable* sacrifices for one another. An inordinate desire to sacrifice (or to be sacrificed for) is unhealthy, of course; sacrifices that are motivated by masochistic or martyristic tendencies are not what I am talking about. Rather, I am referring to the willingness to deprive oneself and do things for the other party under circumstances of personal inconvenience and in a spirit of mutual commitment.

It is important to appreciate that there is also a continuum of mildly pathological factors that are contributory—even in the healthiest marriage. For example, there are healthy marriages where the wife is basically mothering the husband; where extreme shyness is matched with extreme volubility; where an alcoholic is mated with a spouse with a savior complex. The fewer and the less intense these pathological interactions are, the more stable and gratifying the marriage will be. However, as mentioned, I do not believe that they are ever completely absent, even in what most would consider the most stable marriages. Nor do these mildly pathological contributing factors necessarily warrant treatment. In fact, to treat them might weaken the bond and compromise or even destroy an extremely solid relationship.

EPILOGUE

I have written this book in the hope that it may play some part in preventing and alleviating some of the painful psychological problems that children of divorce may suffer. Although divorce does not necessarily cause psychologically harmful reactions in children, stresses and traumas occurring before, during, and after the separation are likely sources of difficulty. Throughout the book I have discussed in detail many of the specific ways in which such children can acquire maladjustive reactions to parental divorce and have described approaches that may help remedy them.

Because of their exposure to these extra traumas and stresses, it is not surprising that children of divorce do not fare as well as those who grew up in intact, relatively stable and happy homes. Children of divorce are likely to be less trusting of human relationships. They may avoid marriage altogether in order to protect themselves from what they may consider a form of enslavement or a relationship doomed to failure. If married they may feel insecure in the relationship with their spouses—expecting rejection and abandonment. Some, having observed the harmful effects of their own parents' fighting, may vow not to fight at all. Such repression and suppression, of course, merely substitute one form of sickness for another. Or, modeling themselves after their parents, they may enter into marriages characterized by violence. Divorce is more likely to occur in the marriages of those whose parents were divorced. Divorce is part of their scheme of things, and there is less family discouragement of this method of dealing with marital difficulties. The more divorce in the family history, the greater the likelihood that younger married people will resort to it when things become difficult. Divorced parents who try to dissuade children from getting divorced are like smoking parents who try to discourage their children from smoking.

There are children, however, who appear to learn from their parents' mistakes. They grow up avoiding involvement in the kinds of sick relationships that contributed to the deterioration of their parents' marriages. Because children identify so with their parents, such rejection of the parental model is neither common nor easily accomplished. However, recognition of the unhealthy parental patterns can be achieved. It has been the purpose of this book to help children, through parental guidance, derive the benefits of such recognition, as well as to reduce the suffering of divorcing and divorced parents and the psychological problems of their children at the time of the divorce and the time after.

There are many children who, even though exposed to a variety of stresses associated with their parents' divorce, still do well. Many have a deep-seated resiliency that enables them to tolerate various traumas without suffering significant psychological disturbance. They seem to be able to bounce back and go on living in a relatively healthy and happy manner. We know very little about the reasons why some children exhibit such resiliency and some do not. Probably the most important factor determining which children will take the healthier route is the amount of genuine love they are receiving from each of the parents. Although I believe that love is not "enough," I still consider love to be the most important determinant of whether children will grow up psychologically stable. My hope is that the guidance contained in this book will complement parental love and help thereby to provide children with what will be "enough"—so that they will be able to tolerate the stresses of their parents' divorce and grow up to lead rewarding and fulfilling lives.

INDEX

About the Author

RICHARD A. GARDNER, M.D. is a Clinical Professor of Child Psychiatry at Columbia University, College of Physicians and Surgeons, and was a faculty member of the William A. White Psychoanalytic Institute. He practices in Cresskill, New Jersey, where he has worked for many years with divorced parents and their children. Author of more than twenty-five books, his titles most relevant to the subject of divorce include *The Boys and Girls Book About Divorce, Psychotherapy with Children of Divorce, The Boys and Girls Book About One-Parent Families, The Boys and Girls Book About Stepfamilies, Family Evaluation in Child Custody Litigation, Child Custody Litigation—A Guide for Parents and Mental Health Professionals, The Parental Alienation Syndrome and the Differentiation Between Fabricated and Genuine Child Sex Abuse*, and his recent *Family Evaluation in Child Custody Mediation, Arbitration, and Litigation*, and his recent *Sex Abuse Hysteria: Salem Witch Trials Revisited*.

Dr. Gardner is certified in general psychiatry and child psychiatry by the American Board of Psychiatry and Neurology. He is a member of the American Academy of Psychiatry and the Law and a fellow of the American Psychiatric Association, the American Academy of Child Psychiatry, and the American Academy of Psychoanalysis. He is listed in *Who's Who in America* and in *Who's Who in the World*.